Bridging the Digital Divide

The Information Age Series

Series Editor Manuel Castells

There is a growing interest in the general audience, as well as in universities around the world, on the relationships between information technology and economic, social, geographic and political change. Indeed, these new relationships are transforming our social, economic, and cultural landscape. Social sciences are called upon to understand this emerging society. Yet, to be up to the task social sciences must renew themselves, in their analytical tools and in their research topics, while preserving their scholarly quality.

The Information Age series is the "Nasdaq" of the social sciences – the series that introduces the topics, the findings and many of the authors that are redefining the field. The books cover a variety of disciplines: geography, sociology, anthropology, economics, political science, history, philosophy, information sciences, communication. They are grounded on original, rigorous research and present what we really know about the Information Age.

Together, the books in *The Information Age* series aim at marking a turn in the academic literature on information technology and society.

Published

Work in the New Economy
Chris Benner

Bridging the Digital Divide
Lisa J. Servon

Forthcoming

The Internet and Everyday Life
Barry Wellman and Caroline Haythornthwaite

The Geography of the Internet
Matthew Zook

Bridging the Digital Divide

Technology, Community, and Public Policy

Lisa J. Servon

Blackwell Publishing

350 Main Street, Malden, MA 02148-5018, USA
108 Cowley Road, Oxford OX4 1JF, UK
550 Swanston Street, Carlton South, Melbourne, Victoria 3053, Australia
Kurfürstendamm 57, 10707 Berlin, Germany

First published 2002 by Blackwell Publishers Ltd, a Blackwell Publishing company

Library of Congress Cataloging-in-Publication Data

Servon, Lisa J.
    Bridging the digital divide : technology, community, and public policy / Lisa J. Servon.
        p. cm. – (The Information Age series)
    Includes bibliographical references and index.
    ISBN 0-631-23241-9 (hbk : acid-free paper) – ISBN 0-631-23242-7 (pbk : acid-free paper)
        1. Digital divide–United States. 2. Digital divide–Government policy –United States. 3. Information technology–Social aspects–United States. I. Title. II. Series.
    HN90.I56S48 2002
    303.48'33'0973–dc21

ISBN 0-631-23241-9 (hbk) 0-631-23242-7 (pbk)

A catalogue record for this title is available from the British Library.

Set in 10.5 on 12.5 pt Palatino
by SNP Best-set Typesetter Ltd., Hong Kong

For further information on
Blackwell Publishing, visit our website:
www.blackwellpublishing.com

I have been truly blessed by the love, support, affirmation, and witnessing I have received from the women in my life. I dedicate this book to them.

Contents

Special Recognition

Although many people contributed directly and indirectly to this book, I am especially indebted to PolicyLink and particularly Angela Blackwell. Angela understood my intentions for this book at a very early stage and gave me the support I needed to focus on my writing for the critical final seven months of this project. Angela and others I worked with at PolicyLink – particularly Josh Kirschenbaum and Radhika Kunamneni, but also Judith Bell, Joe Brooks, and Victor Rubin – truly grasped what I was trying to do, gave me what I needed to do it, and encouraged me to keep moving forward whenever I came up for air. It has been a genuinely amazing experience to complete this piece of work surrounded by people who are committed to an agenda focused on economic and social justice. I consider myself fortunate to have had the gift of working in this tremendous intellectual home.

PolicyLink is a national nonprofit research, communications, capacity building and advocacy organization, dedicated to advancing policies to achieve economic and social equity based on the wisdom, voice and experience of local constituencies. For more information, visit www.policylink.org

What does it profit a man to be able to eat at an integrated lunch counter if he doesn't have enough money to buy a hamburger?

Reverend Dr. Martin Luther King Jr.

Figures

Tables

Acknowledgments

Many people and organizations share responsibility for bringing this book to fruition. Manuel Castells encouraged me to think about the intersection between the information society and the problem of persistent urban poverty. Conversations with him dating back to 1995 planted the seeds that ultimately grew into this work. Completing the book in Berkeley in the spring of 2001 enabled me to meet with him regularly and test out my ideas. Those long conversations in Manuel's sunny office sharpened my own thinking tremendously. I am blessed to have such a generous mentor, colleague, and friend.

My research assistants at Rutgers and in California were truly exceptional. Marla Nelson has been much more of a genuine collaborator than a research assistant. Marla worked closely with me on two earlier studies that fed into this book, conducted fieldwork in Pittsburgh and Seattle, and helped to design and analyze the survey discussed in chapter 3. Our conversations as we drove around Seattle and wrote up our findings shaped my thinking on these issues to a great extent, and I look forward to her finishing her dissertation so that we can continue to work together as colleagues. Raysa Martinez worked closely with me in Harlem and in East Palo Alto conducting fieldwork during the summer of 2000. She transcribed countless interviews, translating many of them from Spanish. She repeatedly surprised me with her ability to pick up on important dynamics between people and within organizations. In addition, Abeni Crooms and Phil Ashton at Rutgers worked doggedly on the survey of CTCs. Lalitha Kamath organized an overwhelming amount of material and was especially helpful in gathering background information for chapter 5.

In California, Radhika Kunamneni provided tremendous assistance in the last seven months of writing – gathering and synthesizing enormous amounts of data, checking facts, and acting as a very balanced sounding board. Her gentle but critical eye and thoughtfulness have undoubtedly made this a better book than it would have been without her. This book is informed by her own vast knowledge of and passion for the digital divide issue. Marisa McNee, an undergraduate at Cal, helped tie up countless loose ends.

Josh Kirschenbaum and Radhika Kunamneni co-authored chapter 7 and conducted the research for that part of the book. They are the first to have made the key connection between the community technology and community building movements, and their continued work is certain to make a powerful impact on the field. Working with Josh was a real treat – his enthusiasm for this issue is truly contagious. Josh was also instrumental in bringing me to PolicyLink – for that, and for his friendship and support, I am eternally grateful.

I received important support from several funders during the five years leading up to publication. A 1995 grant from the Motorala corporation funded my first study of the community technology movement in Austin, Texas where I was teaching at the time. An early paper resulting from that work, co-authored by John Horrigan, set me on this path. John has continued to educate me about telecommunications policy through the writing of this book and has shared data and thoughts resulting from his own fine work at the Pew Internet and American Life Project. The Aspen Institute Non-Profit Sector Research Fund supported a larger study of community technology in three cities: Austin, Pittsburgh, and Seattle. My work on community technology and youth was funded by the Open Society Institute's Individual Project Fellowship Program and the Ford Foundation. OSI's program also enabled me to meet an amazing group of other researchers, many of whom I have remained in contact with. The Milano Graduate School of Management and Urban Policy at New School University awarded me a post as a visiting scholar in Fall 2000, which allowed me to focus almost completely on writing. Special thanks go to Ed Blakely and Edwin Melendez, who made that happen, and to those who attended a talk I gave on this work in November 2000 and who gave me thoughtful comments.

And PolicyLink, in Oakland, California, asked me to be a Visiting Policy Scholar for seven months in early 2001. Being there helped me both to focus on my work and to see clearly how it connected to the larger mission of attaining social and economic justice.

Many people read an earlier draft of this book and provided me with comments, suggestions, and material that helped me to revise it substantially and push it to a new level. In early July 2001, PolicyLink hosted a seminar for local experts, activists, scholars, practitioners, and funders to discuss the manuscript. The truly constructive and engaging conversation that took place between Judith Bell, Eugene Chan, Jerry Feldman, Blanca Gordo, David Gruber, Josh Kirschenbaum, Radhika Kunamneni, and myself, enabled me to make the book sharper and more useful to the target audiences I wanted to reach. Others who read and commented on an early draft include: Lon Berquist, Laura Breeden, Joe Brooks, Steve Cisler, Alec Gershberg, Rahsaan Harris, John Horrigan, David Keyes, Trish Millines Dziko, Grant Mydland, Lodis Rhodes, Steve Ronan, Victor Rubin, Doug Schuler, and Mildred Thompson. I thank them all for taking an interest in my work, for generously giving of their time, and for their own commitment to the community technology movement.

I owe a special debt of gratitude to the organizations discussed within the book that allowed me to study them. Many, many people took the time out to be interviewed and to teach me all they know about this field. The staff and directors of the organizations studied in depth opened their programs, offices, files, memories and, in some cases, their homes to me. They vouched for me to their participants and put me in touch with these participants so that I could interview them. It is difficult, intrusive, and time consuming to allow a researcher to study your program. Thank you all for letting me in. I would like to single out the following individuals here: Magda Escobar, Rahsaan Harris, Trish Millines Dziko, Mara Rose, and Ana Sisnett. Without them and countless others, my work would lack the depth and richness that their experience provides.

Last but not least, I owe a bottom-of-my-heart thank you to friends and family. Writing a book is never a completely pretty or predictable process, and I am grateful to all of the people who understood when I had to go AWOL for a period of days or weeks while I traveled to do fieldwork, buried myself in my writing, downloaded my brain at social events, or simply needed to gain some perspective on my work and on the world. The following people are among the many who supported me directly and indirectly during the time that I worked on this book: Leslie Coffaro, Elke Davidson, Susan Fainstein, Alec Gershberg, Norm Glickman, Robert Gray, Barbara Kaplan, Sarah Mabey, Tracy Meade, Karen Paget, Libby Roderick, Jody Servon, Anne Stuhldreher, Andrew Walker, Ann Williams. All of you continue to inspire me in so many ways.

Foreword

In August 1999, I sat with Manuel Castells at Strada Café in Berkeley talking about ideas for a book on the digital divide. My first book, on US microenterprise programs, was in production at that time – I had had just enough of a lag to have forgotten what a tremendous undertaking it can be to put together a book. I had been conducting research on urban poverty and the technology gap for three years, and it made sense for me to bring it all together into one volume. Little did I know what I was getting into. Writing this book has stretched me in ways I could not have foreseen.

Two challenges faced me as I wrote this book. First, technology (and the digital divide in particular) is a moving target. As I write this, I worry that during the six months between the moment I sit here at my computer and the day the book exists as a physical object everything will change. Keeping the threat of short shelf-life in the front of my mind, I have worked to create a book with messages that last beyond the immediate accuracy of specific statistics.

Second, the range of material that I needed to understand and include expanded endlessly. It sometimes seemed as though I was putting together a giant jigsaw puzzle, and that I never encountered those straight-sided pieces that border the whole. For my chapter on youth, for example, I had to gain a working knowledge of education policy. For the chapter on the information technology (IT) labor shortage, I needed to familiarize myself with the workforce development literature. The chapter on the history of the community technology movement required me to document and condense more than twenty years of amazing work by committed individuals and organizations. Many of these topics warrant much more attention, and I hope this book inspires other researchers to dig more deeply into them. In short, while working on a rather specific topic, I have had to become something of a generalist, a position most academics would rather not put themselves in. I hope that I have done these fields justice, given that others are much more expert than I in these individual areas.

These two challenges – the changefulness of the field and the breadth of topics touched by the digital divide – have made it impossible for me to include all of the good work that is being done across the country and around the world to deal with this pressing problem. I received email every single day of this process highlighting innovative programs and new studies. I believe that the programs and initiatives I discuss throughout this book are representative of the terrific efforts taking place. I apologize for not being able to discuss more of them.

My sincere hope is that I have better defined the digital divide problem, lifted up creative strategies with which to confront it, and that I have raised important new questions that must be addressed as we set an agenda for the next phase of the community technology movement. More importantly, I hope that others will be curious about these questions, will deem them significant, and will be moved to begin the critical work of answering them.

I wrote much of this book in Berkeley, California, from January through July of 2001. My writing room looked out over the bay, and my long afternoon walks in Tilden Park with Hoover helped me to settle my thoughts and coax the better ideas to the surface. Berkeley became, for the second time in my life, a part of me and a part of my work, providing the ideal setting for the kind of focus I needed to pull this book together.

As I complete the final revisions to the manuscript, I sit in a very different place – Manhattan – in a very different world. We have all experienced a tremendous jolt in how we think about our world and our places within it. Since September 11, I have asked myself tough questions about the value and meaning of my own work. Is it as important as I thought it was, this fight to relieve persistent poverty? As a society, we have stated that we are not willing to normalize terror. And yet poverty, inequality, and discrimination remain commonplace, a fact of life. As we continue to deal with the consequences of the unthinkable acts that took place on September 11, we must not forget about the injustices that we have structured into our society. We must not normalize a divided world.

Lisa J. Servon
New York City
November 2001

Series Editor's Preface

The Internet is quickly becoming a fundamental medium of communication and information processing, permeating every domain of economy and society. Because our societies are unequal, so is the diffusion of the Internet. Thus, the notion of the digital divide as a critical dimension of inequality and social injustice in our world. Indeed, most social debates on the Internet, in every corner of the world, start with the denunciation of its potentially evil effects on social exclusion as a consequence of differential access to the global network for countries, social groups, genders, and ethnic minorities. The intensity of the debate often obscures the fundamental issues at stake. Therefore, to understand the interest, and the importance, of the book you have in your hands, it could be useful to define better what is the digital divide.

First of all, there is the simple fact of differential access to the Internet: to be or not to be in the network. This is a fundamental cleavage when we consider the Internet in a global perspective. In 2002, there are only about 7 percent of people on the planet connected to the Internet, in contrast to an average 40 percent in the European Union, above 50 percent in North America, and above 60 percent in Scandinavia. However, within developed countries the differences in access that existed in the early stages of the Internet are rapidly fading away with the widespread diffusion of the medium. Thus, more women than men are online nowadays in North America, and the gender gap is rapidly narrowing in the rest of the OECD countries. To be sure, education and income are correlated with Internet access, and the younger groups of the population are more connected, but the differences are decreasing, as is the difference between rural and urban areas, so that at a higher level of diffusion they may lose significance.

The racial divide is still there, but when it is controlled by education, it shrinks substantially. So, in terms of access, the digital divide is a function of the level of development, which underlines how important it is as a development policy in the new information age, but it also means that it could lose relevance as a source of inequality for developed countries.

However, there are new, and more important forms of digital divide emerging in our societies. One of them is technological, that is the quality of the connection. Broadband is essential to really use the possibilities of the Internet as a communication medium and as an information system. And broadband's distribution is extremely unequal, not only among people from different social status, but among countries. For instance, in South Korea, in 2002, over 50 percent of Internet users have broadband access, in contrast to less than 20 percent in the US. The difference is related to regulatory policies that focus on consumers or on business as a priority. In the US, an excessive deregulation may well lead to a retardation of the US broadband Internet access *vis à vis* Europe and developed Asia, following the same logic that put the US way behind Europe in the diffusion and uses of cellular telephony. Thus, to a large extent, the new digital divide refers to the quality of Internet access.

Furthermore, the more the Internet becomes the key medium for business, for education, for social services, for personal development, and for social interaction, the more the capacity to use it becomes dependent on people's educational and cultural level. In other words, the real inequality starts when we are all dependent on the Internet. Because the cultural ability to determine the information we need, to know where to look for, what to do with it, and to focus it on the performance of the tasks we want to accomplish, becomes the source of social differentiation. Thus, if educational level, cultural level, and capacity for personal autonomy were always key factors in shaping social inequality, their differential effect becomes magnified in the age of the Internet. The more we move into an Internet society, the more education, in the broadest sense, becomes the foundation for equal opportunity, indeed the foundation for a sustainable society.

It is only by identifying the diversity and complexity of the digital divide that policies can be designed to overcome it. And it is only by observing these policies in their real operation that we can assess them, and address the old problems of social inequality and human injustice in our new technological context. Lisa Servon's book deals, rigorously, with both issues. It defines, and conceptualizes, what is the digital divide in different realms of society. Then, it observes what institutions, communities, companies, and people are doing to provide equal chances to everybody in the Internet-based economy. Unlike other studies, it focuses on community-based training programs, but it also analyses work-place programs of technology development, and relates these efforts to the broader institutional context of policy in the public interest. On the basis of her empirical research Servon evaluates prospective policies, and places these policies in their social and political background. The result is an extraordinary blending of good academic research, public advocacy, and sensitive policy proposals. She is not shy of original ideas about what to do, but she always reasons her position, and takes good care of relating it to the results of her research. This is why this book is invaluable, at the same time for students of communities, for researchers on the emerging information society, and for policy makers wanting to know the new social problems they are up against. *Bridging the Digital Divide* provides a much needed bridge between research and policy in the context of the emerging Information Age.

Manuel Castells
April 2002

1

Redefining the Digital Divide

Information technology (IT) has wrought fundamental changes throughout society. IT has instrumented the shift from an industrial age to a network age. We now live in a society in which the production, acquisition, and flow of knowledge drive the economy and in which global information networks represent key infrastructure. How have these changes affected existing power relations and patterns of inequality? Does IT benefit or hinder progress toward social and economic justice?

Clearly it has the power to do both. In addition to altering commerce, education, government, and communications, IT affects the construction of and response to social problems such as poverty and inequality. The very existence of the "digital divide" – or lack of access to IT for certain segments of the population – is evidence of the ability of technology to exacerbate existing inequality. At the same time, technology can bring education to people living far from good schools. It can promote organizing efforts in disadvantaged communities. And it can connect people to a wide range of opportunities. The community technology movement – a grassroots social movement that employs IT to empower historically disadvantaged individuals and communities – demonstrates the potential of IT to serve as a tool of social change.

The digital divide is now recognized as an international issue. High income OECD countries account for over three-fourths of the world's Internet users.[1] In virtually all countries, Internet users tend to be young, urban, male, and relatively well educated and wealthy. In short, the diffusion of technology both within and between countries has been extremely uneven. Current and historical patterns of access

---

1   United Nations Development Programme (2001).

to IT illustrate a significant separation between information "haves" and information "have nots" along lines of race, socioeconomic status, education level, household type, and geographic location.[2] Why has the technology gap emerged as such a prominent issue nationally and internationally? Does it warrant this recent attention? Absolutely. IT affects how we work and what we work toward, how we connect with each other and with whom we connect, and how we make decisions and with what information. Living on the wrong side of the digital divide, as do the persistent poor, means being cut off from these changes and disconnected from the information society.

But the technology gap is only one link in a causal chain that has bound certain groups repeatedly to disadvantage. The digital divide is, therefore, a symptom of a much larger and more complex problem – the problem of persistent poverty and inequality. Widespread access to and use of technology will not solve these larger problems, but it can help to show the way out. Used wisely, technology provides new ways to address this problem. To have any significant effect, however, technology must be enabled by effective public policy in cooperation with concerted efforts by the private for-profit and private nonprofit sectors. One goal of this book is to illustrate and analyze the kinds of arrangements between public policy and communities, using technology, that can lead to social change.

The US government discovered the digital divide in 1995. That year, the National Telecommunications and Information Administration (NTIA) issued the first of four reports under the title "Falling Through the Net." These reports documented the existence and particulars of a digital divide in America that separates people with access to information technology (IT) from those without it.

Community technology centers (CTCs) (known as telecenters in most other countries) have emerged at an increasing pace in the last several years to deal with the digital divide. CTCs are locally based nonprofit organizations that link community residents to IT resources. Thousands of organizations are currently working to disseminate IT to local communities. CTCs work to foster the potential positive benefits of the information revolution while combating its associated problems. CTCs address the digital divide comprehensively and advance larger social, political, and economic goals in the process.

---

2 US Department of Commerce (2000a); Doctor (1994).

Yet when community technology activists talk about the need to narrow the digital divide, they are often met with skepticism. Is IT something people really need, or is it more accurate to think of it as a luxury? Why would low-income people use computers to contact elected officials? They can write letters now, but they seldom do. They can vote now, but the poor are one of the groups with the lowest voter turnout rates. Wasn't the cable access movement supposed to give people a voice? Why has it not made the kind of impact many hoped it would make? Perhaps the Internet, the IT medium of communication, is just the next in a long succession of over-hyped media.

These questions and doubts are legitimate. However, the Internet possesses attributes that make it differ from these other media in key ways. First, the Internet is an open medium that allows broad participation – the shorthand for this characteristic is "many to many." Unlike other media used to deliver information, television and newspapers for example, the Internet allows users both to respond to what exists and to produce their own material relatively inexpensively *if* they possess the skills and access necessary to do so. This "many to many" aspect of the Internet is one of its key cultural features. The Internet's interactive nature creates the conditions necessary "for learning, confidence-building, and self-empowerment."[3] In short, the Internet provides "the capacity for anyone to find his/her own destination in the net, and if not found, to create and post his/her own information."[4]

Second, the Internet enables the creation and support of networks. These networks are organized and maintained for social and economic purposes. The value of networks increases as the number of people who belong to and actively participate in the network increases.[5] The Internet makes joining and remaining engaged much easier, and enables participation across space, thereby increasing the potential for a greater number of users to join. More importantly for the purposes of this book, online networks have the capacity to strengthen and enhance place-based community networks, extending the reach of existing community-based organizations and institutions.

These two attributes – the openness of the Internet and its capacity to support networks – are revolutionizing the way in which individuals, communities, firms, governments, and other institutions and organizations engage with the rest of the world. To ensure that all

3 Sanyal (2000: 146).
4 Castells (2001), ch. 2, p.19.
5 Civille (1995); Brock (1994).

people have the skills and access to participate in the information society is a matter of utmost importance. But before attempting to achieve consensus that this issue must be addressed, we must first agree on the specific nature of the problem.

Redefining the Problem

What exactly is the digital divide? In order to address it, we first need a deep and specific understanding of the problem. Policy makers and the media have thus far defined the digital divide narrowly and incompletely. In short, the technology gap has been defined as a problem of access in the narrow sense of possession or permission to use a computer and the Internet.

This book challenges the current popular conception of the digital divide, which equates inclusion in the information society with access to computers and the Internet. Access to information technology is increasing at a rapid rate. Although some groups of people, namely, African-Americans, Latinos, and the disabled, remain persistently and disproportionately on the wrong side of the divide, the gaps between those who have access to IT and those who do not are rapidly closing. Groups that have traditionally been digital have-nots are now making dramatic gains. Gaps between rural and nonrural households and between seniors and younger people have begun to narrow. Some divides, such as that between women and men, have disappeared altogether.

And yet the larger problem persists. Deep divides remain between those who possess the resources, education, and skills to reap the benefits of the information society and those who do not. Persistent gaps remain between different racial and ethnic groups, people with and without disabilities, single and dual parent families, the old and the young, and people with different levels of income and education. Low-income persons and minorities, particularly when they reside in inner cities, are among the groups being left behind. Table 1.1 illustrates these changes, and chapter 2 takes up this issue in much deeper detail.

Because the technology gap has been defined narrowly, as a problem of access, policies and programs have also been narrowly focused. Proposed solutions to the digital divide tend to begin with making sure that schools are wired and that every household has a computer. For example, in March of 2000, Governor Angus King of

Table 1.1 Dimensions of the digital divide

	Households with computers (August 2000) (%)	Individuals with Internet (November 2001) (%)
General population	51.0	57.6
Gender		
Male	Not available	58.2
Female		57.1
Geography		
Urban	51.5	58.2
Central city	46.3	62.5[a]
Rural	49.6	47.5
Income[b]		
Under $15,000	19.2	12.7
$15,000–24,999	30.1	21.3
$25,000–34,999	44.6	34.0
$35,000–49,999	58.6	46.2
$50,000–74,999	73.2	60.9
$75,000+	86.3	77.7
Education		
Less than high school	18.2	25.9
High school	39.6	48.4
Some college	60.3	63.8
Bachelor's degree	74.0	63.4[c]
Postgraduate	79.0	
Race		
White	55.7	46.1
Black	32.6	23.5
Asian-American/Pacific Islander	65.6	56.8
Hispanic	33.7	23.6

Sources: Computer data from US Department of Commerce (2000a); Internet data from Pew Internet and American Life Project, unpublished.

[a] Pew uses the term "suburban."
[b] Computer and Internet data for income all come from Department of Commerce 2000a.
[c] Pew groups college grad and post-college together.

Maine announced a plan to give every seventh grade student a laptop computer. King stated that he wanted Maine "to have the most digitally literate society on earth."[6] The governor's $65 million plan, however, did not allocate any funds for computer training or for

6 *New York Times*, March 1, 2000.

upkeep of the machines. The focus on simply getting computers to people has resulted in millions of dollars of misspent money. To be fair, some have recently begun to define "access" more broadly. In 2000, for example, the members of the Global Knowledge Partnership met in Kuala Lumpur and defined access to include: physical access to IT; access to training; access to salient local content in the language of the user; and access to the process by which telecommunications decisions are made.[7] Redefining access requires shifting the primary question from who has access to "what are people doing, and what are they able to do, when they go online?"[8]

Clearly, the digital divide is much more complex than a mere lack of computers. Simplistic solutions have therefore masked and perhaps even exacerbated the larger problem. When we provide people with computers, we find that not much changes. IT on its own does not function as a ladder out of poverty. This book defines the digital divide in a broader and more complex way, and suggests similarly broad solutions to deal with the problem. More comprehensive responses based on a more finely textured and nuanced understanding of the problem can be employed to enable disadvantaged groups to participate in today's economy and society, in effect providing the kind of boost necessary to exit poverty.

The way in which a particular problem is defined leads to a specific policy solution. Getting the definition right, then, is key. This introductory chapter redefines the digital divide in order to point the way toward more appropriate solutions. The fact that the technology gap has already been defined as a problem of access creates an additional challenge. It will be difficult to convince key actors to alter their conception of the problem and to expand the toolkit currently employed to address it.

The struggle to create such a change in thinking is worthwhile, however, and informing this change is a chief goal of this book. If we do not reframe discussions of the digital divide, and employ the reframing to create broader solutions, we will have universal access without social change. Policy makers and funders will see that providing access has not altered existing cleavages that separate the privileged from the disenfranchised. The entire issue will be de-prioritized as funders and policy makers move on to search for the next silver bullet to solve the problem of persistent poverty.

7   See also Gordo (2000).
8   DiMaggio and Hargittai (2001).

If the digital divide is not simply a problem of access, what is the appropriate definition? Access is one dimension of the issue. Clearly people need the basic IT tools, computers and Internet access, at their disposal. But access is only the first component.

The second dimension of the digital divide concerns training, or IT literacy – the ability to use IT for a range of purposes, and the knowledge of how and why IT can be used as a key resource. For example, thus far policy has emphasized getting computers and the Internet into the schools, but these efforts have been incomplete and inequitable. Incomplete because teachers are not trained and supported to integrate technology into what they do. And because when IT is used, it is often used for typing exercises and drills rather than to enable the acquisition of the kind of skills and thinking that the information society demands. Inequitable because great differences exist in terms of the way IT is currently deployed in wealthier and poorer schools. Some schools have state-of-the-art computers languishing in unused computer labs because the teachers do not know how to use the technology. Other facilities are wired, but there is no money to purchase hardware and software. As chapter 5 will illustrate, both the computer/student ratios and the IT activities available are much better in well-off school districts than in low-income areas. The training issue extends beyond schools to disadvantaged workers who cannot find work that pays a living wage because they do not have the appropriate skills to work in the information economy. As with any tool, users of IT must understand and have the facility to fully exploit the potential of IT in order to benefit completely from it.

The third dimension of the digital divide has to do with content, both content that meets the needs and demands of disenfranchised groups and content that is created by these groups. The Internet, like most media, is shaped by the first people to occupy its territory, in this case middle- and upper-income white males. When disadvantaged groups do log on, they often find that there is no content there. The kind of information they seek – information that is directly related to their lives and communities and cultures – does not exist. If and when it does, they often lack the skills to find it. Language and literacy issues create additional barriers for these groups.[9] This content dimension is clearly related to the training dimension; IT skills are needed in order to access and create content.

9 Lazarus and Mora, 2000.

Redefining the digital divide, then, requires broadening the concept beyond access to include training and content issues. Access is a necessary precondition but then engenders a need for training in order to use the tools. Once people have facility with the tools, they demand content that serves their interests and meets their needs. The process of redefinition must also be informed by an analysis of how different groups use IT and for what purposes.

Explaining the Divide's Persistence

Several factors help to explain the emergence of the technology gap. These factors interact with each other to keep certain groups stuck in the "information have-not" category.

Market forces

One obvious explanation for the narrowing of some aspects of the digital divide concerns the drop in prices of computers and Internet services. As prices drop, more people are able to afford IT. Although computers and Internet access have become a necessity in many middle-income households, the price of obtaining and maintaining these IT tools puts them into the luxury category for many low-income families. Computer prices have dropped steadily in recent years but remain out of reach for many. As of August 2000, computer ownership in the United States was at 51 percent, up from 24.1 percent in 1994 and 36.6 percent in 1997.[10]

In addition to the initial purchase price, families also need money to maintain their computers, to purchase software and peripherals, and to pay for monthly Internet access. A 1999 study found that when those with computers were asked why they did not have Internet access, the most common response was that the household's occupants did not want such access.[11] The second most common response had to do with cost. The lower a household's income, the more likely the

10　US Department of Commerce, 2000a. These numbers do not reflect how many of these computers are inoperable or obsolete.
11　Wyatt (2001) looks specifically at the issue of non-use of the Internet, making the important distinction between nonusers who choose not to use the Internet, and nonusers who are excluded from using the Internet because they cannot afford it or because they lost access.

respondent was to cite cost as the reason for not having Internet access.[12]

Unequal investment in infrastructure

Unequal investment in infrastructure also contributes to the technology gap. The Internet has been touted as a medium with the capability to collapse distance and to eliminate spatial inequalities.[13] It is becoming apparent, however, that IT is profoundly rooted in geography.[14] Investment in high-end telecommunications infrastructure is much lower in poor urban areas and rural regions than it is in wealthier areas. Wealthier urban and suburban neighborhoods are typically wired and upgraded before inner-city and rural areas.[15] This inequitable provision of infrastructure is a form of market failure: private companies will invest in infrastructure in areas where they are most likely to yield the highest returns on investment. Although it may be unprofitable to invest in the infrastructure of low-income areas, failure to serve these other areas creates an inequitable situation that warrants government intervention.

Graham and Guy argue that "the Internet is showing signs of 'splintering' and unbundling, adding better infrastructure and connectivity to powerful economic 'hot spots' and furthering the relative backwardness of rural and marginalized spaces."[16] Examining the spatial aspect of this issue broadly, on a global scale, Markusen finds a set of privileged global cities, which she calls "sticky spaces", in which intense clustering of Internet activity exists.[17] She contrasts these sticky spaces of production with slippery places that have largely failed to attract and maintain information industries. These sticky spaces drive the information industries. Within metropolitan regions, a similar sticky/slippery spottiness exists on the consumption side. In short, the same places that are characterized by economic poverty also tend to suffer from information poverty; a pattern has developed in which inequalities in physical and electronic spaces mutually reinforce one another.[18]

12 US Department of Commerce (1999: 38–9).
13 See, for example, Mitchell (1995, 1999b).
14 Graham and Marvin (2001).
15 Goslee (1998: 2).
16 Graham and Guy (2001: 5). See also Graham and Marvin (2001).
17 Markusen (1999). See also Castells (1989).
18 Graham and Marvin (1996: 191).

Both of these first two factors, cost and infrastructure, will be exacerbated as broadband takes root and begins to be used on a large scale. Broadband refers to the increased data traffic capacity, or bandwidth, available via cable and phone lines, as well as wireless and satellite transmissions. Broadband technology will enable firms to tailor pricing much more specifically to use, making high quality Internet access more expensive than it is currently. On the infrastructure side, cities and neighborhoods where willingness to pay is greatest (where "willingness" correlates strongly with "ability") will obtain broadband access first.

Discrimination

Discrimination functions as a third factor that reinforces the digital divide. Schools in low-income areas that overwhelmingly house children of color are much less likely to provide quality access, training, and content than are schools in wealthier districts. African-Americans recently protested against CompUSA after corporate officials claimed they did not advertise to the black community because African-Americans did not shop there. In addition, the content and form of hardware, software, and the Internet reflects the culture, tastes, and demands of those who create the products and of the early users – largely middle- and upper-class white men.

Insufficient policy efforts

Existing public sector attempts to address the technology gap demonstrate a failure to understand the complexity of the issue. For example, the E-rate, which provides subsidized IT access to schools and libraries, is not available to community technology centers, which are the only point of access for many low-income users.[19] And, although public-sector efforts to wire public schools is commendable, they accomplish little if not accompanied by funding for appropriate hardware, software, and training for teachers. Little public support exists for training and content. Policy makers' narrow focus on access is insufficient to the problem. There is a disconnect between policy and need.

---

19   The E-rate, which is federal, will be discussed in much greater detail in chapter 4. Some states have made CTCs eligible for subsidies.

Culture and content

People who do not fit the typical IT user profile are unlikely to want to explore cyberspace unless they believe that there is a reason to go there. According to Castells: "Technological systems are socially produced. Social production is culturally informed. The Internet is no exception. The culture of the producers of Internet shaped the medium."[20]

The shape of IT tools and the landscape of the Internet must reflect the needs and interests of diverse populations in order to attract a diverse group of users. Those that have crossed the digital divide have found reasons to do so.

All of these factors – cost, infrastructure, discrimination, policy, and culture – interact with each other to keep certain groups from being able to participate fully in the information society.

Rationale for Closing the Gap

Narrowing the digital divide is important for political, economic, and social reasons. Some consider communications policy to be a civil rights issue.[21] Chapman and Rhodes, scholar-activists, go so far as to assert that "access to the Internet is as important a part of civil life as parks, public transit, libraries, and cultural centers."[22] Although labeling access to IT as a right does not guarantee automatic access, it does usefully reframe the debate "since civil rights demand appropriate public action to ensure that they work in practice and not just exist in principle."[23] In reality, communications policy has not heretofore been framed as such but has rather functioned as a sort of regulatory/social compact between business and government.[24] The important point is that failure to address current imbalances in the ability to use IT may lead to more deeply entrenched imbalances between historically privileged and historically disenfranchised groups.[25] Differential

20 Castells (2001), chapter 2, p.1.
21 Lloyd (1998: 1).
22 Chapman and Rhodes (1997).
23 Carvin (2000: 5).
24 Correspondence with John Horrigan. See also Temin and Galambos (1989) and Horwitz (1989).
25 Doctor (1994).

access and use of IT may actually increase existing gaps in education and access to opportunity.[26] A troubling cycle has begun to take shape, in which the lack of access to information technology and its requisite skills contributes both to an inability to compete in the mainstream economy and an inability to participate in civil society.

Economic rationale

The ability to access and use IT is particularly important given the global economic shift away from manufacturing and toward services and other information-related industries. The two primary characteristics of our current economy are globalization and information reliance.[27] These characteristics mutually reinforce one another. Advanced information technologies enable a global economy in which headquarters, manufacturing, and distribution facilities of a given corporation may be scattered across the globe. Between 1996 and 1999, high technology alone accounted for 25 percent of economic growth and added about 0.7 percentage points to the overall growth rate of the economy.[28] Information technology companies had $800 billion in sales in 2000 and their efforts accounted for 10 percent of the country's gross domestic product.[29]

Politicians use the rhetoric of global economic competitiveness to argue for public and private intervention into the technology gap problem. At the Harlem kick-off event for his 1999 Closing the Digital Divide tour, then Commerce Secretary William M. Daley stated: "We must . . . make sure that America has the skilled workers, the competitive businesses, the digital cities, and the wealth it needs to continue as a world leader."[30] Robert Reich, former Secretary of Labor, argued strongly for investment in training to upgrade the skills of the US workforce as the way to maintain US competitive advantage in global markets. This framing of the issue set the stage for important collaboration across federal agencies. A recent report put out jointly by the Departments of Education, Labor, and Commerce connected global

26   Blakely, Hadi, and Johnson (1995); Goslee (1998).
27   Mandel (1999).
28   Mandel (1999: 5).
29   Information Technology Association of America (2001).
30   US Department of Commerce (2000b).

competitiveness to individual worker earnings. Calling for increased investment in worker education, this report states:

> For America to compete in this new global economy, it can either create low-wage, low-skilled jobs or take full advantage of the Nation's labor force and create high performance workplaces . . . Not only does a better educated and trained workforce create significant productivity gains and better bottom line results for American workers, but the more a worker learns, the more a worker earns.[31]

The Bush administration, however, shows signs of beginning to reverse the trend of increasing support for the agenda to close the digital divide that the Clinton administration initiated. In his first press conference as chairman of the FCC (Federal Communications Commission), Michael Powell downplayed the issue, pointing out that innovative products often reach the wealthy before they spread to the rest of society, and that this did not translate to a divide. He then stated, "I think there is a Mercedes divide. I'd like to have mine."[32] To be sure, the diffusion of IT is not so different from the diffusion of other technologies. According to Rogers, "when the issue of equality is investigated, we often find that the diffusion of innovations widens the socioeconomic gap between the higher and lower status segments of a system."[33]

A mismatch clearly exists between well-paying information economy jobs and the skills of job seekers. An inability of low-income and disadvantaged workers to compete for IT jobs contributes to the accelerating income gap between the wealthy and the poor.[34] The balance of skilled and unskilled workers in the workforce has flipped from 20 percent skilled and 60 percent unskilled in 1950, to more than 60 percent skilled and less than 20 percent unskilled in 1997.[35] Much of the workforce remains unprepared for these skilled jobs. One result is that employers who need high-tech workers – and the majority of these employers are in non-IT fields – are seeking to increase the

31   US Department of Commerce, US Department of Education, US Department of Labor (1999: iii).
32   Stern (2001).
33   Rogers (1995: 125).
34   Holmes (1996: A10).
35   US Department of Commerce, US Department of Education, US Department of Labor, National Institute for Literacy and Small Business Administration, 1999, p.1.

number of skilled foreign workers allowed to work in the US. Raising the H-1B visa ceiling will likely increase productivity, but these gains are unlikely to trickle down to the least skilled.

Wilson makes the important connection between the movement from a manufacturing to an information economy and the increase in concentrated poverty in US inner cities.[36] As the economy has shifted in terms of what is produced, there has been a concomitant shift in where production occurs. Much of the remaining activity has moved out of cities to suburban and rural areas and to less developed countries, where production costs are cheaper. And, at the same time, many jobs have moved away from central cities. New technologies have made it easier for corporations to move many of their operations to the suburbs, resulting in a decrease in jobs, particularly low-skilled "back-office" jobs, in central cities, where poverty is most entrenched. With fewer manufacturing jobs remaining, low-income people are left to work in the second tier of the service sector. Unlike manufacturing jobs, these low-level service sector jobs tend to be nonunion, low-paid, and unstable. They are often part-time or temporary, and seldom come with benefits.

These economic changes have exacerbated the problem of persistent poverty and made the technology gap a more pressing issue. Addressing the digital divide is essential to ensuring that the entire range of workers can benefit from the opportunities the new economy provides. Chapter 6 takes up this issue in greater detail.

Sociopolitical rationale

The digital divide has implications that extend beyond the labor market. The sociopolitical argument for why the gap in access should be closed is that information is a public good to which everyone in society should have access.[37] IT is increasingly a gatekeeper to a whole range of information and resources that "serves to facilitate democratic decision-making, assists citizen participation in government, and contributes to the search for roughly egalitarian measures in the economy at large."[38]

Governments are increasingly going "online," creating more opportunities for citizens to participate in political and civic arenas and to obtain government information and services. No candidate is without a website used for the dissemination of information, and some cities

36   Wilson (1987, 1996).
37   Servon and Horrigan (1997).
38   Schiller (1996: 35).

and states have already experimented with electronic voting and with vetting public issues on the Internet. Unequal access precludes many low-income residents from civic engagement of this kind. For those who lack the technology or the skills to use it, the government presence online may create a wider gap than that which already exists.[39] And a widening gap between the "information rich" and the "information poor" puts our democratic institutions at risk.[40]

IT is also an important tool to strengthen social networks and participation in low-income communities. For example, the Welfare Law Center, founded in 1965, initiated its Low Income Networking and Communication (LINC) project in 1998 to use IT as a vehicle to bring low-income groups into the public debate over welfare policies. LINC has built a communications infrastructure to enable information sharing and collaboration among welfare reform advocates and in addition has created a technical assistance strategy to help low-income groups mount their own organizing efforts.

Further, IT provides the opportunity to bring together groups of users that share common interests but not necessarily physical proximity.[41] Online alliance building through the creation of "virtual communities" is particularly important given the increasing social and cultural heterogeneity among the poor, and thus, the difficulty for community activists to build support for their efforts by relying on spatially proximate constituencies.[42] Denied access to and appropriate skills for IT, low-income groups lack potentially powerful community-building tools and new means of interacting within and outside of their geographic communities. The technology gap reinforces existing patterns of social exclusion.

Technology can further act as a powerful tool to augment the work and extend the reach of community-building organizations (CBOs), most of which have not benefited from the IT revolution. Some have argued that the infiltration of IT into our society, in the form of teleworking, computer games, and Internet chat rooms, actually has the potential to increase social isolation. William Mitchell argues that "At the extreme, electronic management of face-to-face meetings can render some members of society literally invisible to others."[43]

39 Servon and Horrigan (1997: 65).
40 Doctor (1994: 10).
41 Anderson and Melchior (1995); Sanyal (2000).
42 Sanyal (2000).
43 Mitchell (1999b: 95).

Technology has certainly enabled a greater degree of selectivity over who we come into contact with and under what circumstances. But the belief that Internet use decreases social interaction has not been substantiated.[44] And technology also works very powerfully when it is used in a social way. High-tech corporations clearly understand this attribute of the tools they produce. For this reason, firms such as Netscape are housed in campus-like settings that contain fitness centers, restaurants, florist shops, and dry cleaners. The communal corporate environment enables learning, growth, creativity – and work – to occur around the clock.

Community technology centers (CTCs) and telecenters (a term that is used in other countries) have adopted this strategy of collective learning by creating communal spaces in which neighborhood residents can learn about and use IT. People often go to CTCs initially in order to obtain access. They continue to use the centers even after they own their own computers because of what they continue to learn there, and because of the people they have met.[45] Community technology centers are a new form of community institution.[46] Although some argue that ours is an age of declining social capital and the abandonment of many community institutions,[47] it is important to take note of burgeoning manifestations that arise out of the current economic and social reality; CTCs are thriving as places in which people gather, exchange ideas, and build relationships.

Explaining the Urban US Focus

Why focus this study of the digital divide on urban areas within the US? Can the lessons learned from this analysis be applied to other places? The digital divide most certainly affects rural areas as well as urban ones, as the following chapter will show. This book focuses on urban areas for the following reasons. First, over the past thirty years, persistent poverty has become an increasingly urban phenomenon. Second, the work of the community technology movement has been concentrated in urban areas.[48] Although rural issues and problems

---

44   Castells (2001).
45   Chow et al. (1998).
46   Gordo (2000).
47   Putnam (2000).
48   Important exceptions of early efforts, such as Big Sky Telegraph in Montana, exist.

differ from urban ones, many of the lessons and recommendations discussed in this book will be useful in rural areas as well.

The digital divide is also clearly a global issue, affecting both northern and southern countries. Economic globalization has caused every place to feel the effects of restructuring. High-tech manufacturing has been the fastest-growing area of world trade and now accounts for one-fifth of the total.[49] Technology is important not only to a nation's economic health but also to human development. A recent World Bank study shows that technical progress accounted for between 40 and 50 percent of mortality reductions between 1960 and 1990, making technology a more important source of gains than higher incomes or higher education.[50] The 2001 Human Development Report from the United Nations Development Programme report cites benefits for human development from technology in the areas of political participation, greater transparency in planning and transactions, increasing incomes, health, and agriculture.[51]

Different countries are dealing with new technologies in different ways. Existing economic arrangements, political systems, infrastructural conditions, and cultural issues will to some extent determine how each country confronts the technology gap issue. In the US, CTCs initiated at the grassroots level have emerged as the new institutions to address this issue; libraries and schools also play major roles. In Peru, informal economy businesses called cabinas públicas make a profit providing Internet services to the poor living in the shanty towns on the outskirts of Lima. The city of Parthenay, France has set up seven centers called espaces numérisés. UNESCO and the ITU have backed rural multipurpose community telecentres projects in Mozambique, Mali, Suriname, Honduras, Uganda, and South Africa.[52] Finland has made a tremendous commitment to ensuring equal access. And France has just announced a plan that will help to ensure that all citizens will have inexpensive Internet access within five years. The US is certainly not the only place to look for models. But despite the limits of and problems with US policy, the US has begun to deal with key aspects of the digital divide before many other countries have. In addition, the community technology movement is more advanced in the US than in many other places, and the experiences of this movement need to be lifted up and shared. A few cities, like Seattle, have

49 United Nations Development Programme (2001).
50 United Nations Development Programme (2001).
51 United Nations Development Programme (2001).
52 Cisler (1998).

traveled a long way up the learning curve and have begun to institutionalize their commitment to creating a technology literate citizenry.

All countries will face this issue soon enough. Recent research uses
an "Information Society Index" (ISI) which ranks nations based on
several criteria and weights per capita penetration rates heavily.[53] The
theory behind the ISI ratings is that information and communications
technology is available and accessible to all segments of the population.
For these reasons, it is worthwhile to take a close look at the community
and policy responses to these problems in the US, and to consider them
as we think about how to confront the global technology gap.

Bridging the digital divide, even in the comprehensive way that this
book recommends, will not get at the roots of the larger problem.
There is no technological fix for the problems of inequality and
persistent poverty. Providing low-income and low-asset groups with
computers and Internet access will not solve these problems nor will
it magically level the social and spatial inequalities that currently
characterize our regions.

Why then place so much emphasis on this issue and on community
technology centers? Given that resources to solve these problems are
not unlimited, is it not better to use what we have to purchase more
direct relief from poverty? Framing the issue this way, as a choice
between immediate needs and potentially productive assets, is harm-
ful. Doing so sets up a false dichotomy that implies that we must
make a choice. Persistent poverty is a problem of lack of access to
a range critical resources. Solving the problem of persistent poverty
and inequality, then, requires that we satisfy both types of needs –
immediate and long term.

Programs that confront the technology gap provide the kind of
resources that have historically been missing from poverty policy.
With the exception of a very few, small-scale and inconsistently supported programs such as microenterprise development, individual
development accounts, and higher education programs, poverty policy in the US has concentrated on what I call "first-order resources".
First-order resources are those that could be thought of at the base of
Maslow's hierarchy of needs. The bottom two tiers of Maslow's hierarchy consist of physiological needs and safety needs. Poverty policy
has focused on these, and some would argue that it has not done a
great job at that. These resources consist of things like food, shelter,

---

53   Bruno, 2001. Sweden ranks first; the US fourth.

and clothing that enable people to survive from one day to the next. These first-order resources do not include the tools that the persistent poor need to exit poverty, to shift from a survival mentality to a mindset that enables making long-range plans.

Perhaps this recognition should not be surprising, given that poverty policy in the US has not historically emphasized moving people out of poverty. In the early days, it functioned to take care of groups of people, such as widows, who presumably could not take care of themselves.[54] The War on Poverty and Great Society programs successfully lifted some groups, such as seniors, out of poverty. The thrust of the Aid for Families with Dependent Children (AFDC) program, however, was to provide people with enough to get by, but too little to escape their survival mode. Benefits did not increase at the same rate as inflation, and few AFDC families could make ends meet on welfare alone.[55] Since welfare reform legislation was passed in 1996, poverty policy has been conceived of as temporary assistance to help people get through difficult times. The focus of this new era of poverty policy, the core of which is Temporary Assistance for Needy Families (TANF), is to get people off of welfare and into work. For most, that means moving from dependence on inadequate benefits to working poverty. Neither low-wage work nor public assistance is sufficient to support the vast majority of households comprising single mothers with children.[56] TANF imposes time limits that do not take into account the realities of people's live, the vicissitudes of the economy, the impossibility of providing for a family on minimum wage, or the time it takes to require the tools and support needed to move into the workforce. The only bright spot in welfare reform is that it does allow states to experiment with new ways of preparing people for work. Some states have approached welfare reform by providing public assistance with the more comprehensive kinds of support that are needed to move off of welfare in a stable way.

Moving large numbers of people out of poverty will require policy that couples provision of an expanded set of first-order resources with a set of second-order resources geared toward moving people out of poverty, not only off public assistance. Second-order resources have to do with people's ability to accumulate assets, broadly defined, that help them to exit poverty and remain out of poverty. These resources

54 Skocpol (1995).
55 Edin and Lein (1997).
56 Edin and Lein (1997).

Table 1.2 First- and second-order resources

First-order resources	Second-order resources
Food	Post-secondary education
Clothing	Economic literacy
Shelter	Information technology
Housing	Ability to accumulate assets
Primary and secondary education	Soft skills
Healthcare	
Childcare	

include economic literacy, post-secondary education, opportunities to save, and the ability to access and use information technology. Poverty policy in the US has done a poor job of providing some first-order resources – such as quality healthcare, childcare, and primary and secondary education – that are necessary for day-to-day existence. And it has never included second-order resources that truly light the way out. Table 1.2 illustrates first- and second-order resources.

Some have argued that it is frivolous to provide the poor with access to IT before these other needs are met. During a series of remarks in the summer of 2000, Bill Gates told audiences that he had decided to focus the work of his foundation more on children's healthcare issues than on the digital divide, citing the former as a more pressing need. I am by no means arguing that poor children should have computers before receiving inoculations against disease. At the same time, ignoring the "second-order" resources means that we will forever be ensuring that poor people have what they need to survive, but will never be able to get ahead. Resources such as IT can function as ladders with which people can exit poverty.[57]

Second-order resources are important because they create opportunities and enable behavior that allows people to climb the ladder out of poverty. They allow for the creation of networks, nest eggs, and safety nets that buffer people and families during the difficult times that all families encounter.[58] Unless poverty policy incorporates second-order resources, it treats the symptoms of the problem without ever getting at its causes.

---

57 This concept of the "ladder out" derives from Friedman (1988).
58 Oliver and Shapiro (1997: 7).

This book takes a close look at one rung of the ladder out – information technology. IT is a critical resource because it enables full participation in our current society. The skills necessary to work, prosper, and participate in current society are intrinsically bound up with the ability to use information technology tools.

The research presented in this book shows that, although gaps in access to IT have begun to close and will likely continue to do so, deeper and more firmly entrenched gaps remain in terms of what kind of access, training, and content are available for specific groups. Using a computer at school or at work is insufficient. We need to do more to close the gap between those who are using IT tools in sophisticated ways and those who have access but little or no instruction.

On an individual and community-level basis, CTCs are functioning as ladders out of poverty. These locally rooted social experiments employ IT in ways that connect disenfranchised people and communities to the opportunities offered by the information society. In innumerable places, they have demonstrated an ability to operate as effective hooks, drawing people in with technology and then teaching them new ways to think and participate.

The examples of innovative community-based programs discussed throughout this book demonstrate that IT is a tool, not an end in itself. Policy interventions must therefore be geared toward exploiting the potential of IT as a tool to break down historic divides that fall out along the lines of race, gender, and socioeconomic status. If this goal, rather than pure access, drives policy, then social change is possible.

The point is not that technology is the answer, but that it is a critical resource – one of many. Without it, the persistent poor will have one more obstacle to overcome in order to compete for jobs and for policy that reflects their needs and desires. IT tools enable greater civic participation, provide the key to better-paying jobs, and create the conditions for more engaging communication and the formation of networks.

The problems of poverty and inequality are complex, and the forces that combine to create them multiple. Access to IT must be supported as part of a much larger effort to address these historic and deeply entrenched problems. In addition, any effort to use IT as an intervention into these problems, however, must derive from a deep understanding of the complex nature of US poverty and of the specific communities in which the intervention is being undertaken. If low-income populations are to benefit at all from the emergent information revolution they must first participate in it.[59] Ensuring universal access, and coupling it with appropriate training and relevant content, is the first step toward enabling all people to benefit from the information society. Technology is a tool. It has the potential to provide people with skills and information that they can use to move beyond a focus on day-to-day survival. But it is the means, not the end. Without creative and purposive application, it accomplishes little.

Organization of the Book

The book begins with a close look at the digital divide. Having established the reasons for intervention in this chapter, chapter 2 takes a step back to examine closely the parameters of the technology gap. This chapter demonstrates that the digital divide is a dynamic problem and that there is not one divide, but many. Chapter 3 lays out the history of the community technology movement, introducing a typology of community technology programs and exploring the relationship between CTCs and traditional CBOs, and discussing the lessons learned and challenges faced by CTCs. Chapter 4 establishes the policy context by examining public sector efforts to mitigate the digital divide on the federal, state, and local levels. This chapter shows that current policy remains limited, fragmented, and unstable.

Chapters 5 through 8 move to the level of specific communities and particular areas in which community technology has begun to function as a ladder out of poverty. Chapter 5 focuses on CTCs that target youth and explores how organizations that serve low-income youth have exposed children to the opportunities available through IT – providing them with the future orientation to go to college and the skills to obtain good jobs. Chapter 6 examines the IT labor shortage and investigates how community-based IT training programs are moving disadvantaged workers from unemployment or working poverty to earning family wages with less than two years of training. Chapter 7 shows how information technology can be employed to strengthen and extend the existing community development infrastructure, helping resource-thin organizations do a better job of leveraging funding dollars and reaching greater numbers of constituents. Chapter 8 synthesizes key analytical lessons from the preceding chapters and employs Seattle as a case study of the city that has come

59 Sanyal and Schön (1999).

closest to comprehensively addressing the technology gap. Chapter 9 concludes the book with a broader argument about the role IT can play in alleviating persistent poverty.

This book moves beyond documentation of the technology gap to a broader and more fine-grained understanding of the problem and of potential solutions. It illustrates a range of efforts emerging form the federal, state, local, corporate, philanthropic, and private nonprofit arenas that show some promise in terms of dealing with this problem. It is my hope that shining a light on these relatively small initiatives will help to generate momentum and support for the critical task of bridging the digital divide.

2

The Dimensions of the Digital Divide

Like many issues, the digital divide existed long before the problem was named and studied. And, as chapter 3 will show, the community technology movement was initiated more than a decade before public awareness of the digital divide issue had become widespread. It seems that the term "digital divide" was first used in popular media. Jonathan Webber and Amy Harmon claim to have coined the term in 1995, while they were journalists at the *Los Angeles Times*, to describe the social division between those who were using technology and those who were not.[1] Illustrating the early, gendered aspect of the problem, their article used the term to describe "the split between a husband who spent a great deal of time online and the wife who felt alienated from him because of his obsession with computers."[2] The *Falling Through the Net* reports issued by the Department of Commerce redefined and popularized the term. And in May of 1996 the White House began to use the term as the Clinton administration began to formulate an agenda to confront this problem. In a ceremony honoring the Blue Ribbon schools, then Vice-President Al Gore said:

> We've been working with them, and we've tried, at the president's direction, to make certain that we don't have a gap between information haves and information have-nots. As part of our Empowerment Zone Initiative, we launched this Cyber-Ed truck, a Bookmobile for the digital age. It's rolling into communities, connecting schools in our poorest neighborhoods and paving over the digital divide.[3]

1 Larry Irving, quoted at www.rtpnet.org
2 Harmon (1996).
3 Andy Carvin quoted at www.rtpnet.org

Policy makers, researchers, and the media now commonly use this term to describe the gap between those who have access to computers and the Internet and those who do not. The training and content dimensions of the problem discussed in chapter 1 have not yet made it into the popular definition.

Studying the Problem

Research on the digital divide problem has been conducted since the mid 1990s. The US Department of Commerce National Telecommunications and Information Administration (NTIA) studies were among the earliest and have received wide exposure. As the notion of a digital divide has gained national attention, universities, think-tanks and other public agencies have also conducted studies to document the technology gap. Unfortunately, the lion's share of existing research focuses on access; little work explores the training and content dimensions of the digital divide.[4] This chapter lays out the nature and scope of the digital divide relying on data and findings from the following studies.[5]

Falling Through the Net series

In 1995, the US Department of Commerce, through the NTIA, issued the first of four reports titled "Falling Through the Net." Larry Irving, then Assistant Secretary for Communications and Information, was central to this work and became a tireless spokesperson for the Clinton administration's digital divide agenda. The NTIA research grew out of the recognition that existing data[6] on "universal service"

4   A few significant exceptions exist. For example, Lazarus and Mora (2000) conducted important research about content, and other more specific studies look at training in the context of education or workforce development. These studies will be reviewed in later chapters.
5   Other institutions and organizations, such as the Morino Institute, the Education Development Center, and the Benton Foundation, have shaped discussions on this issue in important ways through their listservs, websites, and reports. Although this work does not fit here, it warrants recognition.
6   When the NTIA began its work, data on telephone penetration came from two primary sources: the Current Population Survey (CPS), conducted by the US Bureau of the Census three times each year, includes questions on telephone subscription; and the Federal Communications Commission's (FCC's) Industry

– the primary goal of US telecommunications policy[7] – was lacking in two ways. First, existing data did not enable researchers to examine how patterns of telephone usage varied geographically. And second, it was becoming clear that definitions of universal service needed to be expanded from telephone service to include Internet connectivity. The first NTIA report stated: "While a standard telephone line can be an individual's pathway to the riches of the Information Age, a personal computer and modem are rapidly becoming keys to the vault."[8]

The NTIA therefore contracted with the Census Bureau in 1994 to include questions on computer and modem ownership in the Current Population Survey (CPS) and to cross-tabulate the information gathered according to several specific variables, such as income, race, age, and geographic category (rural, urban, suburban). Since the first report in 1995, NTIA has released three additional reports (NTIA 1998, 1999, 2000). Later reports have expanded on the initial set of variables analyzed in the first study. For example, the most recent report is the first to collect data on access to high-speed Internet services. The *Falling Through the Net* reports represent the most significant effort to document and describe the various aspects of the digital divide to date.

Pew Internet & American Life Project

The Pew Internet & American Life Project explores the impact of the Internet on children, families, communities, the workplace, schools, healthcare, and civic/political life. The Pew project aims to be an authoritative source for timely information on the Internet's growth and societal impact. Specific areas of research include: gender differences in use of IT; online crime; e-government; and the role of IT in urban development strategies. Those reports that are relevant to this book are reviewed here.[9]

Analysis Division uses the CPS data to produce regular reports providing a demographic profile of telephone subscribership in the US.
7   Chapter 4 takes up the issue of, and debates surrounding, universal service in a broader way.
8   US Department of Commerce (1995: 2).
9   http://www.pewinternet.org/. John Horrigan also provided as yet unpublished November 2001 data. Note that Pew data is collected at the individual, rather than the household, level.

Gartner Institute

The Gartner Institute focuses on market research regarding technology for the public and private sectors. Gartner conducts extensive annual surveys of more than 100,000 households to understand how people use and feel about a range of interactive technologies. The institute's digital divide research focuses on moving beyond demographic trends regarding connectivity in order to gain a better understanding of the socioeconomic divisions in the US and how these divisions both affect and can be affected by access to technology.[10]

Tomas Rivera Policy Institute (TRPI)

A Latino think-tank, TRPI conducts and disseminates research aimed at policy makers in order to make them aware of the implications of specific policies and programs on Latino communities. TRPI's information and communication technology (ICT) research examines the impact of telecommunications tools on the economic, social, political, and educational life of Latino communities throughout the United States.[11]

Access and Connectivity in the United States

Telephone penetration

The early *Falling Through The Net* reports examine telephone penetration rates – the traditional measure of universal access – in addition to computers and Internet access. In 1995 the nationwide telephone penetration rate was 93.8 percent, but the poorest households (defined as those with incomes less than $10,000) in central cities had the lowest telephone penetration (78.9 percent), followed by rural households (81.6 percent), and then urban households (81.7 percent). By 1998, the nationwide telephone penetration rate remained unchanged, and by the time the third *Falling Through the Net* report was released there was a slight increase in telephone penetration (94.1 percent).

10 http://www.gartner.com/
11 http://www.trpi.org/

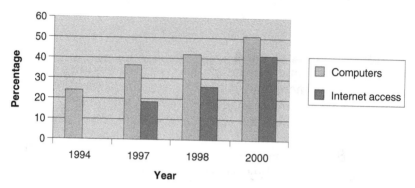

Figure 2.1   Percent of US households with computer and Internet access
Source: US Department of Commerce (2000a)

Computers and the Internet

Although telephone penetration rates have remained relatively stable over the last five years, that same period witnessed dramatic gains in penetration rates for computers and Internet access in US households. In 1995, 24.1 percent of US households had a computer. By 1998, PC ownership increased 51.9 percent (to 36.6 percent), while 18.6 percent of households had Internet access. One year later, 42.1 percent of households owned computers, and 26.2 percent had Internet access. By 2000, PC ownership rose to 51 percent, with 41.5 percent of households having Internet access.[12] (See figure 2.1) The most recent data on overall Internet usage rates comes from the Pew Internet & American Life Project and looks at individuals rather than households. As of November 2001, 57.6 percent of individuals surveyed by Pew had Internet access.

Given these dramatic improvements in penetration rates, why has so much attention been paid to the digital divide? Despite rapid increases in national computer ownership and Internet access rates, a divide persists between the information rich (Whites, Asians/Pacific Islanders, those with higher incomes, those more educated, and dual-parent households) and the information poor (including those who are younger, those with lower incomes and education levels, certain minorities, and those in rural areas or central cities).[13] In some cases, the gap between groups is widening. The following discussion takes a closer look at the many dimensions of the digital divide.

12   US Department of Commerce (2000a).
13   US Department of Commerce (1999a).

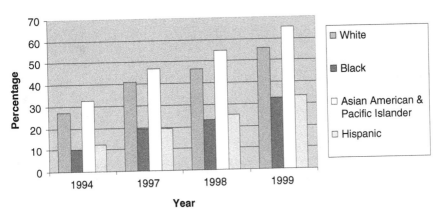

Figure 2.2   Percent of US households with computers by race
Source: US Department of Commerce (2000a)

Race

The release of the first *Falling Through the Net* report showed deep cleavages along racial lines in terms of access to technology (see figure 2.2.). In 1995, Native American households in rural areas had the lowest telephone penetration rates (75.5 percent), while rural Blacks had the lowest computer rates (6.4 percent) followed by central city Blacks (10.4 percent), central city Hispanics (10.5 percent), and urban Blacks (11.8 percent).[14] By the time the second *Falling Through the Net* report was released in 1998, Blacks and Hispanics lagged even further behind Whites in their levels of PC ownership and online access. Although PC ownership for all racial groups increased during the 1995–9 period, penetration rates increased far more slowly for Blacks and Hispanics. For example, in 1998 the difference in PC ownership levels between White

14   The Census Bureau defines "urban" areas as comprised of all territory, population, and housing units of 2,500 or more persons. "Rural" areas constitute territory, population and housing units not classified as urban. This refers to "places of less than 2,500" persons and what the Census Bureau refers to as "not in places" (areas not part of or outside of designated census areas). The NTIA report also uses the term "central city" to define areas or parts of a Metropolitan Statistical Area (MSA) or Primary Metropolitan Statistical Area (PMSA) that meet the standard of the "largest place" or places (based on population and other criteria) within that MSA or PMSA. It should be noted that there is no relation between data for central city and data for urban versus rural. US Department of Commerce (1995).

and Black households was 21.5 percentage points, a wider gap than the 16.8 percentage point gap documented in 1994. The third *Falling Through the Net* report illustrated the same trend: Blacks and Latinos experienced increased connectivity rates, but were not keeping pace with their White and Asian/Pacific Islander counterparts.[15] According to the report, "groups that were already connected . . . are now far more connected, while those with lower rates have increased less quickly."[16]

By the time of the release of the fourth *Falling Through the Net* report, minorities had made significant gains in connectivity, but gaps based on race remained. The gap between Internet access rates for Black households (23.5 percent penetration rate) and the national average (41.5 percent penetration rate) was 18 percentage points, 3 percentage points wider than it had been in December 1998. The divide between Hispanic households (23.6 percent penetration rate) and the national average was nearly the same: 18 percentage points in August 2000, 4 percentage points greater than in December 1998. Importantly, differences in income and education (which will be discussed later in this chapter) account for only about one-half of these divides.[17] The divide in computer ownership rates has stabilized at about 18 percentage points between black households and the national average, and 17 percentage points between Hispanic households and the national average.[18]

Recognizing the importance of better understanding and documenting of the racial component of the digital divide, more specific research aimed at examining racial issues has been initiated. A recent report from the Pew Internet & American Life Project titled *African-Americans and the Internet*, focuses on the ways in which African-Americans use the Internet and how patterns of usage differ between Blacks and Whites.[19] This research is especially important because it helps move the dialogue beyond issues of access.

Pew has found that by November 2001, 48.6 percent of Blacks had access to the Internet, compared to 59.1 percent of Whites and 51.7 percent of Hispanics.[20] These numbers closely mirror the NTIA

---

15   US Department of Commerce (1999a).
16   US Department of Commerce (1999a: 6).
17   US Department of Commerce (2000).
18   US Department of Commerce (2000a).
19   Spooner and Rainie (2000).
20   Rainie and Packel (2001); unpublished Pew data.

Table 2.1   What people do online (Blacks versus Whites)

Activity	Blacks (%)	Whites (%)
Browse just for fun	73	61
Do school research	65	54
Use video/audio clip	60	47
Listen to music	54	32
Look for job information	51	37
Send an instant message	51	44
Play online game	48	33
Participate in chat online	38	23
Look for a place to live	35	27
Seek religious information	33	20
Download music	29	21

Source: Spooner and Rainie (2000).

statistics discussed above. Although the gap between African-Americans and Whites is closing, the report found that Blacks still do not have the same level and kind of access to the Internet as Whites. For example, Blacks with access to the Internet do not go online as often on a typical day as Whites (36 percent of African-Americans with Internet access go online on a typical day, compared to 56 percent of Whites). Additionally, 27 percent of Blacks with Internet access send or receive email on a typical day, compared to 49 percent of online Whites.[21] These differences likely reflect where different groups go online.

Interestingly, the report found that African-Americans are proportionally more likely than online Whites to have used the Internet for information about an important life issue (e.g., employment, housing). Table 2.1 illustrates the differences in online activities between Blacks and Whites.[22] For those African-Americans who are online, the Internet may be providing important information – about jobs and housing, for example – that they are not getting in their communities or through social networks. Additionally, online Blacks use the Internet for entertainment purposes to a much greater degree than their White counterparts.

Other research has focused on Latinos and the Internet. Since the release of the first NTIA report, the Tomas Rivera Policy Institute has conducted research aimed at understanding why Latinos continue to

21 Spooner and Rainie (2000).
22 Spooner and Rainie (2000).

lag non-Latinos in Internet penetration rates, particularly given that there is a growing Latino middle class. In a May 2000 study, the Institute looked at Latinos' language preferences, participation in e-commerce, and activities while connected to the Internet. The report was based on a survey of 1,500 persons over the age of 18 that self-identified as Latino or Hispanic in five large metropolitan areas: Los Angeles, New York, Miami, Chicago, and Houston. The study found that the number one online activity for Latinos is research/information gathering, followed by email, reading news, business/work related activities, and chatting online. Interestingly, over half of all respondents indicated that they access websites that are specifically dedicated to Latino/Latino-American issues.[23] This finding points to the importance of culturally and ethnically relevant content to fulfilling the burgeoning technology interest in diverse communities. Online Latinos are also active participants in online shopping with 43 percent having made e-commerce purchases at the time of the survey.

The study also sampled non-Internet using Latinos to discern their reasons for not using the Internet and what factors might help them gain access. The study found reasons beyond income that help explain lower Internet penetration rates for Latinos. These reasons include the challenge of finding computer classes taught in Spanish, the fact that 80 percent of websites are in English, and the lack of Latino-oriented content. Culture and language are indeed issues for this population.[24]

Another ethnic group that lags in access to information technologies is Native Americans. Native American reservations have historically lacked access to telecommunications services enjoyed by other Americans. For example, there is a large gap between telephone penetration rates on Indian reservations relative to the rest of the United States. According to NTIA, 16 percent of Native American households did not have telephones, compared to 6 percent of non-Native American households.[25] Not surprisingly, Native Americans also trail in computer and Internet access. In 1999, NTIA reported that 19 percent of Native Americans had Internet access compared to 26 percent for the general population.[26] The 2000 NTIA report did not

23 Baretto et al. (2000).
24 Baretto et al. (2000).
25 US Department of Commerce (1999a).
26 US Department of Commerce (1999a).

include separate data on the Native American population because the sample size from that group was too small for credible results.[27] The gap in access to information technologies mirrors other infrastructure gaps that Native Americans have historically faced (for example, to healthcare, public services, roads, etc). Without intervention, the growing overall reliance on information technologies will inevitably exacerbate the persistent poverty and isolation that Native American communities currently face. Greater research and targeted policy and programmatic responses are needed to ensure that Native Americans reap the benefits of information technologies.

Education

The NTIA studies looked at the relationship between access to telecommunications and years of education. For the most part, the fewer the number of years of education, the lower the telephone, computer, and Internet penetration. Over time, connectivity rates across different levels of educational attainment have soared for all educational levels.[28] Yet a significant gap continues to persist. As at November 2001, 83.4 percent of college graduates had Internet access. For those with less than a high school education, only 25.9 percent of individuals had Internet access.[29] Given that technology skills are increasingly important to finding employment in the information age, this lack of access to technology reinforces and excaberates negative outcomes in the labor market for those with limited education.

Income

Much social policy research has documented the interplay between educational attainment and income levels. Not surprisingly, income level, like education, is related to computer and Internet access, with a significant gap persisting between higher and lower income groups (see figure 2.3). As of August 2000, only 19 percent of households with incomes less than $15,000 had a computer, while 86.3 percent of households with an income over $75,000 had a computer.[30] A recent report

27 US Department of Commerce (2000a).
28 US Department of Commerce (2000a).
29 Unpublished data supplied by the Pew Internet and American Life Project.
30 US Department of Commerce (2000a).

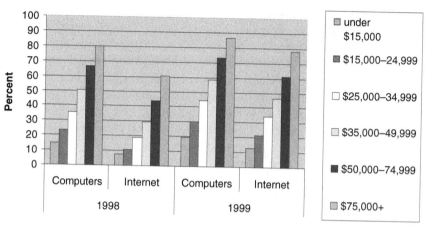

Figure 2.3 Percent of US households with computer and Internet access by income
Source: US Department of Commerce (2000a)

by the Gartner Group found that in 1998 access rates among those in the highest income brackets (persons in households with $75,000 and above in annual income) were more than four times as likely to have Internet access.[31] Pew Internet & American Life Project data from November 2001 show that 34 percent of individuals with incomes under $20,000 have access to the Internet, whereas 85 percent of individuals with incomes over $75,000 have access to the Internet.

Although a technology gap based on income exists, households with lower incomes have registered increases in Internet access at a much faster clip than the national average.[32] The increase in access among low-income households is likely connected to computer and Internet prices dropping. Although still wide, this gap has narrowed in the past two years, with the highest income groups now having online usage levels about two and a half times that of the lowest income group.[33]

Geography

Examining the issue regionally, in 1995 the lowest telephone and computer penetration was in the northeast central cities (89.5 percent,

31   Gartner (2000).
32   US Department of Commerce (2000a).
33   Smolenski et al. (2000).

16.4 percent, respectively), and in central cities (91.2 percent, 22.9 percent) and rural (91.3 percent, 18.6 percent) areas in the south. Modem penetration was lowest in rural areas of the west, midwest, and south.[34] In recent years gaps between rural areas and other areas have also diminished: 38.9 percent of rural households had Internet access as of August 2000, approaching the national Internet penetration rate of 41.5 percent.[35] The 2000 report shows that computer penetration has stabilized across geography when the study controls for income.

Interestingly, interplay between geography and income exists in terms of Internet connectivity. Looking specifically at low-income households – those with an income in the range of $10,000–14,999 – rural households ranked lowest in terms of Internet connectivity (12.5 percent), followed by urban areas (14.8 percent), and then central city residents (15.4 percent).[36] The same pattern holds true for high-speed Internet access: 12.2 percent of central city households had high speed access in August 2000, as against 11.8 percent of urban households and only 7.3 percent of rural households.

Household structure

Another important factor that correlates with computer and Internet access is household structure. Households with two parents and children have much higher rates of computer and Internet access than any other family type. Two-parent households with at least one child under age 18 are nearly twice as likely to have Internet access as single-parent households with at least one child under age 18 (60.6 percent for dual-parent, 35.7 percent for male-headed, and 30 percent for female-headed).[37] Many parents believe that their children need a computer in order to perform well at school. Clearly, two-parent families are more likely to have the resources necessary to purchase and maintain a computer. Single-parent households headed by a male are more likely to have computers than those headed by a female, which is probably related to the fact that men tend to have higher incomes and greater assets than women. It also documents that two-parent families are much more likely to own computers than are other family types.

34   US Department of Commerce (1995).
35   US Department of Commerce (2000a).
36   US Department of Commerce (2000a).
37   US Department of Commerce (2000a).

A relationship also exists between household type and geography. Female-headed households in central cities are much less likely to own computers (34.9 percent) than those in rural (41.6 percent) or urban (43.2 percent) areas. There is also variance by income. For example, dual parent households in high income brackets (greater than $75,000) have a 93.1 percent penetration rate for computer owner-ship, while the overall national penetration rate for computers is 51 percent.[38]

Age

According to the 2000 NTIA report there has been strong growth in computer and Internet penetration rates for all age categories except young children (age three to eight). Individuals 50 years of age and older experienced the highest rates of growth in Internet usage of all age groups, increasing 53 percent between December 1998 and August 2000.[39]

Although rates have improved, seniors continue to be the least likely group in the US to have Internet access. In 2000, the NTIA found that Americans aged 55 and older living in central cities had the lowest rates of Internet access (22.2 percent) followed by older Americans in rural areas (24.6 percent) and then those living in urban areas (26.5 percent).[40] Looking specifically at senior citizens aged 65 and older, Pew found that seniors are coming online at faster rates than other age groups; 18 percent of seniors with Internet access have come online in the past six months.[41] The same study found that fully 81 percent of people who say they definitely will not go online are over 50. Nearly 56 percent of those over age 65 say they will definitely not go online, compared to just 6 percent who say they definitely plan to go online. As of November 2001, Pew found that 77.4 percent of individuals aged 18–29, 67 percent of individuals aged 30–49, 51 percent of individuals 50–64, and 17 percent of individuals 65 and older had access to the Internet. Older Americans who have become

---

38   US Department of Commerce (2000a). The 2000 study does not discuss the interaction between race and household type, but earlier studies showed that these disparities persist when controlling for race.
39   US Department of Commerce (2000a).
40   US Department of Commerce (2000a).
41   Fox (2001).

connected have done so primarily for personal reasons, including staying in touch with children and grandchildren living is far-flung places and finding the Internet to be a valuable resource for obtaining information. The personal motivation of seniors differentiates them from other wired Americans who are often motivated by school or work.

Gender

As recently as the mid 1990s, the population that had access to the Internet was 84.5 percent male and only 15.5 percent female. In December 1998, 34.2 percent of men and 31.4 percent of women were using the Internet. By November 2001, women outnumbered men with access to the Internet; Pew found that 41 percent of men and 42 percent of women had Internet access. The gender gap is now completely closed, at least in terms of access. However, we know less about how men and women use IT tools differently and what impacts this may have on social connections, employment, and a range of other issues.

A Pew report, titled *Tracking Online Life: How Women Use the Internet to Cultivate Relationships with Family and Friends*[42], begins to answer this question of gender variance in IT use patterns. The study found that women are more likely to seek health information, get religious information, research new jobs, and play games online. Men are more likely to use the Web to get news, shop, seek financial information and do online stock trading, participate in online auctions, access government websites and search for sports news. The study also found a number of online activities that men and women engage in equally. These include chat rooms, instant messaging, browsing the web for fun, school- and job-related research, accessing popular culture, online banking, and arranging travel. Interestingly, more women stated that email exchanges improved their connections to family members than did men (60 percent and 51 percent respectively).

Although women are using technology in greater numbers than men to strengthen social relationships, women and men vary in terms of their uses of technology directed toward employment or professional development. Of the approximately 20,000 students who took the Advanced Placement (AP) computer science exam in 2000, only

42   Pew Internet & American Life Project (2000).

15 percent were female while 85 percent were male.[43] Given that careers in the information technology sector are some of the fastest growing and well paid, this gender gap in using technology for employment purposes poses a significant concern. Several organizations have focused on addressing this gender gap in usage. For example, the Institute for Women In Trades, Technology & Science (IWITTS) provides training, e-strategies, publications and technical assistance to the education system and employers to integrate women into technology and law enforcement careers. Likewise, Cisco Systems has created a Gender Equity Initiative to encourage more women to pursue careers in information technology. Chapter 5 discusses some of these gender-specific initiatives in greater detail.

Disability

We have perhaps the least amount of data on access among people with disabilities. This category of analysis was only examined in the most recent NTIA study. As of August 2000, a person with a disability was only half as likely to have access to the Internet as a person without a disability, and nearly 60 percent of people with a disability had never used a personal computer, whereas only 25 percent of people overall fall into that category.[44] Given the potential of IT tools to help the disabled live fuller, easier, and more productive lives, it is surprising and unfortunate that so little attention has been paid to this specific divide. Future research and policy must work to address this dearth of information.

The Evolution of Government Rhetoric

The NTIA reports have gotten the most visibility and the widest diffusion of all research conducted on the digital divide. These reports are important not only because they track the dynamics of the problem, but also because they document the ways in which the language used to describe the issue has changed. The tone of the reports has become progressively more urgent, moving IT from being thought of as an option to being classified as a necessary tool.

43   Cuny and Aspray (2000).
44   US Department of Commerce (2000a).

1995 report

In its 1995 report, the NTIA recommended a long-term strategy of connecting all households to the National Information Infrastructure (NII). More immediately, the drafters of the report recommended focusing on schools, libraries, and other public access centers with the goal of creating "public safety nets" to complement the longer-range goal of "hooking up all those households who want to be connected to the NII."[45]

   This first report began to raise important broader issues. It found that despite large remaining gaps in computer ownership and Internet connectivity at home, disadvantaged users are taking advantage of valuable IT benefits in disproportionately large numbers. For example, low-income users ($10,000–$14,999) in all areas (rural, central city, urban) were among the most likely users of online classes. Minority groups[46] surpassed Whites in percentage of classified ad searches, taking courses, and accessing government reports. And the highest rate of participation in taking online courses was found among those with the lowest level of education. These findings indicate that, given the opportunity, low-income households and minority groups are interested in, and can greatly benefit from, information technologies.

1998 report

The tone of the second report, *Falling Through the Net II: New Data on the Digital Divide*, published in 1998, is significantly stronger. The introduction to that report states that, "Now that a considerable portion of today's business, communication, and research takes place on the Internet, access to the computers [sic] and networks may be as important as access to traditional telephone services."[47] By this time,

45   US Department of Commerce (1995: 4).
46   This chapter uses certain terms that are not used elsewhere in the book. "Minority" is one of them. Wherever possible, specific groups (e.g. Asian, Black, Latino) are used and, if not possible, the term "people of color." "Minority" is simply too imprecise, given that some groups for example, Asians, have very high IT access rates compared to others. In addition, "minority" does not work. Several cities, such as Miami, are now majority Latino or Black. I keep the term in this chapter because it relies so heavily on the NTIA studies, which do use the term "minority"; therefore it seemed important to maintain the category labels that NTIA employs.
47   US Department of Commerce (1998: 1).

Vice-President Al Gore had taken on the NII as a pet issue and had "made it a fundamental goal to connect all Americans to the information infrastructure."[48]

1999 report

By 1999, the year *Falling Through the Net: Defining the Digital Divide* was published, NTIA had shifted from stating that access to IT "*may* be as important . . . as telephone services"[49] to making a much stronger claim:

> With the emerging digital economy becoming a major driving force of our nation's economic well-being, we *must* ensure that all Americans have the information tools and skills that are critical to their participation. Access to such tools is an important step to ensure that our economy grows strongly and that in the future no one is left behind.[50]

The tone of this report was much more imperative. In addition, whereas the first report discussed providing access "to all those households who want to be connected," this third report assumes that universal connectivity should not be elective but should rather be viewed as a national economic necessity. In fact, the third report was issued by the Commerce Department along with two others – *The Emerging Digital Economy* and *The Digital Dilemma: Building Infotech Skills at the Speed of Innovation* – which argued that closing the digital divide was a critical part of maintaining an appropriately skilled workforce.[51]

In this report, the NTIA highlighted for the first time the role played by community access centers, noting that these venues were "particularly well used by those groups who lack access at home or at work."[52] The report also documented that groups with lower rates of home and work access were also "using the Internet at higher rates to search for jobs or take courses." "Providing public access to the Internet," argued the authors, "will help these groups advance

48   US Department of Commerce (1998: 1).
49   Emphasis added.
50   US Department of Commerce (1999: 1). Emphasis added.
51   The issue of workforce development and IT is taken up in much greater detail in chapter 6.
52   US Department of Commerce (1999: 2).

economically, as well as provide them the technical skills to compete professionally in today's digital economy."[53]

2000 report

The most recent report, *Falling Through the Net: Toward Digital Inclusion*, was issued in October 2000. This report adopts a somewhat more optimistic tone, documenting that some of the gaps that appeared worrisome in 1995 have now all but disappeared. The groups that fall into the categories of "information have" and "information have-not" had changed since the NTIA began to track the problem in 1994.[54] The most recent NTIA report added three new dimensions to data collection and analysis. First, the survey included questions about household access to high-speed Internet services. Not surprisingly, the data pointed to large differences in high-speed access based on income and other variables. Clearly broadband is one of the next frontiers of the digital divide. Second, the report analyzed computer and online access by individuals, whereas the earlier reports looked only at household-level data. Collecting and analyzing individual-level data will help to illustrate differences among people within households – a finer-grained approach that will aid the creation of more appropriate policy. And third, the report examined the use of computers and the Internet by people with disabilities.

Two large points become clear from surveying existing research on the digital divide. First, there is not one digital divide but many. A range of cleavages that separate those with access from those without exists, and these cleavages have to do with race, gender, physical location, household structure, and age. The majority of the literature dealing with this problem employs the term, "*the* digital divide," falsely implying that there is one gap. On the contrary, there are specific gaps within the larger gap, and these specific gaps likely have different drivers.

Second, the digital divide is a dynamic problem, not a static one. Some of the groups that were far behind the national averages of computer ownership and Internet use in 1995 have made impressive gains,

53   US Department of Commerce (1999: 2).
54   Although the first report was published in 1995, data on which the report is based were collected in 1994.

Table 2.2 Internet users: a global enclave

	Regional population (as % of world population)	Internet users (as % of regional population)
United States	4.7	26.3
OECD (excluding the US)	14.1	6.9
Latin America and the Caribbean	6.8	0.8
South-east Asia and the Pacific East Asia	8.6	0.5
East Asia	22.2	0.4
Eastern Europe and the CIS	5.8	0.4
Arab States	4.5	0.2
Sub-Saharan Africa	9.7	0.1
South Asia	23.5	Less than 0.1
World	100.0	2.4

Source: Adapted from United Nations Development Programme (1999).

while others remain stuck in an IT black hole. This dynamism, however, may not be as important as it seems at first blush. As access rates increase and larger problems persist, it will be increasingly important to shift our focus beyond access to other, deeper issues.

A Word About the Global Divide

This book focuses on the manifestation of the digital divide in the US. However, it is important to situate the US into a larger context, given that this is an important global issue. How does the United States compare to other countries? The US is doing better than most nations in terms of access to and use of Internet and communications technologies (ICTs). As of 1998, 2.5 percent of the world's population was connected to the Internet, and approximately one-quarter of the digitally connected resided in the United States.[55] The global digital divide is in many ways a divide between developed and developing nations: 90 percent of Internet host computers reside in the highest income nations – these same nations are home to only 16 percent of the world's population.[56] Table 2.2 compares the US to other regions, illustrating percentage of Internet users as a percentage of regional population.

55 United Nations Development Programme (1999).
56 United Nations Development Programme (1999).

If we look at the way in which the digital divide plays out globally, we see that the divide falls along many of the same lines as in the United States. Some of the key factors that determine the use of information technologies on an international basis include:

- *Income* The average Internet user in South Africa has an income seven times the national average. The average Bangladeshi would have to spend more than eight years' income to buy a computer, compared with just one month's salary for the average American.
- *Cost of connection* Monthly Internet access charges are only 1.2 percent of the average monthly income in the US; such charges are 80 percent of the average monthly income in Bhutan and 278 percent of the average monthly income in Nepal.[57]
- *Education* Globally, 30 percent of Internet users have a degree from an institution of higher education.
- *Gender* Women account for 25 percent of users in Brazil, 17 percent of users in Japan and South Africa, 16 percent in Russia, 7 percent in Africa, and 4 percent in Arab states.
- *Age* Most users in China and the United Kingdom are under the age of 30.
- *Language* English is used in almost 80 percent of websites, yet less than one in ten people in the world speaks the language.[58]

Recognizing the critical role that computers and the Internet play in society and the economy, the international community has begun to address the increasing gap in access to information and communications technologies that exists across countries. In July 2000 the G8 countries adopted an information technology charter with the mission of expanding Internet access and Internet-based development around the world. Other international agencies such as the World Bank, International Telecommunications Union (ITU), and the United Nations Development Programme (UNDP) have also initiated new digital divide programs, as well as expanding the scale of existing efforts. The private sector, recognizing that this international technology gap affects productivity and products, has also become involved in this issue. For example, in its annual 2000 meeting in Davos, Switzerland, the World Economic Forum launched the Global Digital Divide Initiative and formed a task force to explore ways to engage stakeholders

57   United Nations Development Programme (2001).
58   United Nations Development Programme (1999).

from around the world in dialogue and action to bridge the global digital divide.

Although the global technology gap is large and widening, information technologies can be powerful tools in the area of human development. This book focuses on the US experience in addressing the digital divide, but it is hoped that lessons can be lifted that will help bridge the global divide. It must be recognized, however, that less developed countries are unlikely to follow the same trajectory as have developed countries. For example, those countries that have only spotty telephone lines may skip that stage and move directly to widespread use of wireless technologies.

The digital divide has changed dramatically since 1995, when researchers began to document and analyze the problem. Significant gains in computer ownership and Internet access have been made across all groups. Divides persist, however, and in some cases continue to grow. Troubling gaps remain between different racial and ethnic groups, people with and without disabilities, single and dual-parent families, the old and the young, and people with different levels of income and education. The gaps in terms of training and content are even larger. In addition, as Internet penetration increases and fails to eliminate inequality, it becomes increasingly imperative to document and study "inequality among Internet users in the extent to which they are able to reap benefits from their use of the technology."[59] The next chapter examines the work that community technology centers are doing to close the digital divide across all of its dimensions.

---

59 DiMaggio and Hargittai 2001, p. 9.

3

The Role of CTCs within the Community Technology Movement

With Marla K. Nelson

The community technology movement works to foster the positive benefits of the information revolution while combating problems associated with the digital divide.[1] This movement was initiated primarily by people who had access to technology, usually through their jobs, and who foresaw the potential negative externalities of leaving large segments of the population behind as socioeconomic systems were undergoing transformation. Like many community-based movements, community technology initiatives were developed to fill a gap unfilled by the public, private for-profit, or private non-profits sectors. The majority of existing community-based organizations (CBOs) did not have the capacity to extend their missions to encompass the technology gap issue and, as chapter 7 will show, CBOs tend to be among the last organizations to benefit from new technology. For the most part, then, community technology centers (CTCs) were initiated by community-minded people with some understanding of technology. Most were started as independent efforts without strong ties to the existing community development infrastructure.[2]

This chapter traces the roots of the community technology movement and documents the process of evolution that led to the current landscape of the field. Although community technology centers are not the only players within the community technology field, the latter part of the chapter focuses on these place-based actors because of their

---

1 Hecht (1998).
2 Chapter 7 discusses important exceptions to this generalization.

tendency to target groups who have been less able to participate in the information society.

History of Community Technology Efforts

The community technology movement consists of four phases. The first begins with the development of the technology that led to what we now know as the Internet in the 1950s. This phase continued until the early 1980s, when we begin to see the first applications of emerging digital technologies as a tool for building communities. During the second phase, beginning in the early 1980s and continuing through to the early 1990s, two tracks developed within the community technology movement: community technology centers and community computing networks. Community technology centers (CTCs) are placebased community technology initiatives, while community computing networks (CCNs) refer primarily to Internet-based strategies. The third phase spanned the remainder of that decade and was characterized by a blurring of the center/network distinction. The fourth phase is the current one, in which a broader range of actors have begun to address the digital divide issue, new intermediaries have been developed, and an innovative set of partnerships has been created. Table 3.1 illustrates these four phases, showing important events and developments that occurred within each phase.

Table 3.1   The community technology movement: key events and phases

	Year	Key events
Phase 1. The roots of community technology	1969	ARPANET (precursor to Internet) created
	1976	Alliance for Community Media founded
	1978	Computer Bulletin Board System (BBS) created in Chicago and Santa Cruz
	1979	Berkeley Community Memory Project (first dial-up computer service, public terminal-based communications service)
	1980	Old Colorado City Electronic Cottage Antonia Stone founds Playing2Win in Harlem
	1981	Penrose Library, Colorado Springs, becomes the first public library in the US to give citizens dial-up access
Phase 2. Centers and networks	1984	"St. Silicon's Hospital and Information Dispensary" – Tom Grunder's medical BBS, Cleveland Domain Name Server (DNS) introduced

Table 3.1 *Continued*

	Year	Key events
	1985	The Well, an online community, introduced in Sausalito, CA
	1986	Tom Grundner establishes the Cleveland Free-Net
	1987	Youngstown, Ohio Free-Net established (second Free-Net system)
	1989	Santa Monica PEN established Inception of World Wide Web
	1980s	PC use becomes more widespread
	1990	Heartland (IL), Tri-State (OH), Medina County (OH) Free-Nets are established ARPANET ceases to exist Tim Berners Lee develops HTML
	1992	Tom Grunder creates NPTN Internet Society founded by Vinton Cerf Number of Internet hosts breaks one million Plugged In founded
	1993	Establishment of a number of FreeNets including: Denver Free-Net, Seattle Community Net, Prairienet (IL), Blacksburg Electronic Village (VA) International Free-Net conference held in Ottawa, CA The Clinton–Gore administration releases, NII: Agenda for Action
Phase 3. Blurring the lines between centers and networks	1994	Netscape introduces first graphical user interface for the Internet First TIIAP awards made by US Department of Commerce
	1995	First *Falling Through the Net* report released documenting the digital divide CTCNetwork founded Austin Free-Net formed AFCN founded NSF funds expansion of Playing2Win Network
	1997	E-Rate legislation passed
	1998	Second *Falling Through the Net* report released Benton's Digital Divide Network Incorporation of AFCN
Phase 4. Confronting new challenges	1999	Third *Falling Through the Net* report released Children's Partnership report published CTCNet offers its affiliates the pilot Leadership Institute
	2000	Fourth *Falling Through the Net* report released Department of Education create the America Connects Consortium (ACC)

Source: Phase I and Phase 2 are adapted from Morino Institute (1994). Timelines for Phases 3 and 4 developed by the author.

As the movement has evolved, a diverse group of actors has made important contributions to the effort to narrow the digital divide. These actors include the public sector, private corporations, and philanthropic institutions, which have fueled the movement through funding. Public schools, community colleges, universities, proprietary schools, and corporations have fostered new training models. These actors will be discussed in other chapters. The fact that the history presented here emphasizes CTCs and CCNs should not be interpreted to mean that they are the most important contributors to this movement. Rather, they deserve special attention because they are creative new organizations and because they have been responsible for much of the innovation in the field.

Phase 1. The roots of community technology[3]

The electronic tools used today to promote community building were created for other purposes. The US Department of Defense began to develop a computer network in the mid 1950s. This work led to the creation of ARPANet (Advanced Research Projects Network), the precursor to today's Internet, in 1969. For over ten years, access to the Internet was limited to an elite group of computer scientists. Access then spread to other academics in order to foster easy and efficient exchange of information. Early users laid the foundation for the open culture of the Internet, operationalizing the belief that "information wants to be free."

Beginning in the late 1960s and into the early 1980s, applications that laid the groundwork for community networking were developed. Most of these early community technology projects relied on the use of a mainframe, which means that these early pioneers tended to work in places where they had mainframe accounts. The National Urban League sponsored a technology center, which consisted of a set of terminals hooked up to a mainframe, in Los Angeles following the 1965 Watts riots. In 1978, Ward Christensen created the first computer bulletin board system (BBS) in Chicago; another BBS called CommuniTree was established that same year in Santa Cruz. Bob Albrecht, a computer professional who left his job to work with computers and children in the schools, created a publication called *People's Computer*

---

3 Correspondence with Steve Cisler provided important information to fill out this early history.

Company, which generated other important early projects. One of these was the PCC center in Menlo Park, California, a public center that housed a terminal connected to a minicomputer, a DEC PDP-8 that ran EduBasic. In 1979, the City of Berkeley initiated the first public terminal based communications service – the Berkeley Community Memory project. Albrecht was also involved with this project, which was founded by Lee Felsenstein and Efrem Lipkin. The group that initiated this project was worried that the increase in computing power would accelerate the divisions between parts of society, which were already seriously divided by the Vietnam War. Community Memory – which placed terminals in housing projects, public libraries, laundromats, a senior center, a university dormitory, and an office building housing nonprofits – is widely recognized as the first community network.[4] Berkeley citizens could access Community Memory from terminals sited in public spaces but could not dial in to the network using a modem. Colorado joined community technology frontrunners in 1980 with the establishment of the Old Colorado City Electronic Cottage. And in 1981, Colorado Springs became the first city with a public library, the Penrose Library, providing citizens with dial-up modem access.

To some extent the community technology movement built on the existing work of people promoting community cable access. A leader in the cable movement was Somerville Community Access Television (SCAT) in Massachusetts, which grew out of the Somerville Media Action Project, founded in 1972, and which has organized for public access to the telecommunications infrastructure. Many community cable access groups, such as Grand Rapids Media Center, have grown to encompass IT as part of their mission. In 1976, the Alliance for Community Media was founded to work for universal access to electronic media by creating public education, advancing legislation and regulations, building coalitions, and supporting local organizing.

The creation of the Public Electronic Network (PEN) system in Santa Monica in 1989 represented an early local government commitment to using IT to achieve broader sociopolitical goals. Introduced by Ken Phillips, director of the Information Systems Department in Santa Monica City Hall at the time, PEN is a public computer network. The PEN system was the first to make available a variety of city records via personal computers. The PEN system also sought to create a public meeting ground where citizens could talk to public officials

4 Beamish (1995).

and civil servants, and where people could chat together about local issues. PEN was free of charge for residents who registered with the city, and more than twenty public terminals were made available in schools, libraries, community centers, elderly housing complexes, recreational centers, and city buildings. The city funded the project with donations of hardware and software from Hewlett-Packard and Metasystems Design Group.[5]

During the mid 1980s, the Internet began to be used to connect people who shared similar interests but were not necessarily proximate.[6] Today, there are countless "places" for people to gather on the Internet. Indeed the use of "community" as an adjective to modify the nouns "center" and "network" refers to a range of types of community. Community technology initiatives encompass at least three definitions of community: community as a physical place; community as a social group that shares common interests; and community as a feeling of belonging or attachment.[7] Because of its focus on how the information society affects persistent poverty, this book deals primarily with the potential of technology to reinforce and build community that is rooted in place. The emphasis in this chapter is therefore on community technology initiatives located in a physical place and space. During this first phase of the movement, community technology pioneers were concerned about democracy and equal access to information, but did not explicitly address poverty and civil rights issues. In the beginning, the community technology movement was not nearly as diverse as it is today.

Phase 2. Centers and networks

The second phase of the community technology movement witnessed a great deal of growth and wide experimentation with different models. This expansion of the movement could not have occurred without the

5   Beamish (1995).
6   Early online communities include the Bay Area-based Whole Earth 'Lectronic Link (the WELL) and New York City-based ECHO. Although people from around the world have joined both of these electronic networks, both have evolved to reflect the places in which they were generated, and both have created ways for local users to engage in face-to-face interaction. In fact, ECHO's mission statement says: "we know that the best online communities are never strictly virtual." Cited in Shapiro (1999: 4). See also Hafner (2001) for a recent history of the WELL.
7   Beamish (1995: 5–6).

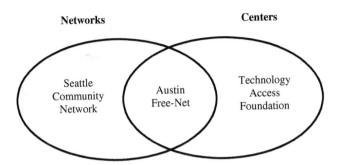

Figure 3.1   The relationship between centers and networks

development and diffusion of the personal computer (PC), which made technology available and accessible to many more people and created the capacity for people to produce much more content from home.

In its second phase, the community technology movement developed along two tracks. One track, community computer networks, grew out of bulletin boards and electronic networks. The other track, community technology centers, or CTCs, has more in common with the work of traditional community development organizations. The creation and proliferation of CTCs began to shift the movement to deal more explicitly with issues of persistent poverty and race. Although community networks focus on the electronic connections between people who share place-based community, centers focus more on the creation of places in which community members can learn about and use technology. All along, supporters of networks and centers have shared the belief that IT offers powerful tools that can be used in the service of community building. Figure 3.1 is a Venn diagram that represents the relationship between centers and networks and provides one example of an organization residing in each section. The Technology Access Foundation (TAF) is a CTC. It is located in a physical space and provides training but does little to create electronic community. The TAF website is dedicated to providing information about the TAF program, not about the larger community. The Seattle Community Network (SCN) is a pure Free-Net. It reflects the City of Seattle but is not located in a specific place. SCN "exists" solely on the Internet and provides a way for Seattle residents to connect to relevant information.[8] The Austin Free-Net was initiated in the network vein

8   See Schuler (1996) for a complete history of SCN and an excellent description of community computing networks.

Table 3.2 Typology of community computing networks

	Free-Net	Bulletin Board	Government network	Wired
Focus	Citywide Community development Access	Neighborhood-wide Community development Access	Citywide or statewide City information	Citywide Physical connection Business
Indicator/ Maintainer	Small group with institutional support	Small group with limited support	City hall or state government	Private/public partnership

Source: Beamish (1995).

but always incorporated an emphasis on the siting of public access terminals. AFN has a staff, offices, a center, and provides training targeted at specific groups. AFN maintains computers and teaches classes at several sites around the city. It also has a website dedicated to providing key information to Austin residents.

Community computing networks

Community computing networks (CCNs) range from simple electronic bulletin board systems, which typically represent one neighborhood and rely on one individual for maintenance, to wired cities such as Blacksburg, Virginia. In 1995, Beamish categorized four major kinds of community networks (see table 3.2). Beamish's typology classifies community networks according to their focus, who initiates them, and who maintains them. These networks range from neighborhood-focused to citywide networks, and are initiated by a variety of actors ranging from community-based organizations to city governments.

People access CCNs either through public terminals located in places such as libraries, schools and senior centers, or via their home computers. The traditional approach of community computing networks has been to foster dial-up connectivity for community users and to use email to encourage community interaction. With a few exceptions, physical place has not factored largely into community networks. Those who support CCNs believe that people need to be able to access these sites, but are indifferent as to whether the use occurs at home, at work, at school, or in public space.[9] Originally, CCN architects wanted to make it easy for people to access the networks they created, but they did not consciously think about using public access terminals as a way for people to come together.

Place is important to supporters of community networks in the sense that these networks reflect and strengthen the place in which they exist. They attempt to address the digital divide by representing all of the residents, not just consumers or those who already have IT access. Community networks' provision of local content differentiates them from other Net-based communities of interest.[10] One criticism of community computer networks is that, despite their intentions, they may not actually represent the entire community but rather reflect that group which adopted technology most quickly. A 1994 survey of Amsterdam-based Digital City, for example, showed that the overwhelming majority of users of the network were young, middle-class males. Although the network was very busy, it was clearly not serving and reflecting the entire community.[11] However, it is incorrect to lump all networks together, as some have made a genuine effort to be inclusive or to broaden their mission. Those that have, have tended to think about place more broadly.

Perhaps the most common type of community network is the Free-Net. Free-Nets have focused on the access and content legs of the technology gap triangle. Free-Nets provide residents of a specific place with an email address and a way to connect to the Internet. In addition, they generally assemble locally relevant content so that residents can easily link to information such as public transit schedules and community calendars. Some Free-Nets also provide a network of public terminals as a way to serve constituents without access at home or at work.

In 1986, Tom Grundner established the first Free-Net – the Cleveland Free-Net. Grundner, an education professor, piloted his idea of using the Internet to build community by first establishing a bulletin board called St. Silicon's Hospital to provide participants with medical and healthcare information as well as to answer health-related questions. Grundner learned enough from that experience to believe he

9 Exceptions exist, such as the Austin Free-Net, discussed above, which was careful to create public centers and strategically sited terminals so that it would be easier for a wider range of people to access the network.
10 Hecht (1998: 2).
11 Beamish (1995: 3).

could expand upon the idea. The project, which was sponsored by Case Western Reserve University, the city of Cleveland, the state of Ohio and IBM, was an ambitious attempt to bring the benefits of technology to all members of the community. The Cleveland Free-Net (CFN) became the model that many other cities followed.[12] Using the metaphor of a physical city, the CFN homepage was organized as a series of buildings or spaces, including the Post Office, the Schoolhouse, and the Public Square. Clicking on any of these buildings provided the user with a list of choices, including content, links to other related sites, and chat rooms and bulletin boards that allowed for interactive information exchange. CFN enabled Cleveland residents to obtain information about their city and to interact with each other. Neighborhood groups could also post their own events. By 1992, CFN had over 40,000 registered users accessing the site more than 10,000 times per day. Over 250 volunteer system operators maintained the system and responded to questions from users.[13]

In the 15 years since Grundner created CFN, many other cities, towns and regions established their own Free-Nets, often using CFN as a model. Although many of these have ceased to exist, others have evolved to meet the changing demands of their communities. Free-Nets – nonprofit, public service information networks servicing local communities – have been an extremely important part of the community technology movement.

Recognizing the importance of Free-Nets to a democratic society – and the capacity challenges associated with creating community networks – Grundner founded the National Public Telecomputing Network (NPTN) in 1989. NPTN served as an umbrella organization to help establish and sustain Free-Nets by disseminating resources (e.g., software and methodology) and creating an opportunity for Free-Nets to network with each other. The three primary goals of NPTN were to:

1   help people in cities throughout the US and the world to establish free, open-access, community computer systems;
2   link those systems together into a common network similar to National Public Radio or the Public Broadcasting Service;

12   Although it was extremely popular for most of its 13 years of existence, the CFN was rendered obsolete by new technology and closed in September 1999.
13   Hauben (1995).

3 help supplement what the local systems are able to produce with high-quality network-wide services and features called "cybercasts."[14]

NPTN declared bankruptcy in 1996. Peter Miller, a community technology activist, cites leadership problems and differences among members regarding how the organization should govern itself.[15] Another organization focused on fostering and supporting the community networking movement is the Association For Community Networking (AFCN). AFCN is a membership association that works to improve the visibility, viability and vitality of community networking through technical assistance, networking opportunities, building public awareness, identifying best practices, encouraging research, influencing policy, and developing products and services.[16]

Originally, a large part of many community networks' missions was to provide free or inexpensive Internet access and email accounts. As the cost of commercial service providers decreased, many community networks, including CFN, ceased to operate. According to Chapman and Rhodes, "One big problem with the early community networks is that they did not actually represent communities in any tangible sense – they were typically just a cheap way for people to get online. When the cost of Internet access plummeted, that rationale evaporated for many customers."[17] In other words, access was not enough. In order for people to maintain an attachment to community technology, they need to believe that they are getting more out of it than cheap access. Those that continue to function[18] tend to have moved beyond the relatively narrow original purpose of community computing networks. Schuler calls the current generation of community networks "both a new type of computer application and a new type of social institution."[19]

Community technology centers

The key difference between networks and centers is that all centers have a physical location. Community technology activists who

---

14 NPTN documents cited in Beamish (1995: 5).
15 Miller (1996).
16 www.afcn.net.
17 Chapman and Rhodes (1997: 2).
18 Shapiro (1999: 4) estimates that "more than a hundred Internet-based community networks in the United States have continued to thrive."
19 Schuler, no date (accessed 11/22/98), p. 1.

support centers believe that there is value added from bringing people together to learn about and use technology. Access is important, but so is social interaction. Steve Cisler of Community Technology Horizons argues that "Part of being community-based is having a physical place to meet. Virtual meetings online can be an effective way of linking up project leaders around a city or around the world, but the need for a meeting hall or building in the neighborhood was paramount."[20]

It is difficult to pin down when the first community technology center (CTC) opened its doors. Some would call the Penrose Library, in Colorado Springs, the first CTC. Penrose was the first library in the US to provide, in 1981, dial-up modem access to patrons. Many believe that Playing2Win in Harlem – a community technology center initiated by Antonia Stone in 1982 – was the first. Playing2Win was certainly the first stand-alone center.[21] In 1990, Stone founded the PlayingtoWin Network, which later became the Community Technology Centers Network (CTCNet), a member organization which now consists of more than 500 CTCs. CTCNet's mission is to support community technology centers so that they can better serve their constituencies. It works toward this mission by conducting research, organizing conferences, and disseminating relevant information to members.

Definitional issues make determining exactly how many CTCs are currently in operation difficult. CTCs range from "mom and pop" shops with two computers with dial-up access via modem, to state-of-the art technology centers with the latest hardware and software, high-speed connections, and advanced training. Although it is difficult to state concretely the number CTCs in existence, community technology experts agree that there are thousands of organizations focused on creating access to technology in a physical location and that associate themselves with the CTC movement.

A word about libraries[22]

To some extent, libraries are a kind of CTC, although not all define themselves as such. Libraries were among the first institutions to offer

---

20   Quoted in Breeden et al. (1998: n.p.).
21   Chapter 5 looks at Playing2Win in greater detail.
22   All statistics in this section taken from the National Commission on Libraries and Information Science, www.nclis.gov.

free access to computers and the Internet to communities. Libraries have also been the focus of important public policy, such as the E-rate, and significant philanthropic programs, such as the Gates Library Program. There are more than 16,000 public libraries in the US serving more than 264 million people. In 1994, only one in ten library systems provided Internet access; by 2000, 95 percent of all library locations provided access to the Internet. Libraries are particularly important in rural areas; as of 2000, 93 percent of public library outlets in rural areas (which constitute 53 percent of all public library outlets) were connected to the Internet. Libraries have also begun to pay special attention to the disabled: 29 percent of public libraries provide hardware or software for accessing the Internet by individuals with disabilities. In addition to providing access, 62 percent of all libraries provide Internet training services.

Phase 3. Blurring the line between centers and networks

"Community technology center" is a broad term that refers to a broad range of public and private organizations and institutions, such as libraries, youth organizations, multiservice agencies, stand-alone computing centers, settlement houses, and various other nonprofit organizations that offer an array of technology-based services and programs to a variety of populations. This shift to an expanded conception of what constitutes a CTC is important because it signals an extension of community technology into areas heretofore occupied by more traditional CBOs and a simultaneous extension of these CBOs into the area of technology. The changing roles of centers, networks, and CBOs raise questions about the continued relevance of these categories as ways of making sense of and analyzing this field.

Although they developed along different tracks, the lines between community networks and community technology centers have become less clear. Distinguishing between the two is not as meaningful or useful as it once was. According to Peter Miller, the development of these two responses to the digital divide "are now taking place in tandem." Miller explains the mutual appeal as follows:

> Those committed to community networking appreciate the value of center-based access as the key approach for providing technology to people who are generally without access, skills, and opportunities to use it. . . . Likewise, those involved with center-based technology access and

programming are appreciating more and more the importance of online communications and resources.[23]

As a result, it has become more difficult to separate "centers" from "networks." This third phase of the community technology movement is also characterized by partnerships between community technology organizations and a range of other actors. For example, AFCN (the membership association for the community networking movement) and CTCNet (the primary trade association serving CTCs[24]) work closely together. AFCN and CTCNet jointly convene national conferences and co-publish materials on issues related to community technology. These two associations are clearly evolving together but have also decided to maintain separate identities.

Phase 4. Confronting new challenges

The current phase of the community technology movement demonstrates that the movement has begun to show signs of maturity. A significant number of CTCs have existed for over ten years, demonstrating that they are serving a purpose and that they have staying power. A greater number of CTCs have expanded their missions to take on training and content issues. And community technology experts and activists have begun to think seriously about issues that affect the institutionalization of the field, such as scale and sustainability. One result of this thinking has been the creation of a relatively new group of intermediaries to serve the movement through a broader dissemination of technology. They will be discussed in greater detail in chapter 7. These intermediaries, along with membership organizations such as CTCNet and AFCN, and other actors such as the Morino Institute, the Benton Foundation, and PolicyLink have begun to promote learning among organizations. An example of this work is CTCNet's Leadership Development Institutes (LDIs), initiated in 1999, which are designed to build the capacity of CTCs by supporting the professional growth of CTC directors and program managers. LDIs are two-day seminars that take place in

---

23   Miller (1999: 1).
24   CTCNet is a "national membership organization that promotes and nurtures nonprofit, community-based efforts to provide computer access to the general public and to disadvantaged populations" (Chow et al., 1998).

several cities around the country and focus on key leadership issues facing CTCs.

Key Findings from Survey of CTCNet Affiliates

In order to gain a better understanding of the community technology landscape, a mail survey was conducted of the 336 US affiliates of the Community Technology Centers Network (CTCNet).[25] The focus was on centers because of their explicit commitment to place and tendency to work in low-income areas. When the survey was conducted in 1999, CTCNet had affiliates operating in 45 states, the District of Columbia, England, Ireland, Scotland, Spain, and the Virgin Islands. Although CTCNet collects basic information on affiliates and has conducted some very valuable research in the field, including a study of the impact of CTCNet affiliates, no one has collected descriptive data from the group of CTCs we surveyed, rendering this data set particularly important for sketching the broad outlines of the field. This work enabled mapping the community technology movement in terms of its geographic distribution and the range of programmatic goals pursued.

The results indicate that the organizations under the CTC umbrella are extremely diverse across a range of variables. Survey respondents included public libraries, YM and YWCAs, community TV and cable access centers, Free-Nets, community development corporations, church organizations, resident and tenant councils, community centers, and stand-alone computing centers. One respondent was a beauty salon that houses a public access terminal. CTCs are broadly committed to closing the technology gap, but they also differ in several key ways.

Target populations

CTCs vary with respect to their target populations – both who they serve and where they choose to locate. Table 3.3 shows that CTCs over-whelmingly serve low-income populations in urban areas. More than

---

25   Appendix A provides a more complete description of our survey methodology, and Appendix B consists of a copy of the survey we administered. Unless otherwise indicated, all statistics presented in this chapter come from this survey. Appendix C contains all survey results.

Table 3.3 Populations served by CTCs

Target population	% respondents
Pre-school children	31.7
School-aged children (5–17)	74.0
Young adults (18–24)	73.2
Parents/adults	76.4
Senior citizens	59.3
General community (e.g., city/county-wide)	69.1
Specific neighborhoods	43.1
At risk	59.3
Low income	76.4
Women	49.6
Others	22.8

three-quarters of respondents target low-income populations and parents/adults. Nearly equal percentages provide services and programs for school-age children (72.1 percent) and young adults (71.3 percent). More than half (59.3 percent) of CTCs offer programs for senior citizens and women. Nearly a quarter (23.8 percent) of respondents serve other specific populations, such as the homeless and the mentally ill, recent immigrants, artists, HIV-positive individuals and people living with AIDS, and fathers who are seeking to get back on track in paying child support.

Geographic location

In terms of geographic area, nearly two-thirds (64.8 percent) of CTCs are located in, and serve, urban areas. Only 14 percent of CTCs are located in rural areas, and only 7.4 percent are based in suburban areas. Thirteen percent identified as mixed, meaning they work in more than one place. Figure 3.2 maps the location of CTCNet's US affiliates and illustrates the clustering of CTCs in the northeast and on the west coast. The uneven distribution of US CTCs likely results from a range of factors. CTCs tend to locate in areas where there is significant high-tech activity and a commensurate demand for IT workers; CTCs are often initiated to respond to this demand by training people. High-tech regions also tend to have a critical mass of technology activists and IT workers who are willing to volunteer time to CTCs. In Seattle, for example, several of the people interviewed for

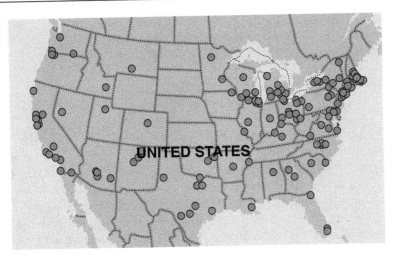

Figure 3.2 Location of CTCNet's US affiliates

this book had made enough money in the high-tech industries to retire early and devote time, energy, and their own finances to digital divide work.

Organizational structure

In terms of their organizational structure, some CTCs are stand-alone centers that were created in order to provide access to IT, while others are part of multiservice agencies that have taken on the digital divide issue. Most CTCs (60.7 percent) operate their technology programs within previously existing CBOs. To some extent, this statistic supports the observation made earlier regarding the increasing overlap between CTCs and traditional CBOs. However, it also includes CBOs that are chasing newly available funding dollars dedicated to technology, and CTCs that use CBO space but are not truly integrated into the work of the CBO. We must be careful not to read too much into this statistic without doing more research to examine the specific relationships between CBOs and CTCs. Nearly one-quarter (24.6 percent) of CTCs are located in housing-project communities. Smaller shares of CTCs offer technology services and programs at schools (19.7 percent) and libraries (13.9 percent). Nearly two-fifths (38.5 percent) of CTCs indicated that they offer their technology services and programs at other locations, including stand-alone computing centers, mobile computer labs, and public-access television centers. Many CTCs offer their services and programs at multiple locations.

Programmatic offerings

CTCs also vary in terms of their IT programming. We deal with each of these purposes separately, below, in order to illustrate the range of activities in which CTCs engage. Although one group of CTCs provides only access, a significant number have recognized that an access-only approach is inadequate to remedy the digital divide. Many CTCs have evolved to include training and the creation of content in their missions. These CTCs, which have a broad understanding of the problem, are on the leading edge of efforts to close the technology gap. Studying them closely elicits important lessons that policy makers and funders can learn from and apply to the more comprehensive effort that is needed to deal with this problem.

Another group of CTCs do not tackle the technology gap directly. Rather, they employ technology to achieve their existing missions. Table 3.5 illustrates the range of programmatic services provided by CTCs. For example, the Austin Learning Academy (ALA) has offered GED and ESL classes for many years and began to integrate technology into its programs in 1988. ALA views technology as a tool that facilitates the work it was already doing. According to Belinda Rojas, director of ALA, "A component of our family literacy is technology, and in the adult education classes, the technology takes on a form that is integrated with the learning that is going on in the classroom. IT is not a separate kind of class where they go to learn keyboarding – no,

Table 3.4 Typology of community technology centers

IT Goal	Organizational Type	
IT goal	Stand-alone centers	Programs within multiservice agencies
Access	HHCAN	Seattle Public Housing
Computer literacy/Training	Technology Access Foundation	BAVC's JobLink
Content	Life/Web journalism project	HarlemLive

Source: Servon and Nelson (2001).

Table 3.5 Services provided by CTCs

Service provided	% respondents
Tutoring/homework assistance	51.6
General/youth development	53.3
Mentoring	35.2
Youth employment/school to career	35.2
Childcare	15.6
Adult education/literacy	56.6
Adult job training	41.0
Community development	46.7
Advocacy	37.7
Technical assistance	48.4
Other	41.8

it's integrated with what's going on in the classroom." ALA's basic educational goals are its primary focus – teaching technology skills is an important by-product that occurs along the way. Nearly half (46.7 percent) of CTCs provide community development functions and 37.7 percent engage in advocacy. Most CTCs engage in more than one type of activity.

Table 3.4 is a typology of CTCs, showing how different goals intersect with different organizational types. Each CTC has its own mix of programming which reflects its mission. The cells of the table are filled in with organizations studied for this book, and which appear as examples throughout this and other chapters. The three basic categories of CTC programming – access, training, and content – correspond to the three components of the digital divide discussed in chapter 1. Some CTCs focus on only one of these areas, although many pursue a mix. There is also a chronological element to these three foci; as the field has developed, community technology activists have recognized the need to expand their missions beyond access to include training and content.

Access

Despite the trend toward expansion of CTC missions beyond access, the most common function of CTCs remains providing unstructured computer access to people who might otherwise have little or no opportunity to use computers and information technologies. General computer access is offered by 87 percent of CTCs, and more than three-quarters (78.9 percent) use technology as a communication tool (i.e., offering access to email). As access providers, CTCs allow community members to drop in and surf the Internet, work on homework, prepare résumés and cover letters, use email, or engage in a variety of other activities. The Hill House Community Access Network (HHCAN), a computing center and network in Pittsburgh, is an example of an access-oriented CTC affiliated with a multiservice agency, the Hill House Association. Although HHCAN offers some structured workshops to provide participants with the skills necessary to use computers, its emphasis is on providing access to neighborhood residents, not training. Carl Redwood (1999), former associate director of the Hill House Association and HHCAN emphasizes the importance of providing unstructured access:

> The free aspect of these centers . . . is very important. I think there is a danger in the technology center movement, particularly as it relates to low-income communities, to assume that we're doing something for people. . . . I think what we have to do is just make resources available to the community and the community will figure out what, when and how to use them. And they may not use them the way the mayor's office or someone else thinks they should use them. . . . But I think it just needs to be open like that.

Redwood and others essentially argue that those who support IT initiatives in low-income communities must remain open to the multiple ways in which these communities may use these tools. Narrow, prescriptive interventions can cut off potentially rich applications of IT resources.

At the same time, most CTCs (including HHCAN) have a broader definition of access than Redwood's statement implies. They not only provide the necessary tools, they also show low-income communities how and why IT tools might be useful to them. A great deal of learning occurs during CTCs' open access hours – it simply occurs informally. CTC staff circulate among users, offering assistance and showing people new websites and software applications. In addition, much learning occurs among drop-in users. CTCs are a new form of community institution where people meet, exchange ideas, and learn. Access-oriented CTCs play a potentially important role in narrowing the urban technology gap, but they are less focused on particular economic or social goals than are training- or content-oriented CTCs. At the same time, many CTCs that provide unstructured access also offer other IT programs. The open-access hours provide a way for participants in, for example, an e-commerce class, to work on their business websites outside of class.

Literacy/training

Many CTCs focus on developing the IT skills of program participants. Those that grow out of the workforce development tradition directly address the economic impacts and jobs/skills mismatch problem discussed in chapter 1.[26] Literacy and training programs range from basic courses in which participants learn how to use email and develop keyboarding skills, to advanced courses in building computers, HTML, Web development and media production.

Despite the wide diversity among CTCs in terms of programming, our survey results indicate that overall there is a strong emphasis among CTCs on education and job preparedness. Some of these CTCs use IT as a tool to deliver traditional material, such as GED and ESL curricula. Others focus more specifically on computer literacy and IT skills. Table 3.5 illustrated how CTCs' program offerings cluster in these areas. Over half of all survey respondents provide adult education and literacy (56.6 percent), general youth development (53.3 percent), and tutoring (51.6 percent). More than 40 percent of all CTCs focus on job training while 35.2 percent work on youth employment and school-to-career services. In line with their emphasis on education and training, 82.1 percent of CTCs use technology to build word processing and keyboarding skills. Over 70 percent use technology to conduct job searches and build résumés, more than half (54.5 percent) offer computer-based instruction, and 47.2 percent provide homework help.

An example of a CTC training people for IT jobs is the Bay Area Video Coalition (BAVC) in San Francisco. BAVC's JobLink program maintains close working relationships with a range of Bay Area employers who recognize the quality of the program and are eager to hire its graduates. The relationships with employers also enable BAVC to understand and respond to the quickly changing skill needs of these employers. BAVC keeps current with new programs and continually modifies its curriculum. The JobLink program has a 95 percent placement rate of its participants in jobs – such as web developers, HTML coders, and designers – that have an average hourly wage of $30 per

---

26   This group of CTCs and the work they are doing to address the IT labor shortage is examined in chapter 6.

Table 3.6 Americans potentially underserved because of Internet content barriers

Type of Internet barrier	Estimated number of Americans affected (million)
Lack of local information	21
Literacy barriers	44
Language barriers	32
Lack of cultural diversity	26

Source: Lazarus and Mora (2000).

hour. Employers hiring BAVC graduates range from high profile IT companies such as Oracle to a wider range of service companies such as Charles Schwab and TravelSmith.

Content

Finally, some CTC programming employs IT as a mechanism to create and deliver content. CTCs that focus on the creation and delivery of content work to address the social impacts of the technological revolution discussed in chapter 1. The goals of these CTCs may include: providing information to the community; fostering a sense of community or personal effectiveness; encouraging collaboration; developing problem solving and strategic thinking skills. CTCs that emphasize content have three distinct purposes: creating material that constituents can use; teaching community members to create this content; and helping community members connect to important information that already exists on the Internet. Not all content-oriented CTCs do all three. Those CTCs that actively foster the creation of new content believe that people should not only be passive consumers of information but rather actively shape the Internet by producing content that reflects and represents disenfranchised communities.

Content-oriented CTCs begin their work from the recognition that the Internet is not currently oriented to low-income communities and that these communities face several content-related barriers. According to Chapman and Rhodes:

The Internet reflects the culture of its principal inhabitants – upper middle-class white males. Thus the global network is dominated by the culture, tastes, preoccupations, styles, and interests of the affluent. A network isn't much good if you don't know anybody who has e-mail;

an online shopping mall holds little allure to someone lacking money and credit cards.[27]

Content-oriented CTCs focus on providing stimulating content about local issues and an opportunity for users to talk with one another. They connect residents to resources and provoke discussion about issues that people care about.[28]

A 2000 report distributed by The Children's Partnership identifies four significant, content-related barriers that affect large numbers of Americans: lack of local information; literacy barriers; language barriers; and lack of cultural diversity.[29] Residents of low-income communities "seek 'life information,' . . . practical information about their local community."[30] Specifically, adult users wanted information about jobs and housing in their communities. Few sites provide this information. Even when this information is available, researchers have found that it is often "still out of reach to users because it is so difficult or confusing to find."

At Project Compute, a volunteer-run CTC in Seattle, volunteers incorporate computers and information technology into their learning programs by teaching participants how to create content. As Anthony Williams (1999), long-time volunteer and sponsor of Project Compute, stresses, "We don't want people to believe that a computer is a computer. We really want people to believe that a computer is a tool." This philosophy manifests itself in Project Compute's Life-Web Journalist Project, the first phase of which was completed in March 1999. As part of the initiative, Project Compute loaned 25 hand-held computers equipped with Windows, an audio recorder, and a digital camera to participants for a six-month period. Participants were to go out into the community, capture stories of interest, and create an Internet website. In addition to helping participants hone their journalism and computer skills, the Life-Web Project provides participants with the opportunity to tell their stories. Project Compute also offers various classes for school-age children, adults and senior citizens, and provides open-lab time for all community members.

Project Compute is deeply rooted in its community. This connection ensures that projects reflect the interests and concerns of the community. According to Lazarus and Mora, "inclusion helps ensure that

27   Chapman and Rhodes (1997: 3).
28   Shapiro (1999: 5).
29   Lazarus and Mora (2000).
30   Lazarus and Mora (2000: 19).

online content incorporates what the community wants and will use, that content acknowledges residents' methods of acquiring information, and that the look and feel of the content works with the user's literacy and linguistic levels."[31] One advantage of the Internet is that it allows for two-way communication in a way that print media and television do not. Users can respond quickly and directly to the information posted and communicate with each other about topics of interest. Content-oriented CTCs exploit this many-to-many attribute of the Internet, creating space for community members to shape what is available to them.

What We Know about Outcomes

What role do CTCs play within the larger community technology movement? To what extent are they narrowing the technology gap? Many CTCs continue to experiment with programming, and most of the existing research that has attempted to evaluate the work of these new institutions is exploratory. Given the range of goals and organizational types discussed earlier and illustrated in table 3.2, it is important not to judge all CTCs by the same standards. A small access lab in a housing project will have different goals from a dedicated training organization. In addition, most CTCs are small, neighborhood-based institutions that have not achieved scale. A clear problem is that these initiatives tend to be fragmented, under-resourced, and reliant on a charismatic leader.[32]

Despite these issues, existing research does indicate that CTCs are filling a critical need for populations that do not have access to computers and other technologies at home or work. The 1999 NTIA study reports that "households with incomes less than $20,000 and Black households ... are twice as likely to get Internet access through a public library or [CTC] than are households earning more than $20,000 or White households" (NTIA, 1999: 78). In a survey of users of CTC services, CTCNet found that CTCs have been a valuable resource for obtaining job skills and learning about employment opportunities, have had a positive effect on participants' goals and experiences, and have fostered a sense of community and personal effectiveness.[33]

31 Lazarus and Mora (2000: 28).
32 Graham and Marvin (2000).
33 Chow et al. (1998).

A 1997 study indicated that most CTC users do not have access elsewhere. Those that do have access elsewhere go to CTCs to use applications and equipment they do not have access to, for social interaction, and for the learner-centered atmosphere.[34] Evaluations of the California-based Computers in Our Future Project, which studied member centers, show that these centers "are reaching groups who have normally been intimidated by technology, and people who have been difficult to attract to the computer-using world."[35] A study of three Canadian community networks found that they "increased user participation in the democratic system, increased access to education and enhanced community development."[36]

Given the networking that community technology facilitates – both physically, at CTCs, and virtually – it seems reasonable to assume that CTCs are promoting the creation of weak ties among participants. Weak ties are connections between acquaintances rather than family members or good friends. Weak tie theory argues that weak ties are more helpful in the labor market than are strong ties.[37] According to Civille, "electronic mail appears to significantly reduce the costs of acquiring and maintaining new acquaintances beyond community boundaries, an ability that those with discretionary time and money tend to take for granted."[38] It is important, then, that some groups that are on the wrong side of the digital divide – for example, African-Americans and Latinos – are using public computer centers more than other groups for job-related purposes.

The fieldwork conducted for this book indicates that CTCs are performing critical functions that help bridge the digital divide. These include providing disadvantaged workers with the skills necessary to work in the IT economy, exposing youth to IT careers and opportunities, and extending the work of traditional CBOs to address issues of social and economic justice.

The high cost of evaluation coupled with the newness of these programs have kept CTCs from doing much evaluation of their own. When asked what they see happening in the programs in which they work, staff members are likely to tell stories rather than to produce numbers. These stories are about connecting people who previously did not know each other; helping people stay in touch with faraway

34   Mark et al. (1997: 3).
35   Cited in Lazarus and Mora (2000: 28).
36   Lillie (1999: 3).
37   Granovetter (1973).
38   Civille (1995: 181).

friends and relatives; watching people learn how to use new technology and create things with it. Ana Sisnett[39] of the Austin Free-Net has observed:

> Age groups working together that did not work together before. For a while antagonistically – looking at each other suspiciously, but then over time they get familiar with each other and they're able to collaborate and help each other out, even if it's something as simple as helping to reload a page, you know? And I've seen people find out as they talk about what their interests are, as they do searches. For example, in a class – "oh, I didn't know that" – and then they might end up walking out of the class talking to each other about something.

Roxanne Epperson,[40] the director of Pittsburgh's New Beginnings Learning Center (NBLC) points to other evidence of success.

> Kids won't leave. At 5:30 when it's time for them to go, you have to make sure there are none hidden in the basement. They hide under the desks. . . . I don't know how their little bodies can fold up, but down in the library there's an opening under one of the shelves, they're all up under there. So that tells me we're doing something right, you know.

Our survey results and interviews with CTC directors show that CTCs are incredibly diverse in terms of both their organizational structures and their missions. The relationships between these differences and program outcomes merit closer examination to determine how successful CTCs are in meeting their goals. This recommendation is particularly tricky to operationalize given the diversity of community technology programs and the range of goals they pursue.

Challenges and Lessons

Community technology centers have proliferated quickly in the US. Although the spread of CTCs is uneven, as figure 3.2 illustrates, CTCs are only one component of the community technology movement. Many other organizations are doing important work to narrow the digital divide. As community-based organizations (CBOs), funders, and policy makers increasingly support, initiate, and become

39 1999 interview with Sisnett.
40 1999 interview with Epperson.

involved in community technology efforts, the lessons learned by CTCs that have already traveled up the learning curve will be important. Additionally, a range of challenges continues to confront program staff at those organizations that have been in existence for a long time.

CTCs lack sustainable funding

As with most community-based organizations, long-run sustainability is a major issue facing CTCs. Nearly two-thirds of CTCs (61.4 percent) explicitly mentioned funding as the biggest challenge facing their organization. Securing funds remains an issue even for organizations with an established track record, making it difficult to plan and program. Most CTCs rely on a patchwork of funding from local, state, and federal government, private foundations, corporate donors, individual contributions, church organizations, membership fees, and cable franchise fees. Private foundations are a particularly important funding source for CTCs. Over 70 percent of CTCs reported receiving some foundation dollars, and nearly a quarter of respondents receive the largest share of funding from private foundations. Slightly fewer respondents (22.5 percent) indicated that local government provides the largest share of their funding.[41] None of these funding sources has made a long-term commitment to the community technology movement, however, putting CTCs in the position of constantly scrambling for money. Many CTCs initiated programs with grants that are unlikely to be renewed. For example, some federal grant programs fund programs once but do not offer repeat funding, leaving CTCs grappling to find replacement funds to keep programs going.

Epperson of NBLC, which has been in existence for over ten years, explains: "Every year you're trying to figure out sources of funding and it's very stressful, it's very stressful. . . . I submitted two grants. . . . If we don't get them, then what are we supposed to do? Are we going to close down in December?"[42] CTCs have found it particularly difficult to secure funding for operating costs,

---

41 Caution must be exercised when analyzing the funding data. Cable franchise fees are a main source of support for CTC initiatives. Respondents listed franchise fees in the "local government," "other," and "private corporations" categories, making it difficult to obtain precise information about this source of funds. We do know from our case study research that franchise fees are a common funding mechanism in many cities.

42 Interview with Epperson, 1999.

curriculum development, staff, and technical support. It is considerably easier to find funders to provide hardware and software. Many fail to understand that these expenses comprise only a part of CTCs' budgets, and that hardware and software need to be maintained and upgraded.

To help cover costs, many CTCs have turned to other revenue sources. NBLC, for instance, has been designated as a community college satellite site. This designation will help the program to generate income, bringing in small yet significant amounts of money to the center each semester while making college courses more accessible to the community.

Some CTCs have begun to partner with other agencies or to charge user fees. However, many programs remain committed to offering free services.[43] As CTCs become more widespread and stable, a major task will be to devise ways for them to become sustainable over the long term. Without long-term funding arrangements, CTCs will be unable to do long-range planning.

Technical assistance is difficult to support

One of the largest problems facing CTCs nationwide is how to support technical assistance. In fact, this issue extends beyond CTCs to schools, workforce development agencies, and other institutions that offer IT programs. CTCs face a constant array of technical problems ranging from the simple – fixing paper jams, setting up printer configurations, and re-creating icons deleted from the window – to the more complex – managing disk space and access, configuring a network, disaster recovery of a server, and controlling viruses.

CTCs provide particularly challenging technical environments. CTCs tend to be understaffed and face high rates of staff turnover, making in-house technical assistance difficult. They often lack the funding resources to contract for technical assistance. Moreover, CTCs generally have a variety of equipment, which is a challenge to manage and support technically, and their computers are used for many activities by many different persons, which raises configuration and security issues.[44] Some CTCs have been able to use local IT workers as a resource to volunteer and provide TA. These arrangements are great when they function. The technology worker benefits by sharing a

43 Beamish (1995: 4).
44 Schroerlucke (1997).

useful skill and feeling good about giving something back to the community, and the CTC benefits from the skilled volunteer labor. However, volunteers, especially those with demanding jobs, are not always completely reliable. Some CTC directors located in the heart of high tech regions have expressed frustration at how difficult it is to get local workers to commit even small amounts of time to CTC volunteer work.[45]

Many CTCs cannot meet the demand for services

Staff at nearly all of the organizations studied discussed the challenge of serving everyone who would like to participate in CTCs' programs. Many staffers claim that their centers and classes are full, even without doing much outreach. Existing demand is greater than the current capacity of CTCs. Over 11 percent of survey respondents also listed this issue when asked about the main challenges they currently face. A shortage of instructors and lack of a well-developed curriculum and computers hinder the capacity of other CTCs. It is particularly difficult to retain staff in this field given the high level of skills required and the fact that nonprofit CTCs cannot compete on wages. As one director of a CTC focused on workforce development said, "Our graduates' starting salaries are far better than what we can pay our trainers." As the Internet becomes even more mainstream, and as familiarity with IT becomes a requirement for an even broader range of jobs, demand for services such as those provided by CTCs will undoubtedly increase. According to the Morino Institute, "there are few worse situations than an enormous build-up in interest that goes unsatisfied or, worse, ineffectively addressed."[46] The challenge to meet this demand is clearly linked to the funding challenge discussed above.

Community technology efforts would benefit from greater integration

Several people interviewed for this research spoke of the need for partnerships to help share information and knowledge among

45 For example, during her lunchtime remarks at the 2001 ITAA conference, Magda Escobar, executive director of Plugged In, relayed how difficult it is to get young people in Silicon Valley, who work in IT, to volunteer at her program.
46 Morino Institute (1994: 10).

2

organizations involved in the community technology movement.[47] Kathy Schroerlucke, a community technology activist in Pittsburgh, notes, "[the Pittsburgh area] is one of the most resource rich areas I've been in – but they're not connected and people don't know how to use them. There's no coordinated effort, so everybody's reinventing the wheel, everybody's doing the same research, everybody's doing the same digging trying to figure out what to do."[48] Gerry Balbier, a program officer at the Heinz Endowments, echoes Schroerlucke's frustration and calls for greater integration among community technology initiatives:

> We're all craving information about how other groups are doing it because we're realizing that we have something to offer as far as our own experience, but we know that other groups are doing things that we haven't thought of or haven't experienced. How do you connect all those sources of knowledge? We've got to get a network going somehow.[49]

Schroerlucke is currently working on a regional community technology collaborative to help coordinate community technology initiatives in Western Pennsylvania. The goal of this collaborative is to make it easier for people to network, obtain the resources they need, and put training and support programs in place. In Austin, where the relatively small size and the character of the city have fostered significant collaboration and cooperation, community technology efforts remain somewhat fragmented. CTC staff believes that the city could do more to broker relationships between existing organizations and to help find resources to sustain community technology programs. In Seattle, the city has set aside a portion of the revenues from cable franchise fees to employ a community technology planner to encourage and foster collaborative relationships among the city's community technology actors. As a result, community technology efforts in Seattle are more cohesive than in most other places.[50]

The funding community must be educated about IT

The fact that CTCs do not fit into any of the traditional categories funders use has made it difficult for CTCs to attract funding. The

47 See chapter 7 for more on this subject.
48 Interview with Kathy Schroerlucke, 1999.
49 Interview with Gerry Balbier, 1999.
50 See chapter 8 for more information about Seattle's community technology efforts.

cross-cutting nature of these organizations, described above, has created problems when the directors of these organizations try to market their programs to funders. A community technology activist affiliated with the Seattle Community Network recalled these difficulties.

> We did try to get funding, especially early on [in 1992 and 1993] from Microsoft and from Boeing and both of them rejected us. We can help just about any organization because what we're doing is providing an infrastructure, an online service. And they told me frankly, "We don't think you are a very good candidate for funding because we can't put you in any category that we traditionally fund."[51]

Increasingly, funders – particularly those associated with high-tech corporations – are identifying the digital divide as an issue in its own right, without feeling the need to tie it to another funding category.

A second problem is that some foundations have not embraced technology themselves. If they do not use and understand IT, they cannot understand its potential for poor communities. Although the funding community has become more active in the community technology arena, Joe Mertz, associate director of the Center for University Outreach at Carnegie Mellon University, says "A lot of foundations are slow to adapt technology. To understand what you're funding and really make leadership judgments, you've got to at least use your email regularly and surf the Web occasionally, know what these things are about. Not that you have to be experts in these things but know what they're about so that you can make decisions about them." In Pittsburgh, community technology activists held a professional development seminar for potential local grant makers to demonstrate the importance of funding community technology efforts, to educate funders and local government about the characteristics of exemplary community technology programs and explain the type of support they should provide. At the same time, the digital divide issue has opened up a new funding vein from the corporate community, particularly IT companies. This funding stream is important and enables high-tech firms to give to a cause that they understand. Helping to narrow the technology gap could also have the positive externality for these firms of creating new markets for their products.

The funding community is traveling up a learning curve with respect to community technology. Whereas funders have traditionally only provided funding for hardware, some have realized the necessity

51   Interview with Aki Namioka, 1999.

of covering the costs of upgrades, technical assistance and staff. Epperson welcomes these changes.

> One thing I've noticed, and I just found this out because of the last proposal I submitted, [foundations are] changing their focus and they're starting to give operating costs now where they wouldn't have before. So that is a blessing . . . I went to meet with the funder, and he gave me a whole list of about five or six other foundations for me to target and they all give operating costs. I'm like, "oh, thank you," because that's critical. How the heck did we run the center without a staff? And we are short-staffed, you know, so we do rely heavily on volunteers.

CTC program staff will need to continue to educate funders about the way IT programs need to be funded and how access to IT connects to a range of other funding targets such as education, economic development, and social welfare.

Conclusion

CTCs play a range of roles. They diffuse technology and IT training to people who have not benefited from the shift to an information society. They function as new forms of community institutions, generating both bonding and bridging social capital.[52] They have triggered the release of a new stream of funding – from public and private, both corporate and philanthropic actors – into low-income communities. But despite the range and diversity of interventions into the problem of unequal access, no systemic solution to the problem exists. The map of CTCNet affiliates illustrates that CTCs are not available in many poor regions. Relatively few poor communities have access to IT through CTCs, and access through schools and libraries is inconsistent. Indeed, the fact that CTCs have tended to spin out from high-tech regions raises a key concern. The uneven development of the community technology movement has the potential to exacerbate the interregional nature of the digital divide discussed in chapter 1. If the goal is to bring the benefits of the information society to all people, a more comprehensive strategy must be mounted.

---

52   See Gittell and Vidal (1998) for a more in-depth discussion of these concepts. Bonding social capital consists of those relationships between people that help them to get by; bridging social capital concerns relationships between individuals which helps them to get ahead.

4

Support for Bridging the Gap

Bridging the technology gap will require not only the innovative work currently underway at local CTCs but also the active engagement of the public sector. This chapter reviews what the public sector is currently doing to close the digital divide and discusses the limits of existing policies and programs. Although the public sector has initiated important work in this area, much of it flows from the narrow definition of the problem discussed in chapter 1. In other words, policy tends to focus on access and does not include adequate recognition of the importance of training and content. The focus on access is not surprising given that universal access has long been the foundation of US telecommunications policy. However, as chapter 1 discussed, the Internet differs in important ways from other telecommunications applications. An access-focused policy works for the telephone, but is inadequate for the Internet.

This chapter analyzes key telecommunications concepts and policies in order to document the current policy landscape, reveal the gaps in existing efforts, and propose recommendations that would enable policy to address this issue more comprehensively. Digital divide policy can be divided into two categories. One category consists of programs that explicitly address this problem and are designed to alleviate it. The other consists of programs in which some of the funding allocated is flexible; that is, state and/or local officials have some say regarding how they use these funds. This chapter focuses on the first category for two reasons: the first is that these explicit programs are the most accurate way to gauge how the federal government views and prioritizes the digital divide issue; and second, the range of programs that provide flexible funding is simply too vast. Some of these programs are mentioned here, and others will be discussed in chapters 5, 6, 7, and 8. This chapter deals only with those policies and programs most directly tied to the digital divide. Workforce development policies, education policies, and other programs that are strongly connected to specific aspects of this issue are discussed in chapters 5 through 7. Although this book focuses on public policy, corporate and philanthropic support for programs to narrow the digital divide have shaped the community technology movement and public policy in important ways. Therefore, this chapter also includes a section on private support.

The Telecommunications Act of 1996

Perhaps the single most important piece of telecommunications policy to be passed in recent years was the 1996 Telecommunications Act (the Act). Congress passed the Act, the first major overhaul of telecommunications law in almost sixty-two years, to remove the legal and economic barriers to competition in the industry. Proponents of the legislation asserted that increased competition would drive down rates, increase consumer choice, and facilitate the development of advanced communication networks throughout the country. Although telecommunications reform was motivated by business interests rather than by the needs of the poor,[1] deregulation was supposed to support universal service to information technologies by making a wider array of services affordable to major segments of the population that had previously been denied access to telecommunication networks. Contrary to the stated goals, deregulation has resulted in the rapid consolidation of the industry. This consolidation has dampened the competition that was expected to emerge. As a result, many customers have experienced price increases in basic phone, cable, and Internet services. In the absence of competition and government regulation, telecommunication companies have little incentive to provide new, high-speed services to rural areas, inner cities, and other high-cost or low-revenue places.[2] The expansion of broadband will only exacerbate this problem.

For the first time in federal legislation, the Act sets forth principles and mechanisms designed to guarantee that a certain set of telecommunication services is available to all at affordable rates.[3] The universal

1 Sanyal and Schön (1999).
2 Wilhelm (1999b); see also McChesney (1999).
3 Benton Foundation (1996).

service rules mandated by the Act seek to: lower basic telephone rates in rural markets, where it is more expensive to provide service; reduce rates for low-income consumers who have difficulty maintaining their telecommunication services; provide rate parity for high-bandwidth urban and rural telemedicine connections; and provide schools and libraries with discounts for basic and advanced communication networks such as the Internet.[4] The Act is important because it set the tone for a great deal of policy. Although it has helped move telecommunications policy forward in important ways, it misses the mark in other ways. For example, the focus on schools and libraries builds on existing infrastructure but does not include the other places, such as CTCs, that low-income people access the Internet.

Federal Policies and Programs Focused on Universal Access

Telephone: Lifeline Assistance and LinkUp America

The Act has preserved and strengthened two programs that serve low-income consumers who have difficulty securing basic telephone service – the Lifeline Assistance Program and the LinkUp America Program. Instituted by the Federal Communications Commission (FCC) in the mid 1980s, Lifeline provides reductions in monthly telephone service charges for low-income consumers who have difficulty getting and maintaining basic telecommunication services. As of 1997, 44 states participated in the program. LinkUp provides federal support to reduce initial connection charges by up to one-half for qualified low-income consumers. The FCC has expanded both programs to make them available in every state, territory, and commonwealth, and has increased the federal contribution to Lifeline support. The FCC also adopted changes that require all providers of interstate telecommunication services to contribute to universal funding mechanisms. Other new FCC rules allow all eligible telecommunications carriers to receive support for offering Lifeline and LinkUp services, thereby expanding the base of companies that contribute to and provide offset communication service rates.[5]

4   Benton Foundation (1997).
5   Benton Foundation (1997).

Low-income households that would otherwise "fall off" telephone networks, or be unable to join them, benefit from these two programs by being able to access essential services such as emergency health-care, and fire and police stations. From an economic perspective, affordable rates for low-income households generate more income than do unused lines. By helping households stay connected to telephone networks, universal service initiatives can make a contribution to fixed costs and lessen the burden on other ratepayers.[6] In recent years, telephone penetration rates have remained relatively constant and at the time of writing stand at about 94 percent. However, 43.5 percent of families who depend entirely on public assistance and 50 percent of female-headed households living at or below the poverty line lack telephone service. African-Americans and Latinos lag about 10 percentage points behind their white counterparts in access to telephones even when income is held constant.[7] These programs are important because most people, especially low-income people and people in rural areas, continue to access the Internet through telephone lines. In addition, policy makers tend to look at and draw upon earlier generations of programs when making new policy.

E-Rate[8]

The newest universal funding mechanism is the E-Rate program. The E-Rate initiative attempts to address the technology gap by defraying connection costs at public education institutions. Although these institutions started to receive small levels of funding from the federal and state governments in the early 1990s, the Act, through the E-Rate program, has substantially expanded that commitment. The E-Rate program provides discounts of 20 to 90 percent on telecommunications services, Internet access, and internal connections for schools and libraries that serve poor and rural communities. The discount provided depends on the income level of the community. It is important to note that CTCs are not eligible for E-Rate funding, even though they tend to serve the very populations this program is designed to reach. This program is particularly significant because it creates an

6   Cooper (1996).
7   www.benton.org
8   For a more complete history of the E-Rate, see Carvin (2000).

important connection between our education and telecommunications systems.[9] Policy makers who supported the E-Rate legislation believed that it would both help to create an appropriately skilled workforce and improve educational opportunity.[10] The E-Rate is also important because it subsidizes important community infrastructure in places that the market might not choose to build.

Funding for the E-Rate program comes from fees collected from long-distance telecommunications providers who received relief from network access fees when the E-Rate was created.[11] Between November 1998 and February 1999, program commitments totaled $1.66 billion; 67 percent of the funds were allocated to urban schools and 11 percent to rural schools. Funding for the second and third years of the program increased to $2.25 billion per year. During the first two years of the program, the largest share of E-Rate funds (58 percent) supported the acquisition of equipment and services for internal building connections: 34 percent was used for telecommunications services and 8 percent helped pay for Internet access.[12] By the end of the program's second year, 70,000 public schools, 5,000 private schools, and 4,500 libraries had participated in the program. As of June 2000, more than $700 million had been awarded to 19,558 applicants. Requests for E-Rate funding for the third year exceeded available funding by more than 100 percent. The need is clearly greater than the dollars available. Also, once these schools and libraries purchase hardware and connections, they then face needs for training and content.

Although a formal evaluation of the E-Rate program has not yet been conducted, several preliminary studies suggest that the program functions as an important tool to bridge the digital divide. First, it has acted as an incentive for states to promote and make investments in telecommunications technologies for schools and libraries. In 1994, 35 percent of all public schools and 3 percent of classrooms were connected to the Internet. By 1999 access had increased to 95 percent of all public schools and 63 percent of all classrooms. The ratio of students per instructional computer also continues to improve – in 1999 the ratio of students to computers in public schools was 6 to 1,

9   Carvin (2000).
10 Carvin (2000).
11 The Schools and Libraries Division of the Universal Service Administrative Company (USAC) administers the E-Rate program.
12 US Department of Education, Planning and Evaluation Service (2000).

and by 2000 the ratio had decreased to five students per computer.[13] Libraries have also benefited from the E-Rate initiative: 95 percent of all public libraries now have at least basic access to the Internet, thanks largely to the E-Rate.[14] Second, the program has had significant impact in reducing the costs of telecommunications services for the neediest educational institutions, and it is likely to continue to do so. It is, then, an important tool to help level the playing field between relatively advantaged and relatively disadvantaged areas. Third, early evidence indicates that the E-Rate program may be producing important spillover effects. A recent survey of organizations that participated in the program[15] indicates that the positive externalities engendered by the E-Rate program include:

- increased involvement in and opportunities for learning;
- greater parental involvement in children's learning;
- increased community interest and investment in the Internet, spurred by the access points created in public schools;
- positive changes in school district planning practices;
- additional dollars leveraged from state governments and private foundations;
- the development of innovative partnerships among diverse community institutions (for example, businesses, community colleges, community centers, museums, and schools).[16]

At the same time, the E-Rate has also caused other issues to surface. Like most policies, the E-Rate has had unintended effects on the positive and the negative side. A recent study of the E-Rate in four midwestern school districts found that:

- professional development needs are increasing geometrically;
- school districts are highly dependent on E-Rate funding;
- the current E-Rate process taxes relationships with vendors;
- "building basics" delay the deployment of information technology.[17]

13   Cattagni and Farris (2001).
14   www.nclis.gov
15   Education and Library Networks Coalition (2000).
16   Education and Library Networks Coalition (2000).
17   Carvin (2000).

Policy makers must learn from and adapt to these early lessons in order to maximize the effectiveness of the program. E-Rate funding should be packaged together with support to meet these other needs.

By helping to build community infrastructure and focusing on the geographic areas that tend to be on the wrong side of the digital divide – poor rural and inner city neighborhoods, for example – the E-Rate does acknowledge and begin to rectify the reality that the market on its own will not fully serve these communities.[18] However, the E-Rate does not go far enough to address universal service needs. Some public interest advocates believe that by targeting one aspect of the digital divide, mainly K-12 schools, the E-Rate program diverts attention from the principle of universal service and divides the universal constituencies into "haves" (schools with a high percentage of children eligible for the school lunch program, libraries, and rural health centers) and "have nots" (every other public interest group from nonprofits to community colleges and community technology centers).[19] Others contend that the E-Rate acts as a powerful disincentive for collaboration with institutions such as CTCs. The Act insists that all recipients of E-Rate funds be libraries, schools, or rural health facilities, excluding many community technology providers from accessing these funds and from working with those institutions that are eligible.

The FCC establishes minimum standards for universal service policies, yet states' regulatory agencies and public utilities are free to broaden definitions outlined in the Act and to recognize community networks and centers as eligible for telecommunications discounts. Thus far, California and Louisiana have authorized discounts for community groups.[20] In North Carolina, NCExChange, a program dedicated to promoting and supporting the effective use of electronic networking technologies by nonprofit organizations and low income communities throughout the state, has been working with the NC Nonprofit Users Group to redefine universal service. Community technology activists have expressed frustration that most community technology efforts are not part of the FCC mandate and that each state must fight to authorize the E-Rate for these groups.

---

18 Carvin (2000).
19 Grunwald (1999b: 15).
20 See section on state public utility commissions below.

Broadband: the Next Frontier for Universal Service

Broadband technologies are currently concentrated in metropolitan areas, and in many instances only a few neighborhoods within a metro area. As the rollout of these new technologies occurs over the next several years, their potential impact on the current technology gap is a very real concern among community technology activists. Chapter 1 listed the uneven development of infrastructure such as broadband as one of the sustaining factors of the digital divide.

As broadband technologies become commonplace, information will become more instantaneously available, real-time audio and video will replace the relatively static text and image files on the Internet, telephony will be transformed, and instant messaging will become the norm. Unless broadband technologies are equitably distributed, the digital divide will be exacerbated – those with dial up connections will be excluded from much of the information that will be available, while others with speedier connections will enjoy the benefits these connections provide. Limiting the definition of access to dial-up connectivity may foster the creation of a broadband divide in the future. As chapter 2 noted, the NTIA has begun to include analysis of access to broadband in its reports.[21]

When the Act was passed in 1996, telecommunications companies argued that deregulation would allow them to more quickly and equitably roll out advanced technologies, including broadband. Consumer advocates have recognized that the deployment of advanced communications networks has not happened to the extent promised by industry. In response to this failure and to the increased recognition of the importance of broadband technologies, community technology advocates have begun to organize around this issue.

One initiative is the Broadband Bill of Rights ("the Bill"), developed by the New Networks Institute in partnership with other consumer advocates. Although some of the statements made in the Bill already exist in state and federal communications law, this declaration reaffirms the principles of telecommunications equity in the face of mergers between and false promises made by telecommunications carriers. The Bill lays out the following 13 rights that consumers should be entitled to:

1   *Access:* Broadband access via local networks to all areas of the public Internet;

21   See US Department of Commerce (2000a).

2 *Choice:* Choice of speed and product (for example, SDSL, ADSL, T-1), vendor, technology, and platform;

3 *Timeliness:* Rapid and trouble free installation of physical infrastructure for broadband access;

4 *Availability:* Guaranteed right to broadband services, regardless of whether they live in an urban or rural area;

5 *Accurate information:* Accurate and timely information from supplier;

6 *Reliability:* High-speed connections that are 99 percent reliable;

7 *Customer services and repairs:* Timely repairs made within a reasonable window of time;

8 *Real broadband speed:* Speed contracted for should work 95 percent of the time;

9 *Enforcement and compensation:* Mechanisms for enforcement of consumer rights;

10 *Broadband true-up:* Telecommunications companies have received massive financial incentives/subsidies to roll out broadband, therefore accountability for their record to date should be required;

11 *Equal access to the customer – marketing priority:* All companies should have equal access to lines, increasing consumer choice;

12 *Divestiture:* Divestiture of conglomerates to promote competition, thereby decreasing costs for consumers;

13 *Competitive broadband bill of rights:* The entire chain of customers, including ISPs, should have equal access to lines.[22]

Although the broadband debate is still in its infancy, it will certainly emerge as a key digital divide policy issue. The current record of telecommunications carriers and the existing geographic inequalities in access to broadband technologies indicate that some form of government intervention will be needed to ensure that all communities have access to the benefits that advanced communications provide.

Other Federal Programs to Bridge the Digital Divide

The programs reviewed here, grouped by federal department, are those with an explicit goal of addressing the digital divide. The residence of digital divide programs in the departments of Commerce,

22 New Networks Institute, http://www.newnetworks.com/broadbandbill.htm

Education, and Housing and Urban Development testifies to the breadth and complexity of this issue. At the same time, the range of departments dealing with this problem points to the fragmentation of the federal policy response, a topic that will be discussed in greater detail at the end of this chapter.

Department of Education

The US Department of Education has several funded initiatives focused on bridging the digital divide in American schools. The Department's Office of Educational Technology (OET) develops national educational technology policy and implements policy goals through its technology programs. Recognizing that progress has been made in access and connectivity in recent years, OET has shifted its focus to assisting the education community to become trained to use technology to improve teaching and learning. The Office of Education Technology administers a range of programs that support educational technology. Some programs, such as the Community Technology Center Program, were developed in response to the emergence of the digital divide, while other programs have been in existence prior to policy focused on the digital divide. For example, the Star Schools program was established in 1988 to improve distance learning, and over time the program has increased relevance due to the presence of a digital divide.

Community Technology Center Program

The Community Technology Center (CTC) Program is a federal initiative that acknowledges the role of community-based organizations and nonprofits in delivering access to basic and advanced telecommunication services. This program supports the development of CTCs that provide access to information technology and related learning services to children and adults. Grants are targeted to public and private nonprofit and for-profit agencies and organizations, as well as state and local education agencies and institutions of higher education. Congress appropriated $10 million in fiscal year 1999 to support CTCs as part of the budget for the Adult and Vocational Education Office of the US Department of Education. The funding dollars increased to $32.5 million in fiscal year 2000, supporting 72 grantees to create new and maintain existing CTCs.

In addition to the Community Technology Center Program, several other Department of Education programs support bridging the digital divide. Although most of these programs focus on supporting the use of technology in K-12 schools[23], some also encourage the development of partnerships between schools and other community organizations. For example, the 21st Century Community Learning Centers, Technology Innovation Challenge Grants, and the Technology Literacy Challenge Fund specifically extend beyond the schools, encouraging school systems to partner with other organizations and to use federal funds to leverage the additional dollars needed to sustain innovative technology programs. The Star Schools program makes grants to a range of education entities to promote the use of telecommunications for improved instruction, literacy skills, and vocational education for underserved populations. The Clinton administration initiated the Teacher Training in Technology program in 1999 to prepare teachers, through collaborative arrangements with institutions of higher education, to use modern learning technologies.

Department of Commerce

The National Telecommunications and Information Administration (NTIA), an agency of the US Department of Commerce, is the Executive Branch's principal voice on domestic and international telecommunications and information technology issues. NTIA works to spark innovation, encourage competition, help create jobs and provide consumers with more choices and better quality telecommunications products and services at lower prices. NTIA is charged with three primary goals: 1) providing greater access to telecommunications for all Americans; 2) advocating for greater foreign market access for the United States; and 3) creating new opportunities with technology.

It is from these goals that NTIA has become the leading governmental actor on the digital divide. NTIA researches and disseminates the *Falling Through the Net* series of reports on the digital divide. NTIA also assists state and local governments, educational and healthcare entities, libraries, public service agencies, and other groups in effec-

---

23   K-12 refers to primary and secondary schools, or elementary and secondary schools. "K" refers to "kindergarten," which in the US is the year before first grade.

tively using telecommunications and information technologies to better provide public services and advance other national goals. This is accomplished through the administration of the Technology Opportunities Program (TOP) and the Public Telecommunications Facilities Program (PTFP). PTFP supports the expansion and improvement of the delivery of public radio and television to underserved areas of the United States, while the TOP program focuses on computers, the Internet, and related information technologies.

Technology Opportunities Program (TOP)

In 1994, the U.S. Department of Commerce's National Telecommunications and Information Administration (NTIA) initiated the Telecommunications and Information Infrastructure Assistance Program (TIIAP). The program name was recently changed to the more straightforward Technology Opportunities Program, or TOP. As described by the NTIA, TOP is a program that provides matching grants to nonprofit organizations such as schools, libraries, hospitals, public safety entities, and state and local governments. TOP funds projects that improve the quality of, and the public's access to education, healthcare, public safety, and other community-based services. Grantees use the funds to purchase equipment for connections to networks, including computers, video conferencing systems, network routers, and telephones; to buy software for organizing databases; to train staff, users, and others in the use of equipment and software; to purchase communications services, such as Internet access; to evaluate the projects; and to disseminate the project's findings.

Since its inception, TOP has awarded 456 grants in 50 states, the District of Columbia, and the U.S. Virgin Islands. Approximately $150 million in federal grant funds has been matched by more than $221 million from local, state, and private-sector sources. Although tremendous benefit has been achieved in low income communities through the TOP program, funding for demonstration programs has actually decreased over time. The TOP program began in fiscal year 1994 with $26 million in funding for competitive grant awards. By fiscal year 2000, only $13.9 million was available. The Clinton administration and community technology advocates worked to increase appropriations to $42.5 million for FY (fiscal year) 2001. The increase in TOP funding for FY 2000 was heartening to digital divide practitioners. More recently, however, the Bush administration has attempted to eliminate the program. At the very least, severe cuts are likely.

Department of Housing and Urban Development

Established in 1965, the U.S. Department of Housing and Urban Development (HUD) works to ensure that all Americans have access to decent, safe and affordable housing. HUD's goals are to:

- create opportunities for homeownership;
- provide housing assistance for low-income persons;
- work to create, rehabilitate, and maintain the nation's affordable housing;
- enforce the nation's fair housing laws;
- help the homeless;
- spur economic growth in distressed neighborhoods;
- help local communities meet their development needs.

HUD has a variety of grants that support affordable housing programs, community building efforts, and economic development projects. Recognizing that access to and training on technology is critical to improve the lives of the populations the agency serves, HUD launched Neighborhood Networks in 1995.

Neighborhood Networks

The Neighborhood Networks program encourages the development of computer learning centers in HUD-insured and assisted housing. Although this initiative is unfunded, as of November 2000 it had supported the development of 641 learning centers currently in operation, as well as 272 centers in the planning stage. Neighborhood Network centers offer a range of technical and nontechnical services to low-income residents including computer training, Internet access, job readiness support, microenterprise development, GED certification, healthcare, and social services. Services available through the centers help residents become more self-sufficient, employable, and economically self-reliant.

Despite the lack of funding, HUD has made arrangements that aid in the creation and maintenance of these centers. For example, HUD has set up a Neighborhood Networks Technical Assistance hotline. Centers can also request assistance online by visiting the Online Networking section of the website. HUD also established a Neighborhood Networks Center-to-Center Mentoring Program. Still, the absence of funding limits the potential of HUD's Neighborhood Networks program. HUD resources are only intended to serve as "gap fillers." Owners of HUD-insured and assisted properties must seek support from state and local government, educational institutions, private foundations, and corporations, placing them in the same position as other CTCs. Owners may borrow funds from financial institutions for hardware, software, and start-up costs provided that the loan is not secured against the property, does not lead to unapproved rent increases, and does not interfere with the services that the property has agreed to provide.

Local HUD resident initiative specialists and asset managers assist owners and residents in developing their Neighborhood Network plans and help them to identify local resources and potential partners. HUD may allow owners to use certain portions of their HUD assistance (for example, budgeted rent increases and special rent adjustments) to cover the costs of establishing a center.[24]

HUD has also begun to partner with other organizations in order to leverage greater resources. For example, HUD joined forces with the National Council on the Aging (NCOA) to train seniors interested in technical jobs. Neighborhood Network staff have also met with representatives of a national youth organization that is managed by a federal agency to discuss ways they can work together to promote youth leadership in communities. Neighborhood Networks National Partners is a list of partner organizations that targets particular populations. In short, this program does a great deal with virtually no dollars. At the same time, HUD could do more. For example, the City of Seattle has located several community technology centers in its housing projects.[25] It seems logical to reach people where they live.

Flexible Funding Opportunities

The programs discussed above represent the lion's share of the federal government commitment to addressing the digital divide program.

---

24 Additional resources that owners can use to fund centers include: residual receipt accounts; owner's equity; funds borrowed from Reserve for Replacement Accounts; funds from rent increases under the Budgeted Rent Increase Process; funds from rent increases under a Special Rent Adjustment.
25 See chapter 8 for more on this.

Additional support, however, exists within programs that provide state and local officials with discretion regarding how the funds are spent. State and local officials have used funds from a range of programs, including the Workforce Investment Act (WIA), Temporary Assistance for Needy Families (TANF), and the Department of Justice's Weed and Seed program, to combat the digital divide. The lessons learned from these state and local experiments should be lifted up and disseminated so that others can learn from them. In addition, federal officials should study those efforts that have borne fruit at the state and local levels, and consider ways to preserve, strengthen, and expand them through more stable funding streams or greater institutionalization.

One example of using Weed and Seed funding from the Department of Justice to support digital divide programs can be found in Pittsburgh. Operation Weed and Seed seeks to "weed" violent offenders, drug traffickers, and other criminals out of target neighborhoods and to "seed" the area with human services and neighborhood revitaliztion efforts. In Pittsburgh these dollars were used to support 33 community technology centers and networks in neighborhoods throughout the city. The community technology efforts in these sites are in various stages of development and cover a range of community facilities including public schools, a public-housing facility, youth tutorial projects at local churches, YMCAs, a substance abuse treatment center, and a community development organization (CDC). The Pittsburgh example illustrates that "nontechnology" dollars are often used to support community technology efforts, making it challenging to determine the scope of digital divide funding. The example also highlights how technology can support community development efforts in diverse ways.

The Comprehensive Incumbent/Dislocated Worker Retraining Program administered by the US Department of Labor (DOL) and the Employment and Training Administration (ETA) is another example of flexible funding that could support digital divide efforts. The program's goal is to test the ability of the workforce development system to create projects or industry-led consortia for the purpose of upgrading the skills of current workers, and designing or adapting training curricula in skills shortage occupational sectors. New and growing occupations in technological fields is one area the Worker Retraining Program supports. For example, Washington State uses dollars from this program to support training partnerships between community colleges and workforce PICs in the areas of networking, systems administration, and related information technologies.

Recent Developments

The election of George W. Bush has called the federal government's commitment to the digital divide issue into question. When President Bush released his first budget request in spring 2001, he proposed a funding increase for CTCs. Yet the increase was far lower than the $400 million that he had proposed for the CTC program during the 2000 presidential campaign. Additionally, it seems that there may be a change in funding priorities for CTCs away from rural areas. The FY 2002 budget also proposes to shift the federal Community Technology Center (CTC) Program, which is currently housed under the US Department of Education, to the Department of Housing and Urban Development. Funds would then be distributed through the Community Development Block Grant program. The budget calls for $80 million to integrate the CTC program with an expanded version of the HUD Neighborhood Networks program. Community technology activists have expressed concern over this proposed change – they see it as a threat to a program that is working well overall.[26]

The future of the Technology Opportunities Program is also uncertain. Bush's FY 2002 budget proposes a dramatic decrease in funding for the Department of Commerce's Technology Opportunities Program (TOP). Under the FY 2002 budget, $16 million dollars is available for TOP, which is one-third of the FY 2001 budget. The proposed changes in federal policy that directly address the digital divide show that this issue has not yet been fully embraced as a priority for government. As a result, federal programs and support remains extremely vulnerable.

State and Local Policy

Public Utility Commissions

Although the Telecommunications Act of 1996 limits local and state regulation in favor of a competitive market environment, devolution creates new opportunities for organization at the state and local levels.[27] In accordance with the Act, each state's Public Utility

---

26 Turner (2001).
27 Kim and Muth (1999).

Commission (PUC) is responsible for designing its state's technology plan. Community involvement in the development of these plans is necessary to protect the public interest. This section examines how public interest advocates in a number of states have advanced universal service goals through regulatory processes approved by the state PUCs.

PUCs and the public interest

State PUCs in California and Louisiana have authorized E-Rate discounts for community groups. In California, community-based organizations (CBOs) that provide healthcare, job training, job placement, or educational instruction are eligible for universal service discounts. Funding for these discounts comes from California's Teleconnect Fund surcharge of 0.41 percent on telephone bills. Although efforts by the California Utilities Commission are important in expanding universal access to include CBOs, many community technology advocates believe that a strictly discount-focused approach is not sufficient to meet their universal service goals.[28] Instead, they argue, provisions should be made for capacity building, the training of CBO staff, and administrative costs.

Louisiana, for example, provides support for a centralized help desk for CBOs and funding for a development officer to raise additional resources from other sources. Louisiana uses state funds rather than surcharges to provide universal service discounts to eligible CBOs.

The New York State Diffusion Fund is another example of a statewide funding pool made available through a state PUC. The $50 million fund, established as part of the performance-based incentive regulatory plan for NYNEX, is administered by the Public Utility Law Project (PULP) through a five-year diffusion program. The purpose of the program is to bring advanced technology to economically disadvantaged areas of New York. Approximately 80 percent of program funds have been earmarked for the NYNEX-installed network infrastructure necessary to support advanced telecommunication applications. The remaining 20 percent has been set aside for grantee equipment and project-related training. The program does not provide participants with assistance for monthly telecommunications services.

28   Schofield (1998).

Project participants have included educational, local government, and healthcare institutions, libraries, CBOs, and small businesses.

In Ohio, a coalition of community groups and consumer advocates formed in response to Ameritech Ohio's application to the Public Utilities Commission of Ohio (PUCO) to change the way in which the company was regulated by the state. The coalition pressed Ameritech for community computer centers, an educational technology fund, general rate reductions for all residential customers, and the establishment of a Universal Service Assistance (USA) program, which would allow low-income residents to get reduced-rate phone service without having to pay a deposit and connection charge.[29] All of these were included in the final agreement. The precedent-setting Ameritech case marked a major victory for public interest advocates. It also marked the first time that community technology centers were included in the settlement of a case by a state PUC.

PUCs operate at the local level as well. Founded in 1999, Digital Vision is a broad-based coalition of business, technology professional groups, and community organizations based in Cleveland, Ohio. In June 2000, Digital Vision successfully advocated for the creation of a $3 million Cleveland Technology Fund using dollars from the City's Public Utilities Commission. The Cleveland Technology Fund focuses on making computers, and related equipment and services, accessible in low-income neighborhoods throughout Cleveland. The Cleveland example helps to show that a city need not have a high-tech economic base in order to create and support efforts to close the digital divide.

Telecommunication mergers

Telecommunication mergers provide windows of opportunity for state PUCs to place conditions on mergers in order to improve access to and diffusion of technology. State PUCs in Ohio and California have opened up the merger review processes to include a discussion of strategies for securing funds for community telecommunications services.[30] On the local level, the City of Seattle extracted 500 cable drops from AT&T when it took over TCI.

The intended merger between SBC Communications and Ameritech will likely be another precedent-setting case for government and

29   Jacobs (1998).
30   Wilhelm (1999b).

community technology advocates. The consolidation would create the largest local telephone company in the United States, with a local calling area covering 13 states. On June 30, 1999, SBC and Ameritech submitted to the FCC a list of conditions to the merger, based on negotiations with FCC staff, aimed at addressing public interest concerns. Public interest advocates have argued that the provisions do not go far enough in bridging the digital divide, but are meant merely to get the companies and the regulators through the merger process. For instance, although SBC has agreed to fund community technology centers and other projects aimed at helping low-income communities gain access to telecommunication technologies in prior settlements in California and Ohio, the FCC has not expanded those efforts throughout the SBC/Ameritech territory.[31]

In Ohio, parties involved with the merger case before the PUCO agreed to several important consumer protections including $3.25 million to fund CTCs and other telecommunications projects in low-income communities and a commitment not to redline city neighborhoods when advanced and broadband services are introduced.[32] When preparing their case for regulators to place conditions on prospective local mergers, community groups should consider the importance of funding for the following: capacity building and infrastructure development in underserved neighborhoods; new computer centers; assessments of community technology needs; and outreach and awareness of CTC programs.[33] Ellis Jacobs, who represented the Edgemont Neighborhood Coalition in the Ameritech Ohio case, suggests that public interest advocates and community-based organizations seeking to address the digital divide through regulatory bodies must educate regulators on the digital divide to build alliances with community organizations, consumer advocacy groups, and civil rights organizations.

Mergers such as the SBC/Ameritech one provide important points of entry to create new policy and help institutionalize mechanisms to close the digital divide. However, because they are reactive and dependent on whether and when a merger occurs, they should not be thought of as primary policy vehicles. Narrowing the technology gap will require much more proactive policy.

During the 1997 merger between Pacific Telesis and SBC Communications, the California Public Utilities Commission, in partnership

31 Breckheimer and Taglang (1999).
32 Edgemont Neighborhood Coalition (1999).
33 Wilhelm (1999b).

with community organizations, were able to negotiate resources for community technology efforts as a condition of the merger. The outcome was the Community Partnership Agreement, through which Pacific Telesis has pledged up to $80 million to support various community technology initiatives. Fifty million dollars has been used to create the Pacific Bell Community Technology Fund, which is managed by the nonprofit Community Technology Foundation of California. As of 2001, $10 million in grants has been distributed by the Community Technology Foundation to support digital divide efforts across the state. The Community Partnership Agreement also supports a universal service initiative and a research fund.

Infrastructure investments

Many states have used state, and sometimes federal (for example, TOP), funding to add physical infrastructure to their telecommunications infrastructure in order to promote access and connectivity. In 1996, Missouri's General Assembly appropriated $6 million for Missouri Express, a three-year capital-improvement project to create community information networks (CINs) across the state. Part of the funding was allocated to increase backbone and bandwidth capabilities for diagnostic equipment. The remainder has helped create and maintain CINs. Missouri Express funds were not given directly to local CINs but were rather used to support these CINs through provision of equipment and general technical support, operation of a reference desk, funding for connections to modem pools, local phone line charges, system administration fees, and maintenance contract costs.

The state of Iowa has underwritten the construction of the Iowa Communications Network (ICN), a fiber-optic network that extends more than 3,400 miles across the state, reaching into all 99 counties. The ICN, a $350 million project, provides the telecommunications infrastructure to make educational, medical, and government services more accessible to all Iowans. This state-administered network provides dynamic interactive video, increased access to the Internet, and enhanced voice and data transmission services. State ownership of the network has been a source of controversy, prompting some law makers to call for the sale of the network or the development of a public–private management partnership. Private telecommunication companies complain that the state-subsidized network unfairly competes for business.[34] Although investments in infrastructure provide a way to increase access and connectivity, some question the appropriateness of using state and federal funds to contribute to the privately owned telecommunications system.[35]

Initiated in 1996, Texas's Telecommunications Infrastructure Fund (TIF) is one of the most significant state-level telecommunications initiatives. TIF's mission is to help Texas deploy an advanced telecommunications infrastructure by promoting connectivity for public schools, higher education, public libraries, and nonprofit healthcare facilities. Priority is given to organizations that address the needs of rural and underserved populations. As of FY 2000, TIF had funded 4,039 projects – both collaborative and single entity, competitive and noncompetitive – amounting to approximately $592.7 million. Until recently, the majority of TIF grants were awarded to public school districts; in 2000, TIF expanded its funding programs to include collaborative community networks, awarding over 30 grants of $500,000 to community networks throughout the state of Texas. TIF also supports technology training programs and encourages the development online content that strengthens education, healthcare, and libraries in Texas.

Franchise Agreements

Local government can advance universal service goals in the negotiation of franchise agreements[36] with telecommunications carriers. Franchise agreements are the arrangements made between government and telecommunications firms regarding the provision of services to a local area. These agreements have historically had terms of 10 to 15 years. Long-term agreements were originally necessary in order for companies to recoup their investments. More recently, franchise agreements have been negotiated for shorter terms, generally around five years.[37] Telecommunications providers may seek a renewal agreement once original agreements expire.

34   Roos (1998).
35   Pigg (1999).
36   According to Grant and Berquist (2000), "A franchise is a license, or contract, between municipalities and telecommunications providers for use of public rights-of-way. Under federal law, municipalities award franchises to cable television systems; and, in many states, municipalities award franchises to incumbent local exchange carriers (ILECs) and competitive local exchange carriers (CLECs).
37   Network Democracy (1999b).

Local authorities may place conditions on telecommunications carriers in the granting and renewing of franchise agreements. In Pittsburgh, for example, community technology activists have requested that the City require TCI to build an institutional network (I-Net) as a condition of renewing TCI's franchise agreement.[38] Franchise authorities may also exact fees from telecommunications providers. For example, the City of Seattle has used a portion of revenues from cable franchise fees to support and implement community technology projects and employ a community technology planner. Although some regard franchise fees as a tax, others view them as just compensation for the use of public property. As Schuler and McClelland explain: "The streets of your town are public property, managed by your local government. The poles on the side of the road and the conduits below the ground are also managed by your local government. These 'rights-of way' and 'pole attachments' are leased to cable TV and other telecommunications companies."[39]

Another example of supporting community technology initiatives through local franchise agreements is in the city of Atlanta, Georgia. Spearheaded by Mayor Bill Campbell, the community technology initiative (CTI) is a program established to improve the quality of life of Atlanta residents by providing public access to and training on computers and the Internet. To accomplish this goal, the City is creating and operating 15 community technology centers throughout Atlanta. The first centers were opened in June 2000.

The CTI is supported by an initial startup fund of $8.1 million from MediaOne, a local cable operator. These funds were acquired through a re-negotiation of the City's Cable Franchise Agreement and the Mayor's Office of Community Technology was created to administer and oversee implementation of the CTI, as well as other related projects. Each of the CTI sites will be based within an existing or planned public facility and Atlanta residents will be able to utilize computer training and services at a nominal cost. Among the services to be provided at the centers are computer and Internet access, literacy training, computerized job searches, and advanced computer skills training (for example, desktop publishing, multimedia, and Web page design). As with mergers, exactions from franchise agreements provide a unique example of how policy makers can harness resources from current activities and steer them toward digital divide issues.

38   See Servon and Nelson (1999).
39   Schuler and McClelland (1999: 21).

Private Initiatives

Philanthropic and corporate support have also been important components of the movement to close the digital divide. Foundation and corporate dollars are more challenging to document than are public programs, given the diversity of possible funding sources. The difficulty in assessing the amount and type of giving is compounded by the fact that some foundations and corporations have discrete technology initiatives, while others fund technology as one component of larger initiatives. Although this chapter focuses on public support for the digital divide, it is important to briefly discuss efforts on the part of the foundation community and the private sector because they play a role in shaping policy. In fact, some foundations, such as Markle and Kellogg, have done their work in this area with the explicit goal of affecting policy.

Philanthropy

Robertson (2001) analyzed the contribution that foundations have made to digital divide efforts and found that in the 1998–99 time period approximately 2,700 "technology" grants of $10,000 or more, with a total value of $332,780,257, were made by 417 foundations. The criteria for being considered a technology grant were: 1) the primary or secondary purpose of the grant is for information technology; or 2) the organizations receiving the funds are classified as an information technology group.[40]

Robertson also analyzed 767 randomly selected information technology grants, and presented three key findings. First, some types of charitable institutions (for example, direct human service agencies) appear to be underfunded relative to IT grants in other areas of the public sector. Second, technology grants are heavily biased toward equipment and do not take into account other costs of technology, such as training, technical assistance, and maintenance. Finally, although a large percentage of grants are going to support interactive online activities, including distance learning and online activism, nonprofits could still benefit from increased support in this area.[41]

40 Robertson (2001).
41 Robertson (2001).

Roberston's findings indicate that the foundation community has followed a similar trend to the public sector digital divide programs with a focus on supporting access to information technology, with less support for training and content development. The emphasis on supporting the physical infrastructure indicates that philanthropy – like the public sector – should take a broader view of what it will take to close the digital divide and how to use IT to achieve broad social goals. Based on her findings, Robertson offers several recommendations for foundations to consider when supporting the use of information technology. These include:

- increase information technology grants for direct service organizations, especially human service, food and nutrition, and housing and shelter organizations;
- budget for the ongoing costs of sustaining technology over the long term as a standard part of information technology grants;
- continue to fund projects that explore innovative ways to use Internet technology to improve the delivery of nonprofit services;
- expand common grant application guidelines to ensure that every project description includes information about the technology required to implement it;
- look for ways to fund technology projects that help nonprofits evaluate impact;
- look for ways to pool technology resources for nonprofits;
- recruit more information technology experts on to foundation boards of directors.[42]

Corporate sector

Another importance source of digital divide support is the corporate sector.[43] As the digital divide gained national attention as a critical issue that society must address, the corporate sector established programs to support the diffusion of technology in low-income communities. Although corporations are an important source of support for

---

42 Robertson (2001).
43 For the purposes of this discussion the foundation arm of private corporations is considered philanthropic while digital divide support from firms falls under corporate sector support. Clearly, the lines between corporate and philanthropic funding are not that concrete, as corporations increasingly have foundations with close ties to company representatives.

the digital divide, it is challenging to quantify and characterize their giving. Corporations often support digital divide initiatives through in-kind contributions of hardware, software, networking technologies, and technical assistance, in addition to cash assistance. And, unlike the Foundation Center, which focuses on tracking the giving patterns of philanthropy, no entity exists that monitors companies in the same manner.

A recent report by the Information Technology Industry Council[44] profiled some innovative digital divide initiatives spearheaded by corporations. The report, which focused on investments in K-12 programs, higher education, lifelong learning, and teacher training programs, looked at programs initiated by large multinational corporations such as 3Com, Agilent Technologies, AOL, Apple, Cisco, Compaq, Dell, HP, IBM, Intel, Kodak, Microsoft, and others. The report found that over $1.1 billion was invested by these corporations in educational technology initiatives alone. This did not include giving in other programmatic areas, and was a small sample of corporations.

Clearly the corporate sector can have tremendous impact on bridging the technology gap. High-tech firms are clearly the most sophisticated users of technology, and through their support their knowledge could inform community technology efforts. At the same time, some question the motivations of corporate involvement in this issue. For example, some donations to schools require the schools to show advertising to the pupils. Donating to schools may also create early consumer loyalty among young people. Similarly, advancements in technology, such as broadband, quickly render earlier technologies obsolete, encouraging new rounds of consumption that feed corporate bottom lines.

Several key corporate actors, such as Bill Gates and Michael Dell, have established foundations that also give to digital divide initiatives. In fact these are private philanthropic endeavors, but they are clearly shaped by current corporate realities.[45]

The Limits of Current Policy

This chapter shows explicitly that an incomplete problem definition of the digital divide has led to policy solutions that are unequal to the

44 Information Technology Industry Council (2000).
45 See Borsook (2000) for a perspective on corporate philanthropy in the high-tech industry.

problem. Policy has emphasized access without adequately supporting training or the provision of content. If the objective of public policy is to bridge the technology gap, then policy must address the components of the problem more comprehensively. In addition to the high cost of access and the information red-lining of rural and low-income communities, the National Community Builders Network identifies four barriers to access in its guide to telecommunication technology: cultural or linguistic inappropriateness of information technology; poor location of access points; lack of adequate training and follow-up support; and uses inconsistent with the needs of the community.[46] Policy to address this issue has been fragmented, slow, and inadequate to the problem. The following problems characterize current policy around the digital divide.

Insufficient support for new and existing institutions

Perhaps the greatest single flaw of policy designed to address the digital divide is that it has failed to recognize and support the new institutions – community technology centers – that are at the forefront of dealing with this issue. With the exception of the Department of Education's CTC Program and scattered state and local programs, policy has focused on attempting to provide access through existing institutions – for example schools and libraries. Although this approach makes sense given existing infrastructure investments, policy has not done an adequate job of helping these institutions to build the capacity necessary to take on this enormous and expensive new activity. For the most part, the overall capacity of schools and libraries in low-income neighborhoods already lags behind those in wealthier areas. Without intensive support, traditional institutions in areas characterized by persistent poverty will have difficulty tackling the digital divide. By targeting traditional institutions, policy does not sufficiently recognize the fact that low-income people disproportionately use CTCs. CTCs fill gaps left by other institutions and programs. Just as the definition of technology must be expanded beyond the telephone, the definition of what kinds of organizations provide access must also be broadened.

46 National Community Building Network (1997: 8).

Fragmentation

Policy to deal with the digital divide is fragmented. This fragmentation is understandable, given that the digital divide issue cuts across a range of policy spheres including education, economic development, and social welfare. However, improved management of public policy, both across departments and between different levels, is necessary in order to comprehensively address this issue. Making sound policy to deal with the technology gap will require coordination and collaboration. At the federal level, some departments have begun to work together on specific issue areas regarding the digital divide, such as workforce development.[47] This work needs to be broadened. In Seattle, the city has created a Department of Information Technology and a position for a community technology planner who coordinates work across other city departments.[48] This approach has worked for Seattle. Other states and cities have begun similar initiatives. The San Diego Technology Alliance has completed a study of digital divide issues in that city, and Austin, Texas is currently working with a group of researchers to map community technology resources there.

Overdependence on opportunities

Many of the significant policy gains that have been made in this area have occurred through telecommunications mergers or through franchise agreements. These advances have been creative and have successfully generated important support for the community technology movement. Cities and states should clearly pursue these opportunities if and when they become available. However, this kind of policy making is reactive and subject to opportunities being available, rather than proactive. In order to leverage the potential of IT tools to create social change, policy must be more tied to these goals and less dependent on circumstances.

---

47 US Department of Commerce, US Department of Education, US Department of Labor, National Institute for Literacy and Small Business Administration (1999).
48 See chapter 8 for a full discussion of the Seattle case, especially table 8.2.

Fragility

Current policy and programs to address the digital divide are fragile and vulnerable to reduction and elimination because of the vicissitudes of politics. Already, the Bush administration has threatened the previous commitment to this issue at the federal level. To be sure, this problem is difficult to deal with: there is no way to guarantee that resources allocated to a particular issue will not be cut. At the same time, it is important to consider ways to institutionalize efforts to address this issue in a way that will help to immunize it against such threats. One way to accomplish this would be to work to link information technology policy concretely to other relevant policy issues such as workforce development, housing, poverty reduction, and education. Doing so will require working through the fragmentation problem identified above.

Universal access does not include IT

Telecommunications policy has historically relied on the notion of universal service. Universal service policies work to extend the potential benefits of telecommunications technologies to low-income and underserved communities.[49] Universal service policies that aim to make telecommunication services affordable for low-income individuals and households are not handouts for the poor but components of a responsible economic and social policy in the information age. Such policies connect citizens to education, health and safety services, employment opportunities, businesses, and government, and allow them to engage more fully in all aspects of political, social, and economic life.[50] Moreover, by increasing subscribership to telecommunication services, universal service policies protect all ratepayers from paying for underused investments in telecommunication networks, reduce the financial burden of subscribership, and increase the value of the networks.[51]

Historically, commitment to universal service has meant providing affordable person-to-person telephone service to rural and low-income consumers through a web of subsidies. Given that telephone

49   Mitchell (1999a).
50   Servon and Nelson (2002, forthcoming).
51   Benton Foundation (1997).

service still is not universal, such subsidies remain necessary. Today, telecommunications technology extends beyond the telephone to include a wide array of voice, data, and video services provided by phone companies, cable operators, and Internet providers. In order to keep pace with recent, rapid changes in technology, the "universal service" umbrella must be expanded.

It has been difficult to generate support among policy makers for programs that treat IT as a necessary resource, such as the Lifeline and Linkup. In order to do so, policy arguments must be crafted that broaden the definition of universal access.[52] The 1934 Communications Act was enacted to "make available, so far as possible, to all the people of the United States a . . . wire and radio communication service."[53] As IT becomes increasingly necessary for people to function as full citizens, computers and the Internet must be included in policies and programs that function to ensure universal access. Leadership for the creation of universal access to IT must come from the federal government. The E-Rate, TOP and CTC programs are a solid beginning, but these efforts must be significantly expanded if the goal of closing the technology gap is to be realized. Despite strong advocacy language in the NTIA reports, public opinion about the need for universal access to IT, and about the importance of CTCs to achieving this goal, remains mixed. Access to information and telecommunication technologies is not yet established as an economic, political, or social necessity.

Insufficient education about the digital divide

Although this issue has benefited from increased publicity in Washington, and in select states and cities, overall awareness about the importance of closing the digital divide remains low. Few cities and states have implemented programs such as those discussed in this and later chapters of this book. The federal government, and most likely the US Department of Commerce NTIA, could play a central role in educating policymakers at the state and local levels about the importance of comprehensively addressing the technology gap.

Although the preceding section focused on the limits of current policy, it is important to recognize the great strides that have been made in

52   Civille (1995).
53   Quoted in Civille (1995: 195).

the last several years. Despite the problems articulated above, a few significant seeds have been sown and have begun to take root. At the same time, the digital divide has emerged as a problem in the wake of broad socioeconomic changes that affect the way we live, work, learn, and make decisions. For the most part, policy has lagged in responding to these changes. New policy is needed that better reflects the socioeconomic transformation wrought by the information society. Despite the progressively stronger rhetoric regarding the importance of access to IT in the NTIA reports, the public sector has not made a firm commitment to fully address the digital divide. Although public support is unquestionably vital to addressing the technology gap, the question of what, specifically, should be the appropriate role of government with respect to this problem remains an open one. The next four chapters deal with topical issues that intersect strongly with the socioeconomic transformation and, specifically, the digital divide. These chapters offer specific policy recommendations to deal with various components of this problem.

5

Community Technology and Youth

Why devote an entire chapter to youth when young people tend to be among the first to adopt new technology? Shouldn't we also be concerned with seniors? With the disabled? With people in rural regions? Of course. This book does not single out other specific segments of the population although much could and should be written about these and other digital divides. The focus on youth in this chapter stems from the fact that this group stands most to lose from being disconnected and most to gain from obtaining access to IT. Young people who are not connected will be potentially cut off from other opportunities IT can offer. Those who are connected will have greater access to college, to well-paying jobs, and to information that will help them more fully participate in civic society.

Research shows that low-income people and people of color are disproportionately part of the digital divide. This means that low-income children and children of color are less connected than their wealthier and white counterparts. The data on youth that we do have comes primarily from the education field and is based on what happens in the schools. Much of this data measures the student/computer ratio, and how much time a student spends on the computer each day. That data, which will be reviewed in this chapter, does show that low-income youth and youth of color are receiving inferior access to and training on IT. But knowing whether there is a computer in a child's classroom, or a computer lab in a child's school, tells us very little about that child's relationship with technology. Although these statistics are important, they only tell the beginning of what we need to know in order to make informed policy decisions. What is most important is how young people use the technology. To obtain this key part of the story, we need to look at the issue on a deeper level, and talk to students and teachers.

This chapter focuses on the role that CTCs play in introducing youth to the world of information technologies, and illustrates that technology is a powerful "hook" that inspires youth to build skills and gain a range of other key life skills. This discussion is based on in-depth fieldwork at three community technology centers: Playing2Win in Harlem; Plugged In in East Palo Alto; and the Technology Access Foundation in Seattle. The findings provide a nuanced understanding of the benefits that information technology can play in the youth development process.

Technology in the Schools

Although the focus of this chapter is on CTCs, a discussion of technology in the schools provides a context for comparison. For youth in lower-income families, the first – and often primary – exposure to computers and the Internet occurs outside the home, usually at school. Schools are in many ways the logical institution through which to diffuse IT to youth. They reach most children and represent a major infrastructure investment. It is relatively easy to generate bipartisan support for programs that reach schoolchildren. Indeed, the Clinton administration's first major digital divide initiative was to wire the schools. Specifically, technology can support the work of schools in several ways including:

- tailoring learning experiences more sharply to learner needs and abilities;
- providing students with access to resources and expertise outside the school, both enriching their learning and extending the time devoted to learning;
- supporting more authentic assessment of a student's progress;
- assisting schools in managing and guiding the learning activities of their students.[1]

In addition to the benefits stated above, facility with IT is an important skill that students need in order to succeed in life and in work. Chapter 6 will show how the information-driven economy requires a

---

1   Glennen and Melmed (1996). www.rand.org/publications accessed 3 October, 2000.

new and different set of skills from workers. Gaining this new skill set requires a process that begins early in a child's education.

Many school systems – and individual teachers – have begun to do incredible work with IT in the classroom. Yet the support needed to do this kind of work on a larger scale does not currently exist. Despite the good intentions of policy makers, IT programs for schools have tended to focus narrowly on access rather than more broadly. This chapter will not deal comprehensively with the issue of technology in the schools – entire books have been written about the subject.[2] At the same time, given that schools are the logical institutional choice for diffusion of IT and that a great deal of policy emphasis has been placed on getting technology into the schools, it seems important to sketch out the most important issues schools face, as well as presenting some positive examples here. Doing so helps to show how youth-oriented CTCs differ from schools with respect to technology, and how schools and CTCs might work together to benefit youth.

The majority of data simply counts numbers of computers and children but fails to ask deeper questions about the quantity and quality of time children spend using computers. Debates around technology in the classroom have been polarized into unproductive conversations about whether computers can and should take the place of teachers. No one who supports technology in the schools believes that technology can do the job of teachers. These debates need to be reoriented toward discussions of how technology can support what teachers do, and what teachers need in order to use IT to prepare their students. Once again, the key issue is not access, but how computers are used to educate children. Conte maintains that we must address the following specific issues: content; curriculum reform; professional development; assessment; equity; and community involvement.[3]

IT is deployed inequitably in the schools

Enormous inequities exist between schools in terms of the IT they have and how they are using it. Schools in wealthier areas tend to have greater resources for technology in the schools than do schools in poorer ones. In 1997–8, schools in the highest poverty areas had only one computer for every 17 students, while more affluent schools had

2 See, for example, Healy (1998).
3 Conte (2000).

one computer for every 12 students.[4] In Maryland, the number of schools reporting that their students regularly use technology to gather information from a variety of sources such as the Internet decreases as the percent of students receiving free and reduced-price lunch increases.[5] Further, a recent study found that schools serving higher-income students generally used computers in more intellectually powerful ways, such as analyzing information and making presentations, whereas schools in low-income districts tended to use computers to reinforce basic skills and for remediation.[6] Although teachers in lower-income schools are more likely to use computers for "remediation of skills" and "mastering skills just taught," a recent study indicates that, at the secondary school level, teachers in lower-income schools see computers as a valuable tool for teaching students to work independently.[7] A report recently issued by the Maryland Department of Education found that "schools in wealthier areas are more than twice as likely as their peers in poorer communities to use technology to gather, organize, and store information. They are also three times more likely to use technology to perform measurements and collect data."[8]

Similar gaps exist between the level and kind of IT access and instruction occurring in predominantly white and predominantly non-white schools. A recent study by the National Center for Education Statistics found that 45 percent of teachers in schools with mainly students of color used computers or the Internet for instruction during class, whereas 56 percent of teachers with mostly white students did.[9] A survey conducted by Market Data Retrieval found that there are, on average, 16.6 students per Internet-connected computer in schools with large minority populations, compared with 8.4 for those with small percentages of minority students.[10] Further, several studies have

---

4   Becker (2000).

5   Specifically, in schools where fewer than 11 percent of students qualified for subsidized lunches, the percentage of classrooms with Internet access increased from 4 percent to 74 percent between 1994 and 1999. In those schools where at least 71 percent of students qualified for subsidized lunches, classroom Internet access rose from 2 percent to 39 percent in that time (statistics cited in Johnston, 2001).

6   Becker (2000).

7   Subject and Teacher Objectives for Computer-Using Classes by School Socio-Economic Status, Center for Research on Information Technology and Organizations.

8   Johnston (2001).

9   Cited in Reid (2001).

10   Cited in Meyer (2001).

found that low-performing students have far less access to computers than do higher-achieving students.[11] At the same time, experimental programs that gear use of technology to the needs of at-risk students have exhibited dramatically positive results.[12]

Computers in the schools can help to narrow the technology gap, but they are only part of the solution. Children from lower-income neighborhoods are as likely to use a computer in school as those from higher income neighborhoods (approximately 30 percent), but children in higher-income communities are more than twice as likely to use a computer outside of school as are children residing in lower-income communities (48 percent versus 23 percent).[13] Therefore CTCs are important access points in low-income communities that augment technology access in schools.

Schools face capacity issues around integrating technology

Teachers legitimately maintain that they are already overwhelmed with what they must accomplish. The idea of having to master and teach constantly changing new technology without any support or incentive seems unreasonable to some. A recent survey by the National Center for Education Statistics found that only 20 percent of teachers feel prepared to integrate IT into their classrooms.[14] In order to use technology effectively, teachers must first be literate and comfortable with a range of educational technologies.[15] Getting to that point requires time, not only to learn the initial applications but also to experiment with new technologies, share experiences with other teachers, and plan and debug lessons using new methods that incorporate technologies.[16] Teachers have precious little free time, which means they will need to be paid for the after-hours, weekend, and/or summer time necessary to learn and integrate IT into their teaching. A Seattle elementary school administrator said: "You have so little time when you are a teacher that, if you are planning around the technology and the technology fails you, you are going to want to stop using the technology, and that happens again and again."

---

11   Schofield and Davidson (1998).
12   Center for Children in Technology, cited in Manzo (2001).
13   Becker (2000).
14   Guernsey (2000: 4).
15   US Congress, Office of Technology Assessment (1995).
16   US Congress, Office of Technology Assessment (1995).

Although this problem is clearly not unsolvable, the administrator's comment does reflect current reality. Teachers and administrators have not been taught to think about how to integrate technology into what they do. Many see it as unreliable and burdensome. The problems of integrating technology are exacerbated with poor-performing kids, disabled children, and those who have limited English proficiency because these populations present additional challenges and require that IT be appropriately tailored to meet these special needs.

The federal initiative to wire schools was an important first step in the process of integrating IT into the educational system, but that process appears to have atrophied. In order for schools to operate as venues for providing experience in IT, teachers and administrators must be trained to use it appropriately. For technology to work well, human infrastructure must be built to complement computers and wiring.[17]

Rather than using IT as a tool to foster creative thinking and problem solving, many schools have employed it as another way to do rote work such as math and spelling drills. Narrow applications such as these have not exhibited great results[18] but these findings should not be taken to mean that IT has no place in the schools. Research on how computers should be used, and what difference they make, is thin. Appropriate outcome measures for assessing the impact of technology-based innovations in schools are lacking; existing research tends to use traditional measures of student achievement, such as test scores, which may not be appropriate.[19] Many of the findings from the CTCs discussed above would not have surfaced using these traditional measures.

Incorporating technology into the schools is expensive

Once schools are wired, they still require hardware, software, and funding for technical assistance, maintenance, and training. Schools deal constantly with limited budgets and competing demands for existing funds. Schools weighing the costs and benefits of spending on technology versus spending on hiring more teachers or preserving an arts program may decide against technology, particularly since there is

17   Conte (2000).
18   Angrist and Lavy (1999).
19   US Congress, Office of Technology Assessment (1995).

little data that strongly supports the use of technology in schools. Because technology needs to be continually maintained and upgraded, schools must budget regularly for these expenses rather than relying on one-time bond issues. The PCAST-Panel on Educational Technology *Report to the President on the Use of Technology to Strengthen K-12 Education in the US* (hereafter referred to as PCAST) recommends that at least 5 percent of all public K-12 educational spending in the US should be earmarked for technology-related expenditures. Current spending is at about 1.3 percent. A recent report documenting five school districts' experiences with funding technology programs identified the four following problems districts often face.

1   Technology must compete for funding with other needs and priorities.
2   Community resistance to higher taxes limits the district's ability to raise additional revenue.
3   Schools lack staff to handle fund raising and administration efforts.
4   Those program components that are most difficult to fund are those that are most heavily dependent on staff positions, for example, maintenance, training, and technical support.

These barriers clearly echo the issues facing CTCs identified in chapter 3. Recent data shows that schools have begun to shift their IT spending from hardware to training and software purchases, a necessary step toward employing IT to its fullest potential.[20]

IT is employed differently at schools and in CTCs

The youth interviewed for this chapter maintained that the way they use computers at CTCs is very different from how they use computers at school. Many expressed that they did not get to use the school's computers very often. Some said their school's computers did not have Internet access. Many said that they used computers only for typing exercises and copying passages of text. Nearly all said that their computer time at school was very limited. The following quotes are representative of kids' responses when asked to compare their use of computers at school and at their local CTCs.

---

20   Market Data Retrieval, "Technology in Education 1999" and "Technology in Education 2000" cited in *Education Week on the Web* (2001).

It is a program that is really boring. They teach you how to type, that's all it does. Sometimes we might do something out of a book, and you have to type a paragraph, and underline, and erase. Really silly stuff. As long as you show up for the class, and she sees you typing, you can show how many words you type per minute, you will pass. It's mostly like a typing course. It is very boring. I learn more here . . .

What is different from here and school? Well, school, involving with computers, we don't get to go in the computers that much because sometimes the Internet don't work, and we don't have a lot of computers that have the Internet.

We didn't have anybody to teach us anything at school, so it was nice to [come here]. Plus, the school didn't have much Internet connections and if they did they were slow. The computers too, they were really slow, and you would just do keyboarding for classes. Those are helpful, but not as helpful as TAF skills.

Parents also remarked on the differences between the school and the CTC.

In her school they would say, "go ahead and type it out," so she will just be pecking whatever they wrote on the paper and do that, but when she comes here they are actually teaching her, and she said there is a lot of steps to learn in order to do her website. But in school . . . they just leave them on their own, so they can't really learn anything from just sitting there pecking.

These comments admittedly come from a very small sample of people, but they are instructive nevertheless. Interestingly, several staff members from the three CTCs studied had worked in schools before moving to technology centers. All talked about the limitations of schools' current use of technology.

[I was working in] one of those schools that had received a grant from SMART to get computers in all the classrooms and for the most part, the teachers had no idea what to do with them. There were maybe two teachers in the school that knew the computers and could really create interesting content. Most of the other folks just had them sitting in the corner, and at some point, the kids would get sent to type something, and they were lucky if they could get any assistance from the teacher. It didn't seem to me that's what you would want to do with computers, ideally.

I work with a lot of schools . . . and they are just teaching technical knowledge. I would make the case that if you are just teaching technical knowledge to kids that are in school, then maybe you are doing that at the expense of giving them an education . . . If you give them the tools for learning then when HTML is gone they are going to master the next generation after that. I think one thing that technology has taught us is that we really are lifelong learners, because you cannot stay in technology if you cannot learn it.

In the schools you just see the most incredible levels of inefficiency, things not working. So the message that this is sending, everything about this environment tells them "you don't count." You know, their housing, their healthcare. They get to school and nothing works, you know, the rooms are locked, and teachers are not there, and one year they might have three teachers because teachers come and go and they get laid off, get rehired, and everything about this environment tells them "you don't count." In a place like this, just looking around, a place where everything works, there is going to be a computer that works, and there is going to be a network connection, and you are going to find your files where you saved them on the server last week. This sends the message that, "yeah, you do deserve this kind of a resource, everyone does, not just the kid in the suburban school that has a great budget and dedicated teachers that are there all the time . . . And maybe that's all they need.

Unfortunately, most schools do not currently possess the capacity to take advantage of what technology offers. Overwhelmed teachers are challenged to take on learning and teaching in an entirely new area. Schools struggle to find funding to support ongoing technology costs. At some future point, schools may be able to effectively incorporate technology into what they do. Until then, youth-oriented CTCs, particularly those located in disadvantaged areas, serve an important function.

Innovative Strategies

The issues currently facing schools do not mean that they should be written off completely as vehicles for the diffusion of IT or as key actors in closing the digital divide. The existing infrastructure investment in schools and the fact that youth spend much of their time at school argue for thinking about ways of overcoming the challenges that schools face in effectively utilizing technology. The following examples illustrate how some schools and school districts have made a deeper commitment to IT.

Technology-focused high schools

One response to the demand for technology literacy and the difficulty of integrating technology into schools has been to create entirely new schools that have a high tech focus. These new schools, which include Tech High in Philadelphia, New Technology High School in Napa, CA, and High Tech High in San Diego, have been initiated to prepare students for work in the new economy. They incorporate technology but also teach students differently and aim to develop a different set of skills. Learning is project based, which means that instead of handing out daily assignments, teachers assign periodic projects with a range of components. Traditional subjects, such as math, English, and history, are integrated to help students make connections between them. At New Technology High School in Napa, which was initiated in 1996, students must master the eight following skills before they graduate: collaboration, problem solving, oral communication, written communication, career building, technological literacy, citizenship and ethics, and content literacy.

These schools have taken a big step back from traditional pedagogy in order to think about how education can best serve students and to what extent the ways in which public schools are educating students prepare them for working in the new economy. Corporate philanthropy, largely from high-tech firms, has thus far provided the bulk of support for these schools, which are expensive. Most high-tech high schools are charter schools, which allows them to accept funding from a range of sources and to employ experimental curricula. San Diego's High Tech High is not covered by a teachers' union contract, which enables the school to pay higher salaries than teachers at the public schools generally command. These higher salaries allow the school to attract teachers with a range of experience not found at most public schools. Cost alone would prevent all schools from following this model. However, there will inevitably be important lessons about the ways in which technology can best be used, and how project-based and hands-on learning work for students. These schools must be closely studied to see what works so that the lessons can be transferred to other schools.

Promising schools

Beyond high-technology high schools, only a small handful of schools have used technology to rethink the traditional approach to education. In 1997, only 13.4 percent of teachers said they believed Internet access had helped students to achieve better results.[21] Those teachers who have creatively integrated technology into their teaching are committed to continuing. They tend to use IT in ways that approach the philosophy of the high-tech high schools, for critical thinking, teamwork, and interdisciplinary learning. Most believe that this way of teaching is more appropriate to the world of work today's students will face upon graduation. According to Conte:

> Traditional classrooms – with their strong central authority, carefully prescribed curriculums, 55-minute classes, homogeneous student groupings, and emphasis on rote learning – may have trained children adequately for the old-style mass-production economy... In the Information Age economy, however, businesses must innovate and customize their products constantly. Because hierarchical workplaces can't adapt to changing market conditions rapidly enough to survive, authority has increasingly devolved to self-directed, interdisciplinary teams. Frequent job changes have become much more common. This environment places a premium on workers who are flexible, innovative, self-directed, and able to solve problems collaboratively.[22]

In order for schools to truly embrace and benefit from technology, there needs to be a commitment at least at the level of the school district. The public school district in Bellingham, Washington has approached the problem creatively and comprehensively. Administrators first created a set of goals that they wanted to achieve with technology. They hired a technology coordinator to oversee the work. The administration also recognized a group of teachers who had already integrated IT into their work and made them mentors for a year so that they could work with other teachers. The initial commitment and careful planning have made Bellingham into a model district; faculty and administrators there continue to create lesson plans for professional development.[23]

---

21 Conte (2000).
22 Conte (2000: 4).
23 Conte (2000).

CTCs and Youth

This chapter is based on research conducted at three community technology centers that target youth: Playing2Win (P2W) in Harlem, New York; Plugged In in East Palo Alto, California; and the Technology Access Foundation (TAF) in Seattle, Washington. These three programs represent the potential of what CTCs that serve youth can accomplish. P2W and Plugged In are both community access centers that have open access hours for all community members and classes for adults as well as a strong focus on youth programming. TAF exclusively provides its services to youth of color.

Playing2Win

Many acknowledge Playing2Win to be the oldest CTC in the country. Toni Stone founded Playing to Win (the name was later changed to Playing2Win) in 1980 and opened its first computer center in 1983; its mission was to encourage community members to learn about computer hardware, software, and related technologies of the time. P2W closed for nearly a year in 1997 as a result of money and management problems, and then reopened in East Harlem. East Harlem residents have the lowest average annual household income in Manhattan, at $14,000, compared with a borough-wide average of $36,000. East Harlem is also one of New York City's top three high-risk neighborhoods in terms of infant mortality, births to teens, child abuse and neglect, childhood asthma, teen school dropout and unemployment, and juvenile felony arrests.

P2W is a project of Boys' Harbor, a 60-year old, multiservice, youth organization serving 4,000 young people and their families annually through direct service. P2W also partners with the Institute for Learning Technologies (ILT) at Columbia University; ILT provides instructional and technical support and facilitates P2W internships for Teachers' College students. These two partnerships, with Boys' Harbor and ILT, ground P2W in the community and tie it to a reputable school of education at a major university; both connections provide P2W with stability that it lacked in its earlier incarnation. P2W's current mission is "to create new economic, social, and educational opportunities for our clients by combining access to technology with effective educational programs."[24] Rahsaan Harris, the executive director of Playing2Win, described the way he perceived the connection between technology and other opportunities.

> I wanted to be able to connect young people to whatever opportunities there are out there in the world, whether that is having access to Ivy League schools if they wanted to, or getting a high paying job, and the new frontier is technology, and if these kids aren't involved in that then they will be shut out of a lot of opportunities. . . . So it wasn't necessarily technology in and of itself, but the fact that that is what opportunity is and I want to be able to connect kids to opportunity.

P2W offers its youth programs to community members aged 9 to 17. Courses are offered in four annual three-month cycles. The center is open only to youth participating in these programs Tuesday through Friday from 3:30 until 5:30. When P2W first decided to focus on youth, the youth programs had little structure. It was thought that the kids, with the help of instructors, could explore the technology and decide for themselves what was important. Program organizers soon found, however, that the kids were spending too much time playing games, using instant messenger, and surfing the Internet. Therefore, staff decided to design more structured, project-based activities. During the period in which the fieldwork for this book was conducted, the following youth programs were operating: Robotics, GirlZone, Uptown Travel Guide, and Youth Entrepreneurship.

The Robotics program was designed for the youngest P2W members because it gives them a lot of opportunity to move around and do hands-on work. Program organizers conceived of GirlZone because P2W was experiencing difficulty attracting girls to the program.[25] Since instituting GirlZone, the number of girls participating in the P2W after school program has increased dramatically. One recent GirlZone project was a "mystery quilt," for which the participants wrote poems about themselves that provided clues to their identities. They also took pictures of each other, scanned the pictures and poems into the computer, and printed them onto fabric which they used to make a quilt. This project was a vehicle for the girls to explore their own identities and also learn about the tradition of quilting.

24 www.playing2win.org, accessed February 26, 2001.
25 This gender imbalance is not true for all programs. TAF, for example, attracts and serves more girls than boys.

During the course of the project, for example, the teacher taught the girls about how African-Americans used quilts as part of the underground railroad to communicate messages to people. They read and talked about poetry in preparation for writing their own pieces. Along the way, the girls also learned how to use digital cameras, PhotoShop, and other computer programs.

P2W's Uptown Travel Guide teaches participants similar IT skills while at the same time helping them to think about their own community in a new way. According to Charles, the instructor for this project:

> After having studied abroad and traveled around the world, I wanted to expose kids – particularly black kids – to travel and what's in their neighborhood and what's not . . . If you look at a lot of tourist guides, the map stops after Central Park, so we are on the border of popular tourism. . . . The primary skill [the kids obtain] is being able to look at things and establish perspective.

This project gets the participants out of the computer center and into the community, causing them to adopt the perspective of what it would be like to be a tourist in Harlem, which helps them to see their neighborhood with fresh eyes. They develop a pride in their community while at the same time creating a useful product and learning to use technology.

In addition to these programs, P2W also houses HarlemLive, an Internet publication produced by Harlem teens. HarlemLive's mission is to "cover events, people, issues, and happenings throughout Harlem while teaching young men and women the processes of reporting, writing, editing, creating digital art, taking photographs, and publishing online."[26] HarlemLive was initiated in 1996 by Richard Calton. Calton had started a similar project from within a school but was frustrated by the limitations of being in a school setting. It was difficult to take the kids out of school without insurance being an issue, for example. Calton also recognized the benefits of working closely with very small groups of students, something that was very difficult in the context of the public schools.

Plugged In

Plugged In is a CTC that has been operating in East Palo Alto since 1992. East Palo Alto is by far the poorest jurisdiction in Silicon Valley,

26 www.playing2win.org, accessed February 26, 2001.

and is home to many communities of color. According to the 1990 Census 53 percent of the population was Hispanic and 36 percent of the population African-American. As of 1990 the unemployment rate in East Palo Alto was 7 percent, compared to 3 percent for the county (San Mateo). For that same year the median family income in East Palo Alto was $29,531, while the county median family income was $46,495.[27] By 1999 the median family income in East Palo Alto had risen to $41,241, but was still far lower than that of San Mateo county's at $69,597 (1999 Claritas Projections).[28]

East Palo Alto is surrounded by the wealth and opportunity generated by the information economy. For the most part, however, its residents remain cut off from the benefits of being so close to a hub of the new economy. Instead, they face only the negative externalities of the Silicon Valley boom, which include horrendous traffic and rising housing costs. In fact, Plugged In recently lost its lease and was forced to move to a temporary building when a core area of downtown East Palo Alto was razed for a new development. Such a move would have threatened the existence of many community-based organizations, but Plugged In has managed to maintain its operations.

In addition to its community access center, Plugged In offers three programs for youth: the Greenhouse, Plugged In Enterprises (PIE) and A La Mode. The Greenhouse, which has a strong arts component, operates as an after-school program Monday through Friday from 3:00 pm until 5:30 pm and serves kids aged 6 through 12. The children are divided into two groups. Each day one uses the computer lab while the other works on an art project; the next day they switch. The two teachers create arts and technology curricula that complement each other. When we conducted our fieldwork, the children were making a music video. During one week, they spent one day together choreographing their dance routine. The next day, half of the group painted watercolor pictures of what the dance should look like, and the other half used a software program to create flip books to illustrate the dance. The next day the groups switched. The Greenhouse project has formed partnerships with two local schools, one elementary and one high school, to reinforce and complement what the schools can do. Greenhouse staff have also created "The Tool Shed," an online resource for

27 1990 Census data.
28 Neighborhood Improvement Initiative, Community Information Packet, revised July 2000, prepared by the Haas Center for Public Service at Stanford University.

arts and technology educators to share ideas and post curricula and projects. Greenhouse staff post the curricula for their own projects in order to share their learning with other CTCs and schools.

Plugged-In Enterprises (PIE) trains teens in the latest web design technology; they then use their skills to operate a web page design business that creates web sites for community members and paying commercial clients.[29] PIE has two components: a training program and a web design business. Each quarter, approximately nine students are recruited from local schools to participate in PIE's ten-week computer training program, which is taught by staff and volunteer professionals from Silicon Valley. After completion of the training component, the students participate in a one-month in-house internship. Those who "demonstrate: improved technical skills; willingness to learn employment skills; and desire to improve themselves are eligible to become members of the production team."[30] The production team meets every weekday from 4:30 until 7:00 pm on Mondays and Tuesdays, and on Thursdays team members work on projects. Wednesdays are reserved for advanced training, and field trips – often to local companies – are scheduled on Fridays.

In addition to learning the technical skills necessary for doing the work, the teens also gain employment experience and professional skills. PIE participants undergo regular evaluations by their supervisors, and their hourly pay is dependent on their skill level and ability to transfer skills to others on the production team as well as to other teens in the community. They also meet with clients, who critique their work. The teens learn how to manage professional relationships, including dealing with criticism, working under deadlines, and juggling obligations.

In 1999, Eric Krock, Group Product Manager at Netscape Communications, volunteered to work with PIE. He was impressed enough with the participants' abilities and maturity that he set up a summer internship program for them at Netscape. The interns helped debug the latest version of Netscape. The company was so pleased with the technical and interpersonal skills of PIE youth that it expanded the program the following summer.

Most recently, Plugged In launched a second program called A La Mode, a graphic design business that targets junior and senior high

---

29 To view examples of PIE work, go to www.pluggedin.org/pie and click the "portfolio" link.
30 www.pluggedin.org, accessed February 26, 2001.

school students. A La Mode utilizes the same business and training models developed by PIE. A La Mode produces greeting and holiday cards in electronic and print form for corporate clients. In addition to learning particular IT tools and programs such as Adobe Illustrator and Photoshop, the students also learn the principles of good graphic design. Plugged In is working to create synergy and overlap between the various programs. For example, A La Mode students produce graphics for PIE websites.

Technology Access Foundation

The Technology Access Foundation (TAF) is the most structured of the three programs studied. TAF was initiated in 1992 by Trish Millines Dziko, a former Microsoft employee who was concerned about the lack of people of color working in IT fields. She started TAF in order to train youth of color to gain IT skills so that they could move into these jobs. Millines recognizes that one reason her program works is because corporate actors have begun to acknowledge the need for people of color to become producers and consumers of technology in greater numbers.

> Now it is like, get more kids into college, and train more kids in [technology]. Well, you know, you still have to train brown children, that's basically what it comes down to. And so now [corporate folks] are realizing that you have this whole untapped potential here because people of color are growing at a very fast rate and not only are they your potential customers, they are also your potential employees, and they finally came to that realization that, yes, you do have to train brown children too. They can call it anything they want, but what it really comes down to is the dollars, and I knew back in the early 1990s that that's what it was going to take to implement diversity in general at corporations. It had to hit their pocketbooks, and not in the form of lawsuits, but in the form of earned income, and you can't earn income if you do not have workers out there developing products.

TAF consists of three programs: TechStart; Connecting Communities of Color (C3); and the Technical Teens Internship Program (TTIP). TechStart works with elementary school children and involves a partnership with the Seattle public school system. C3 works through existing community-based organizations to provide access, training, and equipment. This research focused on TTIP, which is TAF's flagship program.

TTIP is a four-year program for high school students of color. After passing a rigorous application process that includes an interview with TAF staff, admitted students commit to attending classes two days each week after school. TAF maintains a strict 90 percent attendance policy: any student who misses six classes, for any reason, cannot return. For the first year, students progress through a broad, common curriculum, which begins with them taking apart their computer and putting it back together. This first activity is designed to reduce their fear of technology and to demystify the machine. At the beginning of the second year, they choose one of four tracks: multimedia; web programming; computer programming in C; and network hardware repair. Getting into the TTIP program has become extremely competitive; last year nearly 150 kids submitted applications for 40 spots.

After completing their first year, students interview for internships at Seattle corporations; during summer 2000 students were placed everywhere from Microsoft to ESPN.com. In addition to building technical knowledge, the TTIP program emphasizes soft skills development. Youth participants are coached on how to conduct themselves during an interview, and they attend workshops to teach them how to behave in a workplace. Likewise, employers who host interns must attend a one-day workshop that focuses on how to effectively interact with teenagers and how to deal with issues of race and diversity. Internships pay between $10 and $20 per hour, much more than most teens can make working at the jobs traditionally available to them.

TAF staff have found that, at the end of the first year, some participants are not ready to go into the workplace. Millines therefore created an in-house business called TT Creations where students work for 40 hours per week during the summer creating websites for local firms. These students hone their skills, become more socialized to a workplace environment, and earn 9 dollars per hour. TT Creations charges $20–$25 per hour for work that commands more than double that in the market. Many of the group's clients are other nonprofits that might not be able to afford the services of market-rate web design firms.

Millines and her staff have added components to the core technology program to make it a more comprehensive experience. For example, TTIP participants are required to perform 30 hours of volunteer time per year during their second through fourth years in order to teach the importance of giving back to their communities. In addition, TAF contributes $1,000 for every year of training that a student completes to a college fund and encourages the kids to take their SATs and apply to college.

TTIP has grown every year. The construction of a new computer lab, which can handle a larger number of students will allow TAF to better accommodate demand for the program.

Millines sees current efforts to bridge the digital divide as fragmented. TAF is therefore attempting to build a "pipeline model" through its programs. This model enables kids to get early exposure to technology and to continue with it if they remain interested. Many programs focus on a year or a few years; once a child completes the program, there is nowhere else to go. All TAF programs build on each other; for example, children who participate in TechStart are eligible to participate in TTIP, which helps to prepare them for college and the world of work.

Findings from the Three Programs

Technology is a powerful hook

Technology is a powerful hook for kids. It is the technology – the allure of learning to do "cool" things on computers – that gets them in the door of these programs. In the words of the executive director of an organization that partners with TAF: "First of all, the web is totally intriguing to kids. You know, they are like, wow, this is cool, and the idea of having a webpage seems like some unreachable thing . . . And it is like a ground for them to have a voice . . . The idea of [their work] going out into the Internet for the world, for everybody to see is . . . very inspiring."

Once they are in the door, technology becomes the vehicle for learning a whole range of other skills and abilities, from how to express themselves with words and pictures to how to behave in a professional setting. Rahsaan Harris, explaining the allure of HarlemLive, said: "The majority of people come here because the technology is cool. And then all of a sudden they slip into this journalism thing." The participants in these programs are attracted to the power of technology. One HarlemLive participant talked about the power of seeing her writing on the Internet:

The allure of having your work published on the Internet, I think that's something that is like huge and wonderful, that people kind of plug into and that makes them want to come back. Think about how a person must feel to be like, "Oh, I wrote this story and it's on the Internet if you want to go see it." That's awesome. So that kind of keeps people coming, and that is the staying power that HarlemLive has.

Young people understand that IT has gained an important place in the world, and they do not want to be left out of that world.

Youth-oriented CTCs teach kids about responsibility

Teens who are participating in P2W, HarlemLive, TTIP, and Plugged In have become more future oriented. Their involvement in these programs has helped them to think more concretely about their life opportunities. Some poverty theorists have pointed to an inability to defer gratification and to connect present actions to future consequences as factors that contribute to persistent poverty. The work of these youth-oriented CTCs helps illustrate that the problem is not a behavioral one, but rather a lack of opportunity, role models, and exposure to different career paths in low-income communities. One HarlemLive participant found out about the program through an article in a Hip Hop magazine.

I read an article about this kid who was learning HTML at HarlemLive. So I'm like, alright, I'm in the Bronx, it is a train ride away, and I'm going to find out what this place was about. So I came here and it was the first time that I ever used a computer . . . I had dropped out of school a few years ago. I had real trouble coming out. I got my GED though. I'm about to go to get my bachelor's in computer science. I want to sign up for City College. HarlemLive opened up a whole new environment for me, you know? Another road for me to go down instead of just going through the regular door, get this degree, and probably working a 9 to 5 job. I got a chance to go down this road, learn these technical skills, and maybe open up my own business one day. You know, they provided the light.

Many of the participants in these programs have decided to go to college. Although it is impossible to prove what role specifically their participation in programs played in this decision, program staff see a clear connection. Millines of TAF told us:

All of our kids, except for one or two, have pursued higher education. So that's pretty exciting. I know that some kids we had a direct influence, you know, pushing them to get their SATs taken, pushing them to pursue financial aid and things like that, where they didn't think it was possible that they would get enough help from school. So, we have had some direct effect on getting some kids in college, you know, just sort of walking them through the process . . . This year, we implemented Friday and Saturday seminars . . . about getting financial aid, and getting prepared for college, but we decided that we are going to make it a formal part of the program . . . and get the parents involved.

Recognizing the value of these programs helped TTIP participants to make difficult choices about remaining in the program instead of participating in other after-school activities. Asked about the tradeoffs he has had to make, a TTIP high-school junior told us:

Toward the end of the year everybody wanted to play track or basketball, but they were in TAF. Some people dropped out. The ones that really wanted to do it stayed. First I was thinking about dropping out, but then I thought about, I would be wasting education that I wouldn't get nowhere else for free. The chances of me going to college on a basketball scholarship are absolutely slim.

The parents we interviewed noted positive changes in their children, which they attributed to their child's participation in the program. Quotes from three parents follow.

She knows now that you have to keep working at it until you come up with an answer. If anything, she knows that she has to stick with a project. She will go away from it and she will come back. The same thing at home. I see her being more disciplined, and it carries over to other things. For instance, I don't have to bug her about doing her homework anymore, because she knows that she has to have a 2.5 so she could stay in the program. I don't even worry about it . . . It is all making her so sure of herself, and so responsible for herself; it just overlaps, you know?

Being an African-American, you look around at the kids that are interested in doing this, and they are not us. You look around and you try to talk. They are so negative, they don't think they can do it. A lot of them don't have computers. . . . I've been reading a lot and I've been going to classes, and things like crewing and ballet and tap dancing and piano lessons, they say that these are things that discipline you. These are the extras that most of the time minorities or low-income families – they can't do the extra things, but these are the things that round up a child.

Before she began to get a strong interest in computers, I had the computer at home already. She didn't really become as interested as she is right now until she started really getting involved and she saw the advantages of having computer knowledge and what were the different things that she could do.

Participation prepares youth for the world of work

Many of the participants in the TTIP program had worked in minimum wage jobs before their internships; participating in TTIP, PIE, and A La Mode taught them about the difference between doing low-wage service sector work and more highly skilled work, about being respected in the workplace, and about how much money they could make by obtaining marketable skills. When asked what it felt like to receive her first paycheck, one TTIP participant said: "It felt really good, because I also work at Wendy's and it is very different, and I mean, I put basically the same amount of hours but don't get the same. It was nice to see how much."

Another TTIP participant, who works 40 hours each week at her internship and at Sears on the weekends, said:

It is much, much, much better [at the internship]. I'm telling you, it is so sad, too, because Sears, I mostly see kids of color, and it is like labor, and when I think about okay, the job that I'm working right now and the job I'm working at Sears and the way I'm going to college – my goals and stuff – it is kind of sad to see a lot of kids of color quitting school, just quitting after high school to get out and work, and you know, getting minimum wage. It is really sad.

The experience these programs provide also socializes participants toward the world of work – another factor that poverty theorists have pointed to as a critical lack in low-income communities. One Harlem-Live participant described his experience this way:

It gives you experience with being in a work environment, because I don't think that a lot of teenagers get that until they are actually forced into a work environment. People come here and they have to talk on the telephone, they have to greet people, they have to be cordial, they have to not curse, they have to be civil. I mean, it is a work environment, and you have to kind of get used to that and being here is like practice, so that's the benefit.

Youth participation positively affects the family and the community

A child or teen's participation in one of these CTCs also has positive spillover effects on to the family. Many of the children have gotten their siblings involved in the programs. Many become the family computer resource, teaching parents, grandparents, siblings, and neighbors about computers and IT. Three quotes from program participants (the first from a six year old) illustrate this point:

[Being here] makes me want to be a computer teacher somewhere. I'm going to learn a lot when I'm still young. My father doesn't even know much about computers. I have been teaching him, and now he comes here sometimes.

After learning all that I learned over the summer and going back to school I was able to help out those who needed help. It kind of put me ahead. This fall semester I got to work in my class as the student's assistant teacher and I could help other students and other teachers. I can apply all that I know to projects I do in school and take it a step further.

Up at my church they are having this computer room that they want to put together and they need someone to teach people a little bit, or, you know, look over their shoulder once in a while, and they picked me because I know how to work computers. I think that is so deep. . . . I want to get a scholarship for acting, but if I don't, I have computer technology to back me up.

Kids' participation in CTCs also sparks parents' interest in technology. A Seattle school administrator told us:

The parents keep getting left out of it. All the parents come to me now and say well, my kid went to this class. They know what they are doing. Where can I go to get technology training. I tried to research it, and there are not that many places they can go, especially if they are working parents, so that's key.

These kids are not only gaining skills for themselves; they are also becoming resources within their families, at their schools, and in their communities. The technology is the vehicle through which they find their niche.

Structure is important

TAF started out with a very structured program, while P2W and Plugged In have become more structured over time. Although all program organizers recognize that their programs are different from school and should therefore be fun, they also emphasize the importance of learning and building specific skills. Staff at all three programs expressed the belief that youth participants need structure in order to truly benefit from IT. Without such structure, they tend to use the computer for entertainment. They need supervision and instruction to fully exploit its potential. Discussing P2W's shift from open-access to programmed activities, one staff member said:

> It was a lot easier to tell the kids what was expected of them. There were a lot of complaints from the kids at the beginning. They spent most of the time browsing before, and now, well, browsing turned a little bit more interactive. Once we had exhausted the possibilities of that, we started . . . to take it to the next level.

The recognition of a need for greater structure at P2W and Plugged In underscores a finding that has appeared elsewhere in this book: technology is a tool, not an end in itself. As one P2W staff member said, "If you give somebody technology and you teach them to use it like a TV set, I don't see the educational benefit there at all." Many schools and community-based organizations (CBOs) that target youth have recognized that exposing kids to technology is important. Most are just beginning to think through what needs to happen beyond purchasing hardware and software. These youth-oriented CTCs have traveled up the learning curve; what they have learned about the particular ways in which IT functions as a tool for youth can be usefully applied at schools and at youth-serving CBOs.

Participating in a CTC extends a child's web of support

Role models and exposure to a wide range of opportunities are often lacking in disadvantaged communities. CTCs provide kids with a place to go after school and with an expanded group of people to whom they can relate. Again, technology is not the only way to accomplish these objectives but these CTCs show that it is a powerful draw for youth. Many participants spoke about the importance of their relationships with other youth, and about their relationships with instructors in ways that clearly extended beyond traditional teacher–student relationships. One P2W participant described her instructor as follows:

> She teaches the program but she tries to be a friend to everybody. She always listens if I have a problem. I tell her about some of the problems that I'm having in school, and social problems, and stuff like that. They help with things that you might be going through. They try to make it easier so you can make the right decision. I really like it.

Program staff also recognize the role they play in the lives of participants. When asked to talk about this role, one P2W staff member said, "I guess that we are mentors. We are necessary because we talk to these young adults, and we encourage them and empower them." The staff at these programs take an active and personal interest in these kids. Sherry Williams, who is the administrator for the TTIP program, said:

> Some of them don't have parents that take care of them – grandma or auntie is raising them, so they feel bad about that already . . . I make a point to be in the classes during class time and I make a point at snack time to be there to make their snacks because this gives me time to get to know them. School, there is not a lot of support. I always put myself back in their shoes and remember, it was hard being a teenager, and now it is even harder I think.

At the same time, parents are important. Many CTCs have begun to think holistically about serving families rather than serving only youth or parents. The Austin Learning Academy, for example, learned that parents would bring their kids to classes, making it important for that program to begin to create specific programming for the kids. As TAF expands the TTIP program to do more to prepare kids for college, program organizers plan to include parents in more of the activities.

Many kids told us that their parents had found out about these programs and strongly encouraged them to apply. Millines, who lives in the same neighborhood in which TAF is located, regularly gets stopped in the grocery store by parents asking for TTIP applications. CTCs strengthen and add to strong home-based support networks. For those kids without such support at home or at school, the CTC experience fills a critical gap.

Kids can handle a great deal of responsibility

The programs studied here demonstrate both that teens can learn very sophisticated IT skills and that, with proper training, they can handle working in an office environment. One employer, who supervises two TTIP interns, told us: "I would hire these kids again for next summer in a heartbeat if they are interested, and basically if they continue this over four years, they will have jobs waiting for them. They can write their own tickets."

Employers and clients of these programs were universally impressed with the kids' maturity and technical skills. The media tends to focus on problem behaviors of low-income youth, particularly youth of color. These programs illustrate what can happen when we create initiatives that treat youth with respect and connect them to opportunity.

Kids learn more than IT skills

Participants in these programs clearly build portfolios of useful and marketable IT skills. At the same time, these programs also appear to contribute to a range of critical – but hard-to-measure – benefits and abilities, including: self-confidence, determination, teamwork, problem-solving, and exposure. These abilities are essential for success in the twenty-first century economy.[31] With respect to self-confidence, a HarlemLive staff member said: "I see them having more confidence in what they are doing . . . More drive, more confidence, and more enthusiasm about the subject." Asked about the rewards that come

31   CEO forum, March 2001.

with participating in the HarlemLive program, one student said: "Feeling better about yourself, you know, like you actually did something." Rahsaan Harris noted that this self-confidence is manifested in:

the types of conversations that they have, and the level of analyzing things, being analytical thinkers because we talk a lot about controversial topics, and hear people with different opinions. Being in this environment you kind of are forced to be able to express what you feel and defend yourself in the conversation.

Regarding exposure to people and experiences, a HarlemLive participant told us:

I think the benefit is just plain experience. We have small group seminars and guest speakers come in from different places . . . So, just hearing people like that speak to you about their experience in journalism, and these people are mostly people of color, and since we are all people of color, to see people of color in positions of authority and doing things that are beneficial to the community and to the world. And then, just getting the web skills, getting the writing skills, because there is a lot of writing at HarlemLive, getting social skills, communication skills, just being able to talk to people over the phone, explaining to them about HarlemLive.

When asked whether she observed any changes in the kids she taught, Gretchen, who teaches the Robotics class at P2W said:

I think they have all realized they have certain skills that they didn't realize they had before. Whether that's that they are more creative than they thought they were, that they are actually able to use computers better than they thought they could – for some of them actually concentrating and focusing is a problem, so the ones that have been able to sit down and focus for an extended period of time, that has also been a major accomplishment.

Kevin, a P2W staff member, spoke of IT's usefulness as a vehicle for teaching other skills:

[Technology] is a vehicle for communicating a lot of skills that go beyond the computer. Project-based work, accountability, professionalism, you can learn that here, and it is a good match, technology and certain educational ideas, that just go well together, you can get them both from the same environment and that is great.

These youth-oriented CTCs are using IT to engage kids and help them become well-rounded thinkers. The skills they obtain will be broadly applicable, whether or not they pursue IT careers.

Integrating the work of schools and CTCs

The youth-oriented CTCs studied for this chapter offer promising lessons for how technology can be used to educate and excite kids, and prepare them for successful futures, whether or not they decide to pursue careers in technology. Yet these programs suffer from the same problems identified in chapter 3 – difficulty in achieving scale, constant struggle for funding, finding instructors, and serving all of those who want to participate. Many programs that work to bridge the technology divide do a wonderful job assisting the people they serve to improve their lives but lack the capacity to serve enough people in need to make a significant dent in the problem. Some CTC directors, such as Trish Millines, are thinking actively about developing a replication strategy. Most are more concerned with figuring out how to keep their own doors open from one year to the next. CTCs' capacity is limited. Those that target youth serve only a small portion of kids. It may be more productive to derive ways of integrating efforts between schools and CTCs. The answer to this problem may lie in developing more malleable strategies that are easier to bring to scale.

A few promising models illustrate the process of going to scale. ExplorNet is a nonprofit organization dedicated to improving technology-based learning in US schools by equipping schools with the technology and training necessary to prepare students, teachers, and communities for the digital economy. ExplorNet targets traditionally under-served communities, particularly rural areas, and has expanded by emphasizing the development of collaborative partnerships. Through these partnerships, ExplorNet: (1) enhances career opportunities for students through technology training; (2) develops programs that immerse teachers in the use of technology; (3) creates curricula that incorporate Internet and technology use; (4) assists schools in building their technology programs; and (5) evaluates the effectiveness of their programs. The ExplorNet model is currently deployed at schools in North Carolina, North Dakota, South Dakota, Mississippi, and Arkansas.

ExplorNet also employs skills standards, which have aided the replication process. The youth technology training program, for example, incorporates vendor-neutral skills standards which provide youth with technology literacy while laying the foundation for students interested in more specialized vendor-specific certifications. ExplorNet also has a curriculum that focuses on helping teachers integrate technology in the classroom, emphasizing using technology as a tool to help students meet state established academic skill standards. In recent years, teachers have faced increasing pressure to improve kids' performance on standardized tests. Using technology in this way complements, rather than competes with, what teachers are already doing. This focus on skills standards, and using technology as a tool to improve learning – as opposed to an end in itself – are some of the elements that have helped the ExplorNet program to catch on.

Another example of a "scaleable" strategy is Youth Tech Entrepreneurs (YTE). Based in Massachusetts, YTE is an academic and extracurricular activity program currently underway in eight schools. The program focuses on helping youth build a broad range of skills that extend beyond technology. These skills, which focus on entrepreneurship, include: project management, public speaking, customer service, marketing, web design, and computer troubleshooting. Community-focused technology projects provide the vehicle for practicing what they learn. YTE targets both students who might not otherwise be interested in school, and college-bound students who might not otherwise consider technology coursework. At the time of this writing, over three hundred and fifty students have participated in YTE and have fixed hundreds of computers, designed ten websites, built seven computer labs, started web consulting and purchasing services, and worked for 44 employers as computer technicians and web developers.

Current Policy

The E-Rate, which was discussed in chapter 4, is probably the most important federal program for technology diffusion and redistributing funding to poorer school districts. In addition to the E-Rate, several other federal programs acknowledge both the work of CTCs and the needs of schools. Three of these – 21st Century Community Learning

Centers, Technology Innovation Challenge Grants, and the Technology Literacy Challenge Fund – specifically extend beyond the schools, encouraging school systems to partner with other organizations and to use federal funds to leverage the additional dollars needed to sustain innovative technology programs. The Star Schools program makes grants to a range of education entities to promote the use of telecommunications for improved instruction, literacy skills, and vocational education for underserved populations. The Clinton administration initiated the Teacher Training in Technology program in 1999 to prepare teachers, through collaborative arrangements with institutions of higher education, to use modern learning technologies.

At the state level, the primary concerns have to do with equity and teacher training. For most states, school funding formulas are tied to property taxes, which means that wealthier districts have greater resources than do poorer ones. Some states provide specific funding tied to technology to help alleviate this inequity. In Texas, for example, the state provides schools with $30 per student per year for technology. However, wealthier districts spend up to six times as much, making it impossible for the poorer districts to keep up.[32] To deal with the teacher training issue, some states have initiated new programs. Illinois, for example, maintains seven regional learning technology hubs which maintain full-time staff who provide technical assistance and training, curriculum ideas, and technology development plans.[33] In 1990, Texas established the Texas Education Network (TENET), which provides every public educator in the state with an email account, online academic resources, public data, planned forums, and professional support.[34]

Lessons

Partnerships between schools and CTCs can be synergistic

The expertise developed at CTCs can be useful to the schools. Schools can work with CTC staff to learn about how to integrate technology into the classroom and about what sorts of projects have been proven

32 Conte (2000).
33 Conte (2000).
34 Conte (2000).

to work. Likewise, CTC staff can use their programming to build on existing activities within the schools. Also, schools increasingly have valuable infrastructure that often goes unused after hours. Communities that do not have the benefit of a local CTC could potentially create new programs in the schools for adults and kids. Sharing existing resources in this way would also be an efficient use of public funds.

Focusing on youth will help close key digital divides

Chapter 6 demonstrates that it will be necessary to tap the labor pool of women and people of color in order to address the IT labor shortage. None of these programs has been operating long enough to demonstrate whether or not youth-oriented CTCs can be used as an intervention to increase the numbers of women and people of color in IT fields. It is also impossible for us to know whether these particular youths were already predisposed to work in these fields. What we do know is that an overwhelming majority of TTIP, HarlemLive and Plugged In participants are going on to college, and that many of them have decided to major in technology-related fields. Several Plugged In participants have started technology businesses. Developing skills, gaining exposure to new knowledge, and spending time with role models working in these fields undoubtedly shapes the aspirations, goals, and life decisions of these young people. A universal focus on youth will disproportionately help youth of color, low-income youth, and youth living in poor areas.[35] Successfully diffusing technology to youth and ensuring that the quality of IT instruction is consistently high in all schools will go a long way toward closing the technology gap in the span of a generation.

Support School-to-Work legislation

The 1994 School-to-Work Opportunities Act (STWOA), which provides funding to facilitate the education and career preparation of young people during their formative secondary-school years, was scheduled to sunset in 2001. Although this legislation is much broader

35   This universal approach echoes Wilson's "hidden agenda" in *The Truly Disadvantaged* (1987).

than the technology issue, it is an important tool and incentive for the creation of innovative programs and partnerships. Existing research on this legislation indicates that the school-to-work strategy benefits students, teachers, and employers.[36] Funding for this program should be continued.

State IT curriculum standards and teacher technology requirements enable the integration of IT

Technology education is fragmented. Although there is an exciting mix of promising programs, they tend to be small and piecemeal. In many schools, "computers" are taught completely separately from other subjects. They are simply added to the existing curriculum rather than integrated into it. It is time to step back and think in broader terms about the relationship between technology and education. Several states have begun to take the initiative in this area by developing technology standards for the public schools.[37] Twenty-six states have adopted technology requirements that teachers must meet prior to initial licensure.[38] These requirements and standards vary greatly; they are important because they help to institutionalize the relationship between IT and the schools.

Conclusion

More equipment is not the answer to teaching IT skills to youth. Throwing technology at children, in the schools or in CTCs, will not eliminate the technology gap. The CTCs highlighted in this chapter show that technology itself is much less important than how it is used. Using technology wisely requires further research and funding for training teachers and developing curricula. Further research is also necessary to answer such questions as: What sorts of activities is technology most helpful for?, and at what age should technology be introduced? Education scholars have begun to examine these questions.

36 Hughes, Bailey, and Mechur, 2001.
37 Go to Education Development Center website for links to individual states' programs, www.edc.org
38 See *Education Week* (2001) survey of state departments of education for more information on states' programs.

The majority of public schools do not currently have the institutional capacity – the resources, know-how, and incentives – to take on the additional role of teaching IT. As the social fabric of low-income communities has changed and their social buffer has deteriorated,[39] schools have already been required to expand the role they play as social institutions in these communities. Most are stretched too thin to take on IT, which requires both financial support and new training for teachers. Youth-oriented CTCs, particularly those that target low-income youth and youth of color, therefore fill a critical gap. Yet these CTCs do not have the capacity to expand to serve all of the young people who need their services. Until greater capacity is built at either CTCs or schools, these two types of institutions must support and work with each other. In another generation, all teachers will have had much greater exposure to computers and the benefits of using IT to enhance the learning experience. Educational software programs will have likely improved a great deal. We will have a much better sense of how, specifically, to incorporate IT into classroom settings. Until then, youth-oriented CTCs can inform the technology-based work that schools do. Each of the three programs discussed in this chapter has already established relationships with local schools and has plans to extend these relationships.

Currently, both the schools and the CTCs are overextended. Therefore, it makes sense to formulate creative incentives for schools and CTCs to increase the work that they do together. CTCs can help train teachers and make project-based curricula available to schools. CTCs reinforce the work going on in the schools by teaching young participants to think in new ways and by emphasizing the importance of doing well in school. TAF's TTIP participants must maintain a 2.5 grade point average in order to remain in the program. HarlemLive staff take participants on field trips to colleges and talk to the kids about the importance of doing well in school. In addition, some have pointed out that using IT in particular ways helps children to learn and think in ways that are critical to succeeding in the current socioeconomic system. More research is needed to move beyond the exploratory level and understand what happens over time to kids who participate in these programs. Longitudinal work that specifically examines changes in grades, self-esteem, and the future orientation of youth will be important in terms of determining how, specifically, these programs should be supported and what schools can learn from them.

39   Wilson (1987).

6

Training Disadvantaged
Workers for IT Jobs

Workforce development intersects in important ways with the digital divide. Workers who do not have IT skills have access to much less opportunity in the labor market than those who do. Importantly, the area of workforce development also allows for relatively straight-forward intervention. This chapter focuses on the labor market for IT workers, and how innovative programs and policies can be used to benefit both employers, who cannot fill available jobs, and disadvantaged workers, who cannot find good jobs. The focus here is primarily on entry-level IT jobs and workers because of this book's overarching concern for low-income communities in general and disadvantaged workers in particular. "Disadvantaged" refers to those workers who have been largely detached from the labor force, who lack requisite skills, who may face discrimination in the labor market, and/or who are currently unemployed or employed in jobs that fail to pay a living wage.

This chapter makes two primary arguments. The first is that the shift to an information-driven economy enables a concomitant shift in the perception of workforce development activity. Rather than viewing these programs as social welfare, which is how they have traditionally been viewed, they can now be seen as legitimate components of larger economic development strategies. The second is that the current economy, in which there is a high demand for entry-level IT workers, presents a unique opportunity for moving disadvantaged people into good jobs. IT jobs tend to be good jobs. Many require less than two years of training and, as the economy continues to shift in ways that require more IT skills from workers, these opportunities will continue to be available.

Economic Shifts and the IT Labor Market

The shift from a manufacturing to a service and information-based economy has been described in great detail elsewhere; this section touches only on the issues most directly relevant to this chapter.[1] First, information plays a different and larger role in the current economy than in previous economic incarnations: information is now both a product of the new economy and an increasingly more important input to production processes.[2] These structural shifts in the economy have impacted the sectoral composition of regions and the way in which production processes are organized across space. For example, regions that were dominant in manufacturing have declined unless they have been able to remake themselves.[3] New cities and regions in which IT plays a large role – Silicon Valley, Seattle, and Austin, for example – have grown substantially and have become leaders in the new economy. Internationally, a few cities – New York, London, and Tokyo – have achieved an uber-status as megacities.[4] And less developed countries have become important as places in which to locate parts of the production process that can benefit from low-skilled labor and loose environmental regulations.

How have these changes affected the labor market in terms of entry-level jobs? The effects can be described in terms of a "skills mismatch" and a "spatial mismatch."[5] First, there has been a significant decrease in the availability of low-skilled, stable manufacturing jobs. These jobs used to offer relatively stable, dependable work at living wages and with benefits. The shift from a manufacturing to a more service-oriented economy has changed the kinds of jobs available. Low-end service sector jobs tend to be lower-quality jobs: they are often unstable or temporary, pay low wages, and offer few if any benefits. Although many cities have carved out new roles as service centers, the service sector tends to be highly polarized in occupation and wage structure.[6] As a result, the shift away from manufacturing has tended to benefit college-educated professionals and high-end service

---

1 Castells (1996); Bluestone and Harrison (1990).
2 Castells (1996).
3 For example, Pittsburgh, formerly a steel town, has encouraged and fostered the growth of IT activities, with some success.
4 Sassen (1992).
5 Servon and Nelson (2001).
6 Bluestone and Harrison (1982); Sassen (1992).

workers.[7] Many inner-city residents displaced by structural changes in the economy have found new jobs in the service sector, but these jobs tend to be low wage, unstable, and without benefits. "As a result," Atkinson argues, "cities face the challenge of bridging a growing gap between the skills required for employment in advanced services concentrated in urban cores and the limited skills that many entry-level big city residents bring to the job market."[8] IT has directly exacerbated the "skills mismatch" between higher-end jobs in central cities and the low-skilled urban labor force living there as technological literacy is added to the skill set needed to join the information economy.[9] Even low skilled tasks require proficiency with the use of telephones, fax machines, and computer equipment.[10] The result is that inequality persists, while many jobs in IT fields go unfilled.

The spatial mismatch has to do with economic and spatial restructuring that has resulted in a loss of stable, well-paid employment opportunities for low-income urban residents. Advances in IT have lessened locational constraints enabling firms offering low-skill jobs, particularly in manufacturing and routine services, to leave the inner city for the suburbs and, in some cases, overseas locations where production costs are lower. Meanwhile, segregation and discrimination have prohibited the poor and minority populations from following these jobs to the periphery, creating a "spatial mismatch" between low-income urban residents and employment opportunities.[11] IT will likely facilitate the further decentralization of economic activity, exacerbating the spatial mismatch, particularly as teleworking becomes more common and firms develop new ways of transmitting producer and personal services electronically.[12] Some fear that the continued reconfiguration of spatial patterns, made possible by IT, will further cluster the affluent while leaving the poor trapped in places with few good job and services.[13]

The rise of the IT sector, however, has opened a unique window of opportunity. The Information Technology Association of America estimates that the current demand for IT workers is 901,589, and that

7   Kasarda (1985).
8   Atkinson (1998: 157–8).
9   Atkinson (1998).
10 US Department of Commerce (1999b).
11 Teitz and Chapple (1998).
12 Graham and Marvin (1996).
13 Mitchell (1999b).

425,358 will go unfilled. Many of these positions are entry level. For example, technical support people (which are entry-level positions) are the most in demand, constituting one-quarter of all new positions in the field.[14] IT jobs tend to be relatively good jobs. According to a recent report issued by the US Department of Labor, "real average wages in the high-tech industries increased 19 percent since 1990, compared with a 5 percent average increase for the private sector as a whole. The average high-tech job pays 78 percent more than the average non-high-tech job – $53,000 compared to $30,000."[15]

Many jobs experiencing high growth do not require a four-year college education. Harrison and Weiss cite research showing that for the period 1992 to 2005 "only one of eight higher than average growth occupations will require a college degree, whereas fully two thirds will require no more than a high school diploma."[16] A 1999 study put out by the Department of Labor found that the majority of jobs currently being created require less than an associate's degree, but often require other skills.[17] According to these researchers, "the alleged disappearance of low-skilled job opportunities in America has been exaggerated. There is, and will continue to be, considerable room in the economy for workers with modest formal schooling."[18]

Although not all of these high growth jobs are in IT or in well-paying sectors, many entry-level IT jobs also require less than a four-year college degree. At the same time, entry-level IT jobs do require specific skills, and the rapidly changing nature of the IT economy requires that IT workers continually upgrade their skills.

Furthermore, if we look at other occupational sectors we see that technology literacy is now viewed as part of the bundle of skills a worker must bring to the workforce. The Economic Policy Institute found that attainment of computer skills "tends to widen pay differences between educational groups more so than in the past."[19] In this new economy, "good jobs require analytical research skills, not simply the ability to read and write and follow instructions."[20] The Secretary of Labor's Commission on Acquiring Necessary Skills (SCANS) outlines the following set of five competencies for the high-performance

14   Information Technology Association of America (2001).
15   US Department of Labor (1999: 3).
16   Harrison and Weiss (1998: 10).
17   US Department of Labor (1999: 5).
18   Harrison and Weiss (1998: 10).
19   Quoted in Civille (1995: 202).
20   Civille (1995: 202).

worker: using resources; dealing with interpersonal relationships; working with information; working with systems; and working with
technology.[21]

The Demand for IT Workers

The ITAA estimates that approximately 10.4 million people are part
of the IT workforce.[22] The demand for IT workers is being experienced first in those cities – such as Seattle, Austin, Boston, and San
Francisco – that have economies that are heavily dependent on technology industries. IT corporations deciding where to locate a new
facility weight the quality of the workforce heavily in their decision
matrices. For example, in a recent survey of industry leaders in
San Francisco's Multimedia Gulch, access to *a qualified labor pool* was
cited as the most important reason to locate in San Francisco.[23] The
multimedia industry's demand for a mix of technical and creative
talent induces firms to locate in San Francisco, even though the cost
of doing business would be significantly lower in other areas.
However, although survey participants stated that access to a qualified labor pool was the reason for doing business in San Francisco,
these same firms found it challenging to find qualified staff (including entry-level employees).

But the demand for workers with IT skills is not isolated to traditional IT industries. Given the transformation of business practices
resulting from the effects of information technologies, universities,
banks, hotels, and insurance corporations all need technical support,
MIS managers, and system administrators. According to ITAA, there
are 10.4 million IT workers in the United States – 9.5 million of which
are employed by non-IT companies. That is, non-IT companies employ
ten times more IT workers than do IT companies. Not only are non-
IT companies the largest employer of the IT workforce, theses companies also have the highest unmet demand for skilled IT workers.
Non-IT companies estimate an increase in demand of 643,257 workers,
compared to 258,332 for IT companies.[24] A report issued by the Council
on Competitiveness cites a 1997 survey in which nearly 70 percent of
CEOs identified the skills shortage as the number one barrier to

21 Quoted in Civille (1995: 203).
22 Information Technology Association of America (2001).
23 Cooper & Lybrand (1998).
24 Information Technology Association of America (2001).

Table 6.1   IT demand and gap by job categories

IT career cluster	All companies 50+ employees	
	Demand	Gap
Tech support	218,238	107,624
Database development/admin	110,104	46,166
Programming/SW engr.	134,637	69,292
Web development/admin	120,982	56,957
Network design/admin	186,613	85,534
Tech writing	17,461	8,526
Enterprise systems	75,177	32,026
Other	26,437	13,362
Digital media	11,940	5,871
Total	901,589	425,358

Source: ITAA (2001).

growth.[25] Non-IT firms also account for the majority of new demand for IT workers. [26] A 2000 survey conducted by the Employment Policy Foundation found that one-third of polled businesses said they would move operations overseas if qualified workers were not available in the US.[27] The shortage of IT workers has spread from cities with economies heavily dependent on IT to other regions. Table 6.1 illustrates the demand and gap for IT workers by job category.

Interestingly, ITAA's estimates of demand and gap in IT workers are down significantly from a year ago. In 2000, employers believed that they would demand 1,608,499 workers and be unable to fill 843,328 of these jobs. The current statistics depicted in table 6.1 show that the gap has been cut nearly in half. These new figures reflect the downturn in the market which began in late 2000 and extended through the first part of 2001.

Industry spokespeople, like investors, were overly optimistic about the growth potential of very thin firms. The drop in demand should be thought of as a correction, not as the beginning of a long-term

25   Quoted in Congressional Commission on the Advancement of Women and Minorities in Science, Engineering and Technology Department (2000).
26   Information Technology Association of America (2001: 12).
27   Center for an Urban Future (2000: 4). Chapple and Zook (2000) argue convincingly that the likelihood of massive movement of jobs overseas has been exaggerated, but the issue of a shortage of workers with the necessary skills to fill available IT jobs remains important.

decline in demand for workers with IT skills. An upward trend in this demand will likely continue.[28] Although this sizable change clearly demands closer analysis, the fact remains that demand for IT workers is very strong, and the gap is significant. The continued need for IT workers is evidence that a fundamental shift in the type of work being performed across sectors is underway. [29] Programs to train disadvantaged workers for IT jobs, then, need not be thought of as social welfare, but rather as a way to fuel an economy hungry for skilled workers. According to Bruce Bernstein, the need to train low-skilled workers for available jobs is "an economic necessity, not a social prerogative." This shift in thinking is important. The perception of workforce development programs, especially those that target public assistance recipients, is often that it is social work rather than economic development. Framing the issue as an economic development issue rather than strictly a social welfare one is more likely to generate bipartisan public sector support as well as key backing from the private sector.

The demand for IT workers is likely to grow as the new mode of production continues to be absorbed and assimilated across institutions and industries.[30] According to Castells, "the generalization of knowledge-based production and management to the whole realm of economic processes on a global scale requires fundamental social, cultural, and institutional transformations that, if the historical record of other technological revolutions is considered, will take some time."[31] As this process of transformation continues, the demand for workers with IT skills will only grow. A Department of Commerce report projects that, by 2006, nearly half of all workers will be employed in industries that produce or intensively use information technology, products, and services.[32]

What is Different About the IT Labor Market?

Classifying IT workers

Attempting to define and describe the IT labor market is challenging given the diversity of ways in which digital technologies are utilized.

28 Foster-Bey (2000).
29 Information Technology Association of America (2000: 11).
30 Meares and Sargent (1999).
31 Castells (1996: 91).
32 Cited in US Department of Labor (1999: 60).

The most narrow definition of the IT labor market would include only "core" IT occupations: computer scientists, computer engineers, systems analysts, and computer programmers. These professions constitute the high end of the IT labor market. Core IT jobs require the most education and skills and pay the most. Workers with these skills are in the greatest demand.

This narrow definition of the IT labor market fails to reflect the fact that as the economy becomes more digitized, virtually all occupations involve some use of information technologies. Although this chapter will not discuss the way in which traditional sectors of the economy (e.g., administrative, retail sales, etc.) have been transformed by the adoption of information technologies, it is important to note that the IT labor market is much broader than core IT occupations. There is a large gray area between computer scientists and salespeople who use computers, and this gray area is occupied by a broad range of emerging IT occupations.

Recognizing the breadth of IT-related occupations, the Northwest Center for Emerging Technologies (NWCET) has developed eight career clusters that both expand the frame to include a larger universe of IT jobs and make more precise distinctions between types of IT work. The NWCET clusters enable a finer-grained approach to research and program design for IT-based workforce development. Using these eight IT career clusters can help provide better answers to key questions such as: What IT jobs are most in demand? What skills are required to perform these jobs? What are the best methods for providing and acquiring these skills?[33]

According to the ITAA, the former, narrower scope, which is still used by other research organizations, misses "the dramatic impact that the Internet, e-commerce and other influences have had on the nature of jobs and work." The NWCET job categories are as follows:

Database development and administration

The creation and management of structures, tools, forms and reports that help companies understand their data. Work functions include needs analysis, database design, testing, and maintenance.

Digital media

The process of bringing sound, video, graphics, animation, and text together to create digital media products. Delivery platforms include

33   Information Technology Association of America (2000: 8).

websites, videos, computer games, and CDs. Work functions include needs analysis, visual and functional design, media production and acquisition, and design implementation and testing.

Enterprise systems analysis and integration

The integration of complex and numerous information technology systems to create comprehensive customer solutions. Work functions include defining customer requirements, determining systems solutions, providing strategic direction for systems configuration, technology management, and implementing enterprise-wide systems.

Network design and administration

The development of networks that connect users to computer systems via cable, fiber optics, and wireless communications. Work functions include design and analysis, configuration/implementation, testing, administering, monitoring and management of networks.

Programming/Software engineering

The translation of business problems into codes a computer can understand through the use of various programming languages. Work functions include: needs analysis, developing structures, designing, developing, implementing, and testing computer programs.

Technical support

Assisting customers diagnose and correct computer systems problems. Work functions include trouble shooting, customer service, hardware/software installation, configuration, upgrades, systems maintenance and monitoring.

Technical writing

Documenting, explaining, translating and interpreting technical information for a variety of audiences. Work functions include writing, editing, and publishing of technical documents for products, product training, internal systems, web-based training, and more.

Web development and administration

The creation, maintenance, and development of websites. Work functions include content and technical analysis, development, implementation, and maintenance of web applications/site design, and managing web environments and enterprise-wide web activities.[34]

What is an entry-level IT worker?

An important aspect of the IT labor market has to do with changing requirements for entry-level jobs. As the technology required to do particular jobs becomes less complicated and as institutions other than four-year colleges increasingly demonstrate an ability to train people for these jobs, employers have changed or decreased what is required to obtain a job. For example, Chapple and Zook describe the process by which particular occupations, such as the computer support specialist and the web developer, have matured to the point that skill levels required for entry-level positions have been reduced.[35]

The shortage of IT workers has clearly played some role in these shifts as well. Employers are willing to lower their requirements when they are desperate for workers. As these jobs become more institutionalized, it becomes easier to figure out how to train people for them.

At the same time, even "entry-level" IT workers require some training. The term "entry-level" is used here to refer to those jobs that require a two-year associate's degree or less. The focus here is on those jobs that disadvantaged workers could be moved into in a relatively short amount of time, and relatively inexpensively.

The education/skills distinction

The current economy clearly demands more and different skills from workers than did the manufacturing-driven economy. Qualifications for many IT jobs are measured not in terms of degrees but rather in terms of specific skills and abilities. The distinction between skills and education has become more important.[36] A skilled worker in 1950 was unlikely to require additional training throughout his career. Today, the skilled IT worker must constantly upgrade her skills in order to remain productive. Lifelong learning has become the norm, yet an

---

34 Northwest Center for Emerging Technologies (1999).
35 Chapple and Zook (2000).
36 Northwest Center for Emerging Technologies (1999).

Table 6.2 Salary and training for emerging IT occupations

Emerging occupation	Salary		Training		
	Beginning	Experienced	Deliverable	Avg. time	Avg. cost ($)
Telecommunications installer	$7–15/hr	$15–22/hr	Certificate	9 months	400
			AS degree	2 years	720
Technical writer[a]	$12–33/hr	$20–65/hr	Certificate	1 year	200
Technical support rep.	$8–15/hr	$12–34/hr	AS degree	2 years	720
PC technician	$8–18/hr	$12–35/hr	Certificate	2 semesters	300
			AS degree	2 years	720
Network administrator	$15–20/hr	$18–35/hr	AS degree	2 years	720
Network technician[a]	$10–24/hr	$11–35/hr	Certificate	1 year	200
			AS degree		720
Computer programmer[a]	$12–31/hr	$20–60/hr	Certificate	3 semesters	250
			AS degree	2 years	720
Web designer[a]	$12–40/hr	$25–115/hr	Courses	4 months	400
			AS degree	2 years	720
Webmaster[a]	$10–20/hr	$15–40/hr	Certificate	3–9 months	300
			AS degree	2 years	720

[a] Indicates high-demand occupations.
Source: 21st Century Workforce Commission (2000).

infrastructure of policies and programs to support this norm is lacking.

Workers in many emerging occupations require specific training, but they do not necessarily need higher education. Although the three occupations projected to grow most quickly between 1996 and 2006 all require at least a bachelor's degree,[37] many new IT jobs require less in the way of degrees. Table 6.2 illustrates the salaries and training requirements for several emerging IT positions that demand two years or less of training.

According to several recent studies, hiring managers overwhelmingly focus on capability rather than formal qualifications like degrees or certifications.[38] ITAA's survey of employers found that "a good

37 US Department of Labor (1999), citing Bureau of Labor Statistics projections, p. 20.
38 Chapple and Zook (2000); ITAA (2000); Harrison and Weiss (1998).

knowledge base in relevant areas came out as the single most important high level qualification (62 percent), followed by hands-on experience (47 percent)."[39] Responses of hiring managers to the ITAA survey indicate that "many routes lead to in-demand IT skill levels."[40] Harrison and Weiss cite research showing that "what employers say they want is people with better, more reliable schooling in job-relevant skills, not necessarily people with more schooling, per se."[41] An important characteristic of the new economy is its ability to take on workers who have technical proficiency and computer skills regardless of whether they have formal degrees.[42]

At the same time, employers responding to the ITAA survey expressed a preference for candidates with degrees from four-year colleges. Murnane and Levy suggest that employers tend to view a bachelor's degree as a proxy for "a set of advanced academic skills, a strong work ethic, and general analytical and teamwork skills required in the workplace."[43] Although employers responding to the ITAA survey preferred candidates with a four-year college degree, they also saw the value of shorter-term, targeted skills training. For example, some community colleges and community-based training programs can deliver applicants with solid skill packages in a relatively short amount of time. However, the extent to which employers will accept applicants coming through such community-oriented training systems remains to be seen.

IT job ladders

Just as there are multiple entry points into IT jobs, there are also multiple tracks within the IT sector. The traditional concept of a "job ladder" may not be as applicable in the information economy as it was in the manufacturing economy. A report recently issued by the Center for an Urban Future decreed that "the days of the gold watch are over: The average person can now expect to change jobs many times during the course of his or her life. Yet the current job training system doesn't serve the average person at all."[44] At the same time, some training programs that focus on IT have identified routes leading from

39　Information Technology Association of America (2000: 19).
40　Information Technology Association of America (2000: 18).
41　Zemsky, cited in Harrison and Weiss (1998: 12).
42　Chapple and Zook (2000); Moss and Townsend (1999).
43　21st Century Workforce Commission (2000: 50).
44　Center for an Urban Future (2000: 4).

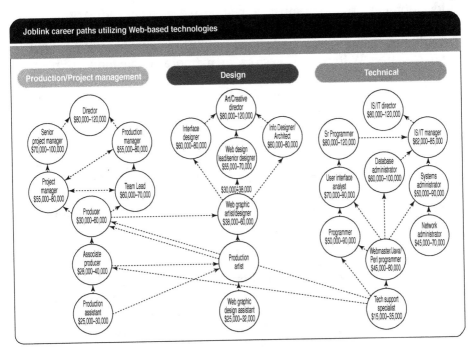

Figure 6.1   Bay Area Video Coalition job ladder

entry-level jobs to higher-paying, more advanced jobs. Patterns of advancement in IT careers differ for people working in IT versus non-IT firms. Workforce development institutions are beginning to play an important role by identifying "entry-level occupations that pay well, offer opportunities for advancement, and require only short-term training."[45] Also, whereas traditional career ladders took place within a single firm, IT ladders can rely on a range of firms and other organizations with, for example, a worker coming back to a training program between positions in order to acquire additional skills. Figure 6.1 illustrates how an IT worker might move between jobs and organizations.

Moving Workers Into Jobs

The IT sector is characterized by rapid change. This rapid change carries with it three primary implications. First, workforce

45   Chapple and Zook (2000: 5).

development programs must be responsive to what industry needs and constantly update curricula to provide the skills demanded by employers.[46] Second, the traditional concept of "job ladders" is called into question. Within the IT sectors, many more people move from job to job more quickly, which also makes traditional measures of job training effectiveness, such as job retention, potentially less appropriate. Obtaining and keeping a job for a long time is not necessarily a good measure of whether a job training program works. And third, workers must become lifelong learners. Training must be seen less as a one-shot deal – graduates of training programs will likely continue to need training after placement in order to keep their skills current.

Four types of institutions offer relatively short-term training (less than two years) in IT-related areas:[47] community-based training programs (CBTs); community colleges; employer-led training programs; and proprietary schools. These institutions offer a variety of programs and serve a wide range of populations. Although all of these training institutions occupy important niches in the landscape of IT training, community-based training programs and community colleges have placed the greatest emphasis on targeting, training, and placing disadvantaged workers in and for IT occupations.

Community-based training programs

Community-based training (CBT) programs focus explicitly on assisting disadvantaged populations to find employment. These organizations fall into two basic categories. One category consists of traditional workforce development organizations that have recently added IT training to their roster of services. Take, for example, Training, Inc. based in Newark, NJ. Training, Inc. has been providing workforce development training and services to low income communities since 1986. In 1995 this program began offering information technology training for the following jobs: PC technician, software applications specialist, and office support assistant.

46   I use Harrison and Weiss's (1998: 5) inclusive definition of workforce development as consisting of "a constellation of activities from orientation to the work world, recruiting, placement, and mentoring to follow-up counseling and crisis intervention."
47   Although four-year colleges offer a range of IT training, this chapter focuses on shorter-term training programs, as these are the ones most likely to be accessed by disadvantaged and transitioning workers.

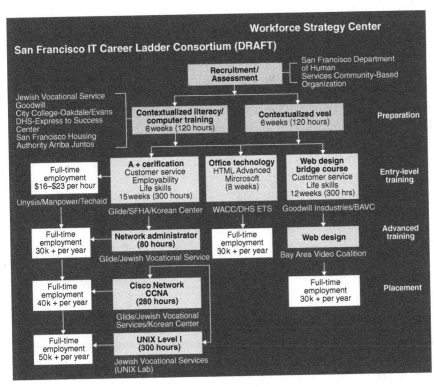

Figure 6.2 San Francisco IT career ladder consortium

The other category consists of organizations focused on creating access to technology, that moved into employment-oriented training to capitalize on the opportunity to help their constituents find employment. Playing2Win, which was discussed in depth in chapter 5, is an example of a "technology-oriented" CBT. Founded in 1983, Playing2Win was created with the goal of providing access to computers and the Internet for the underserved Harlem community. Over time this program added technology training to its menu of course offerings, and has been successful in connecting low-income residents to jobs. The unifying thread among all CBT programs is a commitment to assisting low income and low skilled workers find employment.[48] Figure 6.2 illustrates how a range of organizations providing IT training in the Bay Area has been coordinated by the Workforce Strategy Center.

48   Chapple and Zook (2000).

CBT programs have demonstrated significant promise in training disadvantaged workers for entry-level jobs in the IT sector. Some of these programs work specifically with populations thought to have significant barriers to work. OpNet is one example. Founded in 1997, OpNet's mission is to create economic opportunities in the new media industry for low-income young adults, with an emphasis on women and people of color. OpNet maintains close connections with industry, and has demonstrated success in training and placing low-income San Francisco Bay Area residents. OpNet works to forge strong business–community partnerships to benefit both the new media industry and low-income communities. For example, local businesses host internships for OpNet trainees, participate in professional development workshops, and help shape the program's curriculum. Their participation helps create a program that is reflective of industry needs, and ultimately leads to the development of a skilled labor pool. This industry–community partnership also helps OpNet garner the resources and knowledge needed to effectively connect low income communities to jobs.

Although CBT programs have demonstrated success in training disadvantaged communities, their ability to tackle the larger problem is somewhat restricted. First, these programs tend to operate on a relatively small scale. Second, like many community-based organizations, they tend to have exceptional, charismatic leaders. Both of these factors raise questions about whether these strategies can be replicated and/or brought to scale. At the same time, these programs serve an important function by creating pathways to IT employment for some of the most disadvantaged communities. At the very least, these programs must be studied more closely in order to determine: what they do well; who specifically they serve best; and what happens to graduates in the medium and long term.

Community colleges

Community colleges offer several advantageous characteristics as training institutions. They are economical, tend to be conveniently located, offer flexible schedules, and have a history of serving underrepresented minorities, adults, and immigrant populations. Research conducted thus far on community colleges that provide IT training has been largely exploratory, and the findings are mixed. In the ITAA's survey of IT employers, which asked them to rate four-year colleges, private schools, short courses, informal training, and community colleges, community colleges did not score as well as four-year colleges and private schools. The authors of the report recognize, however, that the relatively low score may reflect the fact that many community colleges do not offer specific IT degrees. A study by the Urban Institute similarly found that employers do not recruit at community colleges. The same study also found, though, that community college graduates "do not face any limits to their career mobility once they are hired."[49] Stoll posits that regulation and bureaucratization at many community colleges, coupled with the fact that many are disconnected from industry, has shaped employers' perceptions.[50]

It would be wrong, however, to label all community colleges in the same way; there are important exceptions. For example, in their excellent study of IT training programs, Chapple and Zook found several community colleges that appear to have effective programs. These colleges tended to have established computer science departments and committed faculty members. These community colleges have figured out ways to maneuver around the problems identified above. The Urban Institute study explored the issue of how community colleges find out what employers want and how they incorporate their findings into the curriculum.[51] The authors found that community colleges typically have an advisory board made up of industry representatives who advise the college on curriculum; suggested changes must be approved by a committee. The frequency with which this committee meets varies greatly and has much to do with how responsive course offerings are to industry needs. State regulations dictate some of this bureaucracy, so it would be useful to study more thoroughly differences in state regulations. Some anecdotal information exists. Iowa Western, for example, offers new classes on a temporary basis until they are approved; Bellevue Community College in Washington State administrators do not specify what software will be used for particular classes, giving them the opportunity to update or change what they will use without going through the approval process.[52] A recent report to the Ford Foundation cites De Anza Community College in California and the Borough of Manhattan Community College as examples of community colleges that have also overcome bureaucratization issues.[53] Some community colleges – for example, Seattle Central and Colorado Community Colleges – are members of

49   Lerman et al. (2000: 23).
50   Stoll (2000: 8).
51   Lerman et al. (2000).
52   Lerman et al. (2000: 16).
53   Chapple and Zook (2000).

Workforce Investment Boards (WIBs). Their participation on these boards ensures that they maintain close connections with industry and local government.

A small number of community colleges have moved beyond industry advisory boards to creating more formal connections with employers. Some of these partnerships have been initiated by particular corporations. In 1997, for example, Microsoft launched the Working Connections Program, committing $7 million to develop IT programs in community colleges. IBM created its S/390 University Program to enable colleges – both two- and four-year – to teach mainframe hardware and software. These programs tend to deliver high quality programs that produce a particular kind of graduate for a specific job. Some wonder, however, whether graduates will have mobility or whether their skill sets may lock them into one job. Some employers have taken a broader view of what is needed to increase the supply of appropriately skilled workers. For example, SPRINT works with the Metropolitan Community Colleges and local agencies in Kansas City to increase the number of underrepresented students in IT careers. SPRINT's program provides scholarships, tutoring and other support to these students.

The Urban Institute study concludes that community colleges can potentially play an important role in training people for IT jobs. The authors cite high levels of enrollment, low graduation rates, and large numbers of older students to "suggest that community colleges are functioning as retaining institutions rather than primary training institutions."[54] In order to make more specific recommendations about how to use community colleges to address the IT labor market problem and the digital divide, we need first to gather best practices information from the group that seems to be successful and then determine whether and how such programs could be replicated at other community colleges.

Employer-led training programs

Given the current shortage of IT workers, employers are faced with a choice either to "buy" workers away from other firms or to "build" them themselves through internal training. For the most part, employers rely on their employees' obtaining basic training from external sources; in-house training tends to focus on company-specific

54 Lerman et al. (2000: 26).

skills.[55] Although many IT companies are reticent to invest in training because of the frequent job switching and poaching common to the industry, other forward-thinking companies recognize that they must be part of the solution to the IT worker shortage by investing in training programs. Such an investment in training also serves longer-term strategic goals such as building a market for their technologies and capturing market share.

Perhaps the best known of these programs is Cisco Systems' Networking Academy Program, which is available in 50 US states, Washington, DC, and 121 countries worldwide.[56] Launched in 1997, the Academy program is a partnership between Cisco Systems, education, business, government, and community organizations. The curriculum focuses on teaching students to design, build, and maintain computer networks. It is an eight-semester (560 hours), web-based, hands-on curriculum that is taught mainly in high schools and colleges, but also in some community organizations. Currently there are more than 157,000 students enrolled at 6,596 academies worldwide. As of summer 2000, the Academy had 10,000 graduates.

It should be noted that not all Networking Academies target low income or disadvantaged workers. Like most employer-led programs, it was created because it positively impacts the company's bottom line. At the same time, the Cisco program has done more than most employer-led training programs to reach underrepresented communities. Cisco does this primarily through partnerships with community groups and international organizations. For example, as of March 2001 there are 100 Networking Academies in 26 of the 34 Empowerment Zone communities. To encourage the development of Networking Academies in Empowerment Zone communities, Cisco donates all of the networking equipment necessary to educational institutions that establish centers in these neighborhoods.

The corporate sector appears to be recognizing the increased need for training. In a 1994 survey, 54 percent of establishments reported providing more formal training than they had in 1990; only 2 percent reported a decrease.[57] Another study documented that business investment in education and training rose more than 33 percent between

---

55 Chapple and Zook (2000).
56 www.cisco.com/edu
57 US Department of Commerce, US Department of Education, US Department of Labor, National Institute for Literacy and Small Business Administration (1999: 15).

1990 and 1998.[58] Twenty-one percent of employer-based training focuses on computers.[59] However, most training efforts are not targeted at disadvantaged workers.

In addition, many corporate actors have chosen to focus their contribution to training on the K-12 school system. For example, 3Com's NetPrep GYRLS program provides network training to high-school girls to encourage them to enter IT fields. The Dell Foundation launched a program in 2000 to help children prepare for the digital age. Although these efforts are clearly important, there must also be a greater investment in workforce-oriented training programs. Employer led training efforts are fragmented; there is a lack of coordination across companies, though they could achieve greater scale were they to collaborate.

The primary benefits of employer-led training programs are that private corporations tend to have the resources to invest in these programs and they can target the training very specifically to their needs. From the perspective of potential employees, this second benefit can be a limitation. Some believe that graduates of employer-led programs are trained too narrowly and that they face difficulty transferring the skills obtained to other work situations.

For-profit post-secondary institutions, proprietary schools, and private technical institutes

For-profit post-secondary institutions (which include private technical institutes and other proprietary schools) account for approximately 5 percent of enrollment in two-year institutions.[60] Although many of these schools offer two-year Associate degrees and certifications, for-profit secondary institutions cost more than community colleges. These institutions have been around for decades. For example, DeVry Institute, one of the first and largest for-profit post secondary schools, was established in 1931. The focus of these institutions has been to provide career-oriented educational programs in business, technology, and other related services. These for-profit institutions operate close to the labor market, altering their course offerings with changing

58   21st Century Workforce Commission (2000: 57).
59   US Department of Commerce, US Department of Education, US Department of Labor, National Institute for Literacy and Small Business Administration (1999: 16).
60   Bailey, Badway and Gumport (2001).

employment patterns and skills shifting. For example, when the DeVry Institute first opened its doors the school focused on radio, television, and sound systems. Over time, DeVry has expanded to include computer technology, electrical engineering technology, telecommunications management, and a host of other programatic areas. The ITAA survey found that IT companies rated proprietary schools as an effective source of IT training because the perception is that these schools focus on specific skills and require few unnecessary classes. IT-related technical institutes have mushroomed in recent years. Although these institutions appear to be an effective source of short-term, specialized training, they are also very costly to participants, limiting their usefulness as a strategy to train disadvantaged populations.

Overall advantages and disadvantages

The four types of programs that train people for entry-level IT jobs have different advantages and disadvantages. Table 6.3 lays these out explicitly, along with some other descriptive information about each of these delivery mechanisms. Although IT training programs located in CTCs and community-based organizations have done some impressive work, it is unclear whether, in fact, they have "enormous potential for increasing the number of people who can participate in the knowledge-based economy."[61] Even the largest of these programs is operating on a relatively small scale. Further work needs to be done to determine whether and how these programs can achieve greater scale, who specifically they reach most effectively, and how dependent they are on "charismatic leaders" and "well-ingrained institutions."[62]

Many important questions remain unanswered because the data simply do not exist. How many people are trained each year through each of these types of programs? How many of these programs exist and where are they located? Can programs meet the demand for services? Are some programs more effective than others at placing graduates? At providing training that keeps a worker employable over the long term?

Across the board, those programs that have thus far demonstrated success in producing graduates and placing them in jobs share the following characteristics:

61 Chapple and Zook (2000).
62 Harrison and Weiss (1998: 7).

Table 6.3 Programs that deliver entry-level IT training

Program type	Relative cost	Target population	Length of program	Advantages	Disadvantages
Community-based training program	Free or low cost; training costs are usually covered by public or private sector grants	Low-income; disadvantaged or displaced worker	Various, programs range from a few sessions to several months of intensive training	Serves low-income people; strong connections to community; economical; little bureaucracy	Small-scale; replicability issues; charismatic leader syndrome
Community college	Low cost	Geographic focus, with enrollment open to the general population	2 years	Economical; many locations; flexible scheduling; history of serving underserved groups;	Bureaucracy impedes flexibility
Employer-led program	Various; free to expensive, depending on the program	Wide ranging, depending on the goals of the program	Varies	Skills taught are relevant; eliminates the middleman; replicable	Narrow skill set; fragmentation across programs; questionable transferability of skills to other employers
For-profit post-secondary institutions/ Proprietary schools	Relatively expensive	Various; general enrollment for those who can pay	1–2 years; longer for advanced degrees or certificate	Strong connections to industry; replicable	Expensive

- strong ties to industry;[63]
- after-placement services for graduates;
- ability to quickly modify curriculum.

The primary challenge faced by all training programs is an acute shortage of faculty to do the actual teaching and training. The shortage of IT workers has created a situation in which those with the skills to teach these courses have little economic incentive to do so. Those programs located in community-based organizations and CTCs also have difficulty sustaining funding and meeting demand for services.[64]

Relevant Policy Efforts

Policy also clearly affects the IT labor market. Some relevant policies were discussed in chapters 3 and 5. This section deals with those federal and state policies that relate most directly to the workforce development issue.

The H-1B visa program

One response to the IT labor shortage is the H-1B visa program. This program admits foreign skilled workers to the US in order to fill jobs not being filled by US workers. Although not all foreign workers who enter the country under the H-1B program are IT workers, estimates indicate that the program currently fills 70,000 IT jobs, roughly 28 percent of the average annual demand for IT workers.[65] Approximately 460,000 H-1B visa recipients currently work in the US. In 1990, Congress imposed a 65,000 cap on the number of H-1B visas issued. In 1997, that cap was reached for the first time. The corporate sector has successfully pressured the federal government to increase the number of H-1B visas available for each of the past several years; each year the new limit has been reached. In 2001, the cap was reached in March. Table 6.4 illustrates the annual increases in the number of H-1B visas allowed into the US.

---

63 Bliss (2000) makes that case that it is important to distinguish between "business-backed" and "employer-led" initiatives, arguing for the latter, which engage employers in all facets of employment training.
64 Servon and Nelson (1999); Chapple and Zook (2000).
65 US Department of Commerce (2000: 51).

Table 6.4 Number of H-1B visas, 1997–2001

Year	Number
1997	65,000
1998	65,000
1999	115,000
2000	115,000
2001	195,000

Source: Tech Law Journal and United States Congress, S.2045, American Competitiveness in the Twenty-First Century Act.

Legislation is currently pending that would amend current H-1B visa regulations. The "American Competitiveness in the Twenty-First Century Act" (S.2045) would authorize an additional 80,000 visas this year, 87,500 in 2001 and 130,000 in 2002.[66]

The primary accomplishment of the American Competitiveness in the Twenty-First Century Act of 2000 is that it raises to 195,000 the cap on the number of available H1-B visas, a type of temporary visa used to recruit established mid- and upper-level scientists (mainly information technology experts) from foreign countries. Controversy associated with this bill was unrelated to the fact that the academic community, government, and nonprofit organizations no longer have to compete with private industry for these temporary visas. S.2045 was introduced on February 9, 2000, by Senator Orrin G. Hatch (R-UT). The bill was amended several times before the Senate passed it by a vote of 96 to 1 on October 3, 2000. The House also passed the measure on October 3, 2000, by a two-thirds majority voice vote. On October 17, 2000, then President Clinton signed the bill into law.

The "Helping to Improve Technology Education and Achievement Act of 2000" (H.R.3983, also known as the "HI-TECH Act) would increase the caps on H-1B visas to 200,000 through 2003 and increase funding for technology training and K-12 education. It would also increase the H-1B application fee by $500 and earmark the additional funds generated for education and training. Both pieces of legislation have enjoyed strong bipartisan support. H.R.3983 has been referred to the House Education and Workforce Committee, the House Judiciary Subcommittee on Immigration and Claims, and the House Science subcommittees on Basic Research and on Technology.

66 http://olpa.od.nih.gov/Legislation/2american.htm

Already, training grants through the H-1B program have supported innovative work. The US Department of Labor recently awarded an H-1B grant of $1.3 million to the Communications Workers of America (CWA) to train workers in Washington, DC and Alameda County, California. Cisco Systems donates networking curriculum, lab equipment, and training to CWA's Training Centers, and Stanly Community College provides the learning infrastructure, educators, and accreditation. This type of partnership – between industry, government, the community college system, and labor – brings together the strengths of various stakeholders and is much more likely to make a significant dent in this problem than would any of these groups working independently.

The H-1B visa program helps to fill demand for workers right now, but it is a stopgap measure. A longer term solution to filling these jobs with US workers is needed. Even if annual increases continue in the number of H-1B visas allowed into the country, this solution is unlikely to meet the labor shortage in IT jobs by itself.[67] In addition, H-1B workers are likely to work in the most skilled jobs within the IT industry. These jobs create a complementary demand for lower-skilled IT workers, and that demand is currently going unmet.

Labor is often thought of as a relatively immobile input to production, especially as compared with inputs such as capital and raw materials. But labor does not necessarily need to be mobile in order to be globalized. This globalization of the labor force occurs either by offshoring parts of the production process or by bringing foreign workers to the US to work. First, firms can and do locate in a range of places worldwide in order to take advantage of specific skills or the particular cost structure of a local labor market. One reason for the relative decrease in manufacturing jobs in the US is the offshoring of a great deal of manufacturing activity to places in which labor is cheaper. Clearly, it is not that we have stopped making things. This aspect of globalization of the labor force has to do with multinational corporations expanding abroad to capture the lower cost of unskilled labor in other countries. Technology abets this disintegration of the Taylorist production process; for example, it is now easy for designers in one country to communicate with those who produce the designs in another very quickly.

Second, employers' demand for increases in the H-1B visa program shows that firms are soliciting and obtaining labor from other countries – thus far the US has had no trouble filling all of the allowed H-1B slots. This aspect of globalization involves fewer, but more highly

67   Stoll (2000: 15).

educated workers, the "core" IT workers discussed at the beginning of this chapter. Castells points out that only "a tiny fraction of the labor force, concerning the highest-skilled professionals" is globalized, while "the overwhelming proportion of labor . . . remains largely nation-bound."[68] Raising the H-1B visa quota means generating more jobs for the second tier of IT workers – those who have particular skills but are not as highly educated as the first-tier workers – which requires figuring out how to train the current workforce for these jobs.

Workforce development and welfare policy

Workforce development policy has long been identified as a form of social welfare policy. This perception arises because workforce development programs are often targeted at the unemployed and welfare recipients, creating the commonly held belief that these people either need remedial training in "soft" skills or need to be cajoled into working.[69] Workforce development proponents argue that these programs should instead be viewed as part of economic development policy because they help to maintain an available and appropriately trained workforce.

Several factors currently convene to make the link between workforce development policy and economic development stronger.[70] First, the labor shortage in IT fields has engendered a useful sense of urgency among employers. A report issued by the Center for an Urban Future maintains that "job training can no longer be dismissed as a feel-good favor to the downtrodden. It is now, at every level, a business necessity."[71] Second, the Clinton administration passed the Workforce Investment Act (WIA) in 1998 with the goal of coordinating over 163 job training programs funded through a range of government agencies. WIA emphasizes the importance of skills training and is characterized by the following goals: coordination of services; universal access; work first; consumer choice; and employer participation.[72] Third, 1996 welfare reform that replaced Aid for Families with

68   Castells (1996: 234).
69   This is not to say that soft skills are not important. In fact, Chapple and Zook (2000) show how critical it is to package soft skills training into larger IT training programs. Many programs (e.g., DeVry) market their inclusion of soft skills as a selling point.
70   See also Gruber and Roberts (2000).
71   Center for an Urban Future (2000: 1).
72   Kleiman and McAuliff (2000).

Dependent Children (AFDC) with Temporary Assistance for Needy Families (TANF) makes getting welfare recipients into the workforce a much higher priority than it was previously.

Both TANF and WIA share another important characteristic: they give much of the control of the programs to the state and local governments. Job training and welfare policy have nearly always been federal issues, which makes these recent changes significant. Some places have taken the opportunity to use WIA and TANF funding to train workers for IT jobs. In effect, then, there are many, many different ongoing experiments in each of these policy areas. This devolution allows states to tailor their policy responses to their particular economies and workforces. Some states have responded to the changes in legislation more creatively and entrepreneurially than have others. Some have thought about these two programs together rather than dealing with them in separate policy categories. In New York City, for example, TANF funds are being used to provide UNIX training to public assistance recipients.

Washington State has a booming high-tech sector and declining core industries, such as lumber and aerospace. Most workers who have been laid off do not have the skills they need for available IT jobs. In response, Governor Gary Locke created two programs. The first, Worker Retraining, guarantees 18 months of training to anyone who has been laid off. The training is designed to move workers from declining industries to those experiencing fast growth. The second program, Pre-Employment Training (PET) is delivered through the state's community college system, which works with employers to identify jobs for graduates. As soon as they are able, participants enter the workforce, but they continue to attend college to strengthen their skills foundation. Although early results from the program look promising, state officials are continuing to fine-tune the system. For example, Governor Locke has set aside $10 million for "job coaches" to raise the wages of PET participants and other low-wage workers and to help with the issue of job retention. Locke also shut down an underused training program operating through unemployment offices, demonstrating a willingness to experiment with a mix of initiatives.[73] Other states, such as Texas and Indiana have also launched creative initiatives based on their particular issues.

73 Description of Washington State programs taken from Center for an Urban Future (2000).

Nebraska's Applied Information Management (AIM) Institute is another example of an innovative IT workforce development program. The AIM Institute is a nonprofit membership organization created by a consortium of business, education and government entities to support and promote business growth related to information technology. Recognizing that a skilled IT workforce is critical to Nebraska's competitiveness, a critical focus of AIM's work is on information technology training. Through independent training modules and partnerships with high schools, universities and colleges, AIM develops model technology curriculum and training opportunities for residents of Nebraska.

Some states have also recognized the importance of a basic competence with technology for welfare recipients who are being moved to the workforce and are creating programs that provide these people with IT skills.

National Science Foundation: ATE and ITWF

The National Science Foundation (NSF)[74] funds the Advanced Technology Education (ATE) program, which promotes improvement in technological education at the undergraduate and secondary-school levels. ATE works toward this goal by supporting curriculum development, facilitating professional development of college faculty and secondary school teachers, and creating internships and field experiences for faculty, teachers, and students. ATE also brokers relationships and partnerships between two-year and four-year colleges, and funds a granting program called Centers of Excellence in Advanced Technology which supports projects that develop educational material, disseminate information, and engage in professional development for educators. The Northwest Center for Emerging Technologies (NWCET), which has been mentioned elsewhere in this chapter, is a Center of Excellence and has received over $5 million in grants from the ATE program since 1995. ATE specifically targets women, underrepresented minorities, and persons with disabilities.[75]

NSF also initiated the Information Technology Workforce program (ITWF), a research program that focuses on projects addressing

74   The NSF is an independent US government agency. Its mission is: to promote the progress of science; to advance the national health, prosperity and welfare; and to secure the national defense.
75   Congressional Commission on the Advancement of Women and Minorities in Science, Engineering and Technology Department (2000: 33).

research questions related to the underrepresentation of women and people of color in the IT workforce. The genesis of this program was the recognition that, in order for the US to maintain its global leadership in IT, there would need to be a continuous supply of well-trained engineering and computer science professionals. ITWF targets women and people of color as key populations that can help to increase the supply. The program funds research in three primary areas: environment and culture; the IT educational continuum; and the IT workplace.

IT training tax credits

The Technology Education and Training Act (TETA) has recently been proposed at the federal level. This legislation would provide tax credits to employers who provide training to their employees. The Technology Workforce Coalition argues that IT training tax credits will: increase personal income tax revenue from new employees; increase local sales tax revenue from new employee spending; increase corporate tax revenue from increased employee productivity; and develop necessary skills in non-IT businesses. In the meantime, some states have begun to move ahead with their own legislation in this area. Arizona was the first state to pass such legislation (HB2442). Similar legislation is pending in six other states, and four states have organized discussion groups to create legislation for next year.

Recommendations

This section lays out recommendations directed at training programs, and at the public and private sectors.

For training programs

Work with employers

Existing research shows that workforce development initiatives work best when they include strong ties to employers.[76] "These arrangements are most likely to create the kind of workforce development

---

76 Harrison and Weiss (1998); Stoll (2000); Chapple and Zook (2000).

policy and institutions that are sufficiently flexible to modify training to the specific demand for skills."[77] Flexibility and the ability to quickly respond to changes in skills demanded are clearly characteristics that any IT training program must have. It is not surprising, then, that the ITAA found that hiring managers value on-the-job training more highly than any other training.

For the private sector

Invest in training

The private sector has a great deal to gain by investing in training. The high value employers place on on-the-job training (OJT) means that the workplace is a primary site for the design and location of pro- grams. Research on the effects of employer-based training show that firms providing formal OJT raise their productivity by roughly 10 to 15 percent, on average.[78] Another study found that employers get more bang for the buck by investing in education than by investing in capital stock. Firms whose workforce had a 10 percent higher than average educational attainment level had an 8.6 percent higher than average productivity level, while firms with a 10 percent higher than average level of capital investment had only a 3.4 percent higher than average payoff.[79] Folding training into the workplace also makes sense from the perspective of workers. Focus groups of workers interested in continuing education cited lack of time and high cost as two of the biggest barriers to taking courses outside of work. Many high-tech companies have begun to invest in training, particularly at the K-12 level.

Create and participate in regional consortia

Another response involves regional consortia of firms joining forces to provide training. Some literature uses the term "coop-etition" to describe how rival companies cooperate when it is in their mutual

---

77   Stoll (2000: 2).
78   Cited in US Department of Commerce, US Department of Education, US Department of Labor, National Institute for Literacy and Small Business Administration (1999: 7).
79   US Department of Commerce, US Deparment of Education, US Department of Labor, National Institute for Literacy and Small Business Administration (1999: 7).

interest.[80] An example is the Alliance for Employee Growth and Development, a joint training trust to which AT&T, Lucent Technologies, the Communications Workers of America, and the International Brotherhood of Electrical Workers (IBEW) belong. The Alliance consists of more than 200 labor/management committees that "help identify educational needs, coordinate training, and build enrollment."[81] The Alliance also offers a range of training and learning opportunities that are tailored to local and individual needs. For example, participants can get involved in Alliance-sponsored on-site, offsite, and distance learning training programs. The Alliance offers tuition assistance and special services for dislocated workers. In addition to technical skills training, the Alliance also offers support services such as financial planning, career planning, test preparation, and certifications.

For the public sector

Support entry-level IT worker training

Public investment will be critical to maximizing the potential of the new economy. The rationale for public investment in training is that we cannot remain competitive as a nation without an educated and appropriately skilled workforce. Investment in human capital is needed in order to fuel the economy and create opportunities for historically disadvantaged groups to take advantage of the current demand for workers. This kind of investment in training will also assist workers who lose their jobs to adjust to labor market changes caused by increased trade and globalization.[82] The federal government has some programs in place, but these need to be expanded and updated. The employer fee for H-1B visa petitions is currently $500, much of which goes to training. Given that demand for these workers has thus far been relatively inelastic, that fee should be increased as a way to increase funding for effective programs.

---

80 21st Century Workforce Commission (2000: 29). In addition, Harrison and Weiss (1998) maintain that "an important theme that has emerged from [the workforce development field] during the past 12 years is that firms must learn to strategically cooperate as well as compete with rivals (pp. 7–8).
81 US Department of Commerce, US Department of Education, US Department of Labor, National Institute for Literacy and Small Business Administration (1999: 23).
82 US Department of Labor (1999: 75).

Create specific incentives for small firms

It is clearly more difficult for smaller firms to take on the added cost and burden of in-house training. Government incentives could help remedy this problem. For example, Section 127 of the IRS tax code, which makes employer-provided educational assistance tax-free to both the employer and the employee, is temporary. Section 127 should be permanently extended. State government can also create incentives for private corporations to invest in IT training.

Change regulations around education and training

The labor market has changed, but many government programs and policies have not changed along with it. For example, traditional government loans and grants can only be used toward degree programs. Lifelong Learning Tax Credits provide some assistance, and their expansion should be explored. Further, unemployment insurance (UI) recipients lose their benefits if they enroll in training that has not been approved by the state. Given that more people are receiving valuable training through alternative programs, there needs to be some shift in policy in this area. Existing policy does not reflect and work with the current reality.

Target women and minorities for IT training

The ITAA points to "the underrepresentation of women and other minorities in the IT workforce" as a key factor contributing to the shortage of IT workers. Table 6.5 illustrates the racial/ethnic distribution of the science, engineering, and technology (SET) workforce in 1997, showing that relatively few women, African-Americans, and Hispanics work in these fields.

By 2050, "the US population is expected to increase by 50 percent, and minority groups will make up nearly half the population."[83] Given that these groups make up an increasing proportion of the labor force, it makes sense to take action to prepare these groups for the requirements of the current economy. The need for skilled workers is so great that employers literally cannot afford to discriminate. Moving minority and women workers into these fields now will also create the positive spillover effect of creating networks and ties that will have long-lasting effects into the future.

---

83   US Department of Labor (1999: 2).

Table 6.5 1997 gender and racial/ethnic distribution of US and SET workforce

	US workforce (%)	US SET workforce (%)
White male	41.7	67.9
White female	34.7	15.4
Black	10.3	3.2
Hispanic	9.2	3.0
Asian and other	4.0	10.2
American Indian	—	0.3

Source: Congressional Commission on the Advancement of Women and Minorities in Science, Engineering and Technology Department (2000).

Table 6.6 Computer science degrees awarded to women by level

Academic year	Ph.D. awarded	% women	MS awarded	% women	BA/BS awarded	% women
1992–93	997	13.3	4,523	—	8,218	—
1993–94	1,005	15.6	5,179	19.1	8,216	17.9
1994–95	1,006	16.2	4,425	19.7	7,561	18.1
1995–96	915	11.7	4,260	20.0	8,411	15.9
1996–97	894	14.4	4,430	22.3	8,063	15.7

Source: Cuny and Aspray (2000).

The percentage of women earning computer science degrees has dropped steadily since 1984; women were 37 percent of degree recipients in 1984 compared to 28 percent in 1994. According to the Department of Commerce, only 1.1 percent of undergraduate women choose IT-related disciplines compared to 3.3 percent of male undergraduates.[84] If we follow the IT workforce pipeline, we see that the under-representation of women continues from those pursuing computer science degrees through all levels of the workforce. Table 6.6 illustrates the drop-out rate as women move from college through post-college degrees in computer science. According to Catalyst Associates, a non-profit research organization based in New York, only 8.1 percent of women occupy executive positions (senior VP and higher) at major technology companies, compared to approximately 12 percent in other sectors of the economy.[85] Women also make up nearly 60 percent of the working poor in this country, and minority women are more than twice as likely to be poor as white women.[86]

84 Cuny and Aspray (2000).
85 Congressional Commission on the Advancement of Women and Minorities in Science, Engineering and Technology Department (2000: 40).
86 US Department of Labor (1999: 4).

A report issued by the Commission on the Advancement of Women and Minorities in Science, Engineering, and Technology Development identified several barriers that exist for women, underrepresented minorities, and persons with disabilities at various places along the SET pipeline. These include: inadequacies in precollege education; lack of access to higher education; narrow and inflexible workplace environment; poor public image of science, engineering, and technology fields.[87] According to this report, "the lack of diversity in SET education and careers is an old dilemma, but economic necessity and workforce deficiencies bring a new urgency to the nation's strategic need to achieve parity in its SET workforce."[88] Policies that address these barriers must be developed in order to move women and underrepresented minorities into the IT workforce. Such policies would range from improved elementary education to creating mentor relationships between IT professionals and college students majoring in related fields to providing members of these groups with early work opportunities in IT fields. The private sector can certainly share some of the burden for this work. In fact, were the number of women in the IT workforce increased to equal the number of men, the gap in supply versus demand for IT workers would close.[89]

Increase attention to and funding for K-12 education

This chapter is geared primarily toward understanding and solving the current shortage of IT workers. However, this issue is unlikely to go away soon. Although chapter 5 examines youth specifically, primary and secondary education is important enough to warrant mention here as well. In order to mitigate against future problems, there must be greater investment in primary and secondary education, particulary for underrepresented minorities who often attend poor-performing schools. Three recent initiatives may provide some assistance in this area. The International Society for Technology in Education developed the National Educational Technology Standards (NETS), which outline technology skills that can be incorporated throughout the K-12 curriculum. And the Techforce Initiative, developed through a partnership between the Education Development Center, ITAA, and the National

87   Congressional Commission on the Advancement of Women and Minorities in Science, Engineering and Technology Department (2000).
88   Congressional Commission on the Advancement of Women and Minorities in Science, Engineering and Technology Department (2000: 5).
89   Freeman and Aspray (1999).

Alliance of Business created an "IT Pathway Pipeline Model" which integrates technology into students' learning beginning in primary school.[90] Third, Intel, Hewlett Packard, and Microsoft have joined forces on a project called Teach to the Future, which will train 100,000 US classroom teachers to integrate computer technology into existing curriculum. These three initiatives, although welcome, do not address the more basic problem of schools that deliver chronically poor performances in basic subjects such as math and reading.

Partnerships

In addition to the above, it will be critical for existing training programs, the public sector, and the private sector to partner with each other in order to devise effective ways of addressing the IT labor shortage and moving available workers into existing jobs. Promising examples of such partnerships already exist.

California's Employment Training Panel[91]

The Employment Training Panel (ETP) is a California state agency created in 1982 as a cooperative business–labor program to retrain workers. ETP's purpose has been to fund training that: 1) meets the needs of employers for skilled workers, and 2) meets the needs of workers for good jobs. Since its inception, ETP has trained over 336,000 workers using over $645 million in funds. ETP is funded through the Employment Training Fund, which is one-tenth of 1 percent of subjects' unemployment insurance wages paid by every private, for-profit employer in the state and some nonprofits also. This fund generates between $70 and $100 million each year. Companies are eligible to apply for ETP funding if they are paying into the state's Employment Training Fund (ETF) and:

- are hiring and training unemployed workers who are receiving unemployment insurance benefits (UI); and/or
- face out-of-state competition and need to retrain current employees; and/or
- need to upgrade workers in areas where there are demonstrable skills shortages; and/or

---

90   Education Development Center (2000).
91   Description of ETP comes from www.etp.ca.gov/program/program.cfm.

- have special, unique training programs in areas such as defense conversion, entrepreneurial training, and new industries.

ITAA partnerships

ITAA has initiated a range of partnerships with industry, academia, and community groups in order to increase the number of IT workers. Several of these partnerships focus specifically on populations that are underrepresented in the IT industries. RITA, a joint venture with Women Work!, is executing a plan to help women in transition achieve self-sufficiency with IT job training and placement. ITAA works with a group called Community Options to train and place people with disabilities. And the National School-to-Work Office has funded ITAA to work with the National Alliance of Business (NAB) and the Education Development Center (EDC) to facilitate, support, and promote IT employer participation in school-to-work efforts.

Conclusions

The current high level of demand for entry-level IT workers, both from IT and non-IT firms, presents a unique opportunity for integrating workforce development and welfare initiatives into economic development goals. Collaboration will clearly be key to solving the current shortage of IT workers. Creative partnerships between industry, government, educational institutions, and the private nonprofit sector have the potential to help industry fill jobs that will fuel the economy while at the same time creating new opportunities for groups that have historically experienced labor market discrimination. These partnerships can operate to increase and improve the flow of information about employers to job seekers and vice versa.[92] If it is true that disadvantaged workers do not lack employment opportunities, two challenges remain. The first involves training the available pool of workers for these jobs. Doing so requires figuring out what the best mechanism is for delivering this training, and determining what subset of workers can be easily trained. The second challenge concerns ensuring that these jobs pay a living wage.

92   Holzer (1996) cited in Harrison and Weiss (1998: 34) asserts that job seekers and employers lack sufficient information about each other, leading to the current state in which certain groups experience more unemployment and underemployment than others.

7

The Organizational Divide

*With Josh Kirschenbaum
and Radhika Kunamneni*

Scholars and activists have begun to recognize that, in order for low-income communities to benefit fully from IT, the next generation of technology policy must support two additional pillars – the creation of local content[1] and the increased technology capacity of community-based organizations. Community content and technology capacity are closely related. Building the technological capacity of local community-based organizations (CBOs) will enable both the generation of relevant content for low-income communities and strengthen the ability of CBOs to achieve their existing missions. Community-based organizations are rich repositories of local information, but they lack the technology capacity to share and fully employ this local knowledge. CBOs also have the relationships necessary to reach groups that are currently excluded from the information society. We call this lack of technology capacity among CBOs the "organizational divide."

This chapter discusses the current connections and missed opportunities between the community-building and community technology movements. Although these grassroots movements have evolved relatively separately, enormous potential exists for them to work together in mutually beneficial ways. We discuss an exemplary set of CBOs that are currently using technology to create community-based content and to extend their reach. These CBOs are using IT tools to do work in the following six categories: advocacy and online organizing; community information clearinghouses; networking and online communities; innovations in service delivery; interactive database development; and community mapping.

---

1 Content is discussed in greater detail in chapter 3.

Although policy and programs to address the digital divide have helped to support CTCs and bridge the access component of the digital divide, the access-centered approach pursued by both public and private funders has done little to promote the development of relevant content for low income communities or to bring technology resources to community based organizations. Addressing these gaps must be a key part of any comprehensive approach aimed at narrowing the digital divide.

Chapter 2 showed that the digital fault line falls along historic social and economic divides. As digital technologies transform the workplace, educational institutions, financial systems, and social spaces, communities that lack access will be further marginalized from full participation in society. Policy solutions to the digital divide must build on the existing infrastructure of the community-building movement. Grassroots social movements have traditionally worked to bridge persistent economic and social divides and promote a more equitable and democratic society. These movements, led by community development corporations (CDCs), social service providers, activists, organizers, and residents, have created a vital community infrastructure[2] in disadvantaged neighborhoods around the country. If one goal of bridging the digital divide is to strengthen low-income neighborhoods through the application of information technology, then it is critical to understand how this existing community infrastructure, with its connection to local constituents, can complement and work with the community technology movement. Community organizations are the gatekeepers of local information and are therefore the appropriate actors for creating local content that is relevant and useful to low-income residents. These organizations and their resident constituency bases possess the wisdom, knowledge and experience to use IT tools to build social and economic equity.

These local community-based organizations are rich repositories of information, but they are technology deficient. The network of community technology centers discussed in chapter 3 evolved somewhat separately from the community building infrastructure. Although nearly 61 percent of CTCs responding to the survey discussed in chapter 3 are housed within existing community-based organizations,

---

2 Community infrastructure includes residents, activists, community development corporations, social service organizations, affordable housing developments, faith institutions, business owners, schools, etc. working together and independently to address poverty and racism.

most use computers and the Internet to provide access to their constituents. Few use technology to create content, and the examples of CBOs that have employed technology creatively to strengthen their prevailing work are rare. Important exceptions exist, however, and these exceptional CBOs are the focus of this chapter. Most of the resources provided to CTCs do not support building the technology capacity of community-based organizations. Building this kind of capacity will be challenging; CBOs historically have been the last to benefit from technological innovations and have struggled to find ways to use technology as a tool to advance their missions.

CBOs' Relationship to Technology

As the digital divide for individuals gained national attention during the late 1990s, it was framed as a problem experienced at the individual and household level. It was not long before the nonprofit sector recognized that it was experiencing a technology divide of its own. Few community-based organizations have the resources or technical capacity to maintain computer systems and generate community-based content. In response to this "organizational divide" several nonprofit technical assistance (TA) providers and technology TA providers created the National Strategy for Nonprofit Technology (NSNT) to address the organizational divide from a national perspective. In 1998, NSNI, a leadership network of nonprofit staff members, funders, and TA providers, developed a blueprint for how the nonprofit sector can use technology more effectively and creatively. The blueprint highlighted the challenges facing the nonprofit sector in the late 1990s.

> Most nonprofits are hesitant to use technology and are ill-informed about the impact it could have on their work . . . funders are reluctant to invest in efforts that seem unrelated to program delivery, and . . . technology assistance providers are ill-equipped to provide the kind and scale of support necessary to transform the nonprofit sector's use of technology. Also, research indicates that there are disparities in nonprofits' access to and use of technology – namely, that many nonprofits in low-income communities and in communities of color are underserved with respect to technology acquisition and use.[3]

3 The Planning Partners for a National Strategy for Nonprofit Technology (1999: 2).

An inability to use technology in their work has effectively penalized nonprofit organizations by making them unable to meet potential increases in demand for services, to demonstrate program successes, to compete with for-profit enterprises, and to communicate effectively with their constituencies.[4] Lack of facility with technology has also distanced these organizations from the new economy.[5] Shorters has developed a classification system for understanding the range of "technology cultures" in nonprofit organizations. Organizations, regardless of mission, budget, or size, can be classified with respect to their relationship to information technology into one of four distinct categories:

1 **Unnecessary** failing to see the benefits of technology and avoiding it as much as possible. No Internet access and limited computer use.
2 **Necessary evil** having a limited use of technology. Limited Internet access and limited computer use.
3 **Necessary good** viewing technology as a necessary part of their work. Have Internet access and computer use.
4 **Strategic advantage** believing that their effective use of technology will give them strategic advantage. Using both the Internet and computers as strategic tools.[6]

Most CBOs reside in the "Necessary evil" category and are far from making technology a part of their strategic tool kit. This observation is supported by a 1999 study by Wired for Good, where Silicon Valley nonprofits were asked to name the three most frequently used methods of communication. The top three responses included telephone (77 percent), in-person meetings (70 percent), and hard copy memos (45 percent). Email was near the bottom of the list at 28 percent and sharing files across a computer network ranked even lower at 18 percent. CBOs are chronically understaffed and underresourced. Most have not attempted to generate the funds or allocate the staff time necessary to integrate technology into their work despite the clear potential benefits. As a result, a capacity gap around information technology in the nonprofit sector has developed and continues to challenge the sector.

4   The Planning Partners for a National Strategy for Nonprofit Technology (1999).
5   Shorters (1999).
6   Shorters (1999).

Building the Technology Capacity of CBOs

Those CBOs that have recognized and responded to the need to gain technology capacity have done so in one or more of the three following ways: by working with technical assistance providers; by partnering with community technology centers; and/or by generating entrepreneurial initiatives of their own. The first avenue is by far the most common. Collaborative efforts with CTCs and home-grown strategies are more rare, but have important potential for wider use.

Technical assistance providers

The technology technical assistance (TA) available to nonprofit organizations consists of three types of organizations: traditional technical assistance providers; a new breed of IT-focused TA providers; and institutions of higher education. Taken together, these organizations constitute a new level of infrastructure to support the use of technology by the nonprofit sector.

Traditional nonprofit TA providers

An increasing number of traditional nonprofit TA providers have added information technology services to the menu of supports they offer to community based organizations. For example, Compass Point Non Profit Services in the San Francisco Bay Area, has provided management and training classes to the community sector for decades. Recognizing the need for IT-specific assistance, Compass Point now offers technology services in addition to its existing menu of services and organizes an annual conference on nonprofits and technology. These traditional nonprofit TA providers have a deep understanding of the needs and challenges of the community serving sector, and can leverage this experience to offer technology services specifically tailored to CBOs' needs.

Technology-specific TA providers

The shift to an information-driven economy has generated a new type of technical assistance organization with an explicit focus on supporting the use of technology by the nonprofit sector. Organizations such as NPower in Seattle[7] and CompuMentor in San Francisco serve the important function of connecting nonprofits to technology in relevant ways. For example, since 1987, CompuMentor has served over 23,000 nonprofits and schools with a range of person-to-person computer services. These include matching skilled volunteers with schools and nonprofits, technology planning (TEAM) and consulting. The organization recently launched TechSoup.org a one-stop information resource for nonprofit technology issues. TechSoup provides information on hardware, finding the right software application, guidelines for selecting an appropriate database, planning your organization's network, and how to get funding.

Within this category of TA providers, national groups (such as National Council of Nonprofit Organizations, CompuMentor, the Benton Foundation, the Rockefeller Technology Project, the Progressive Technology Project, OMB Watch's Nonprofits Policy and Technology Project, and the National Strategy for Nonprofit Technology) tend to play research and clearinghouse roles and connect nonprofits to local service providers that can provide direct assistance. In some cases, these organizations provide direct service (CompuMentor) and support public policy campaigns (the Benton Foundation). At the local level, programs like Compass Point (San Francisco), NPower (Seattle and New York City), and Technology Works for Good (Washington, DC) provide service by dispatching staff to organizations, linking technicians (often known as circuit riders) to organizations and offering technology courses for organizations.

Institutions of higher education

Community colleges and universities increasingly serve the important role of providing technology assistance to nonprofit organizations in the regions in which they operate. These institutions of higher education – which are resource rich in terms of hardware, software, and human capital – provide an important community service through assistance to nonprofit organizations. At Carnegie Mellon University in Pittsburgh, an undergraduate course titled "Computer Science and the Community" has initiated unique partnerships between the university and CBOs throughout the city. The course pairs computer science students with community-based organizations to develop the technology capacity of the organizations. Students work with the

---

7   Chapter 8, which focuses on Seattle, discusses NPower in greater depth.

CBOs to: identify their technical needs and problems; discuss options for meeting those needs and solving the problems; and help integrate technology into the organization's programs. The students teach their troubleshooting techniques to the partners so that the knowledge is transferred, and by the end of the semester the CBO is able to do much of the troubleshooting independently.

Community technology centers

As described in chapter 3, community technology centers (CTCs) have made significant strides in narrowing the technology gap. However, many of these community technology centers have been created independent of the existing community infrastructure; their missions gravitate toward technology access and training rather than toward neighborhood revitalization. Some community technology efforts have begun to provide resources beyond access and training by connecting to larger neighborhood revitalization efforts. In a few cases, mature CTCs have provided technology capacity building assistance to community-serving organizations. These emerging connections between the community building and community technology movements over the last five years demonstrate the potential role CTCs can play in strengthening the existing community infrastructure. The community technology movement has the potential to be a significant resource in providing technology TA to CBOs.

Entrepreneurial efforts of CBOs

The third way that CBOs obtain technology capacity is through their own entrepreneurial efforts. Recognizing the importance of technology to their work, some CBOs have been successful in acquiring the necessary resources to integrate it. These bootstrap efforts are often spearheaded by a charismatic and technology-committed leader, and are often supported through the acquisition of public (for example, NTIA's TOP program) or private foundation dollars to build capacity and develop content. However, as discussed in chapters 3 and 4, funding for this kind of work is much more difficult to obtain than is funding for access.

The majority of nonprofit organizations have not traditionally used information technology as a tool to promote their work and have not been exposed to the recent innovations and potential of the Internet. CBO staff tend to consider technology in isolation from or in competition with other program tasks rather than as a tool that can support all of the organization's work. For example, many nonprofits remain unaware of training labs in their own neighborhoods and of TA providers at either the local or national levels. This isolation may lead organizations to acquire the wrong technology and training that leads to further frustration and greater isolation from using technology as a tool. As the technology TA field matures, more outreach and education is needed so that community-serving nonprofits can learn about the benefits of information technologies and move from the "unnecessary" and "necessary evil" categories to the "necessary good" and "strategic advantage" categories.

Promising Practices

Innovative examples of community-serving organizations using technology as a strategic tool to support their work have recently begun to surface. These entrepreneurial organizations have overcome significant challenges and utilized an array of mechanisms to support their efforts to incorporate technology into their programmatic activities. We have identified six primary activities that community-based organizations support through the use of information technologies. Table 7.1 summarizes these activities and provides examples of CBOs using technology for each purpose.

We have separated these activities here for ease of analysis, even though great overlap often exists between them. For example, the information gathered through a community mapping process may be an important tool in an advocacy campaign, or a community information clearinghouse might be powered by an interactive database to provide information to its constituents. In addition, CBOs tend to first adopt simpler applications that lie closest to their core work, such as databases to support evaluation and outreach, and listservs to enhance advocacy, taking on more advanced applications such as mapping after building confidence and witnessing the power and potential of IT. Following is a discussion of how exemplary CBOs currently utilize technology to strengthen their work. Highlighting these local community successes in utilizing technology to promote equity will enable the creation of a set of best practices.

Table 7.1 Innovative community-serving organizations using information technology

Type of activity	Organization	Issue area	IT tools
Advocacy/Online organizing	Welfare Law Center, Community Voices Heard, Make The Road By Walking	Welfare reform, promoting participation by low-income communities	Website, listservs, Internet, training, technical assistance
	1000 Friends of Oregon	Sprawl and other environmental issues	Listservs, email, other electronic tools
Information clearing-house	CDCNetwork	Community development, affordable housing	Internet, email, online resource bank, other e-business tools
Online communities/networking	Grace Hill	Building social capital, neighborhood revitalization	Web-based Time Dollar Exchange system, computer mentoring, online resource bank
	Technology Access Foundation	Organizational development for youth-serving agencies	Virtual Private Network (VPN)
Innovations in service delivery	Sexual Assault Crisis Center	Support services for survivors of sexual violence, advocacy	Online support group (similar to a "chat room")
Interactive database development	East Bay Works	Employment and training services	Web-based data systems, online job training resource bank, individualized email accounts
	Cabrini Connections	Tutoring and mentoring	Web-based data systems, GIS technologies, resource bank mentoring services and best practices
Community mapping	Neighborhood Knowledge, Los Angeles	Neighborhood revitalization, advocacy, public policy	Interactive Electronic Monitoring System, GIS, training for residents
	National Neighborhood Indicators Project, Boston Community Building Network	Neighborhood development, community building	Various information systems including GIS, resource banks, interactive databases

Advocacy and online organizing

For decades the fields of community organizing and advocacy have worked to rebuild civic life and to transform the power structures that impede the building of strong, empowered communities. A primary strategy that community organizers have used to achieve these goals is the creation of institutions and mechanisms that allow people excluded from decision-making processes to advocate for the redistribution of power and promote greater public participation.[8] The Internet and other emerging communications mediums hold the potential to facilitate and strengthen community organizing and advocacy by: allowing a greater number of people to access and exchange information about their communities and public policies; achieving a larger scale and efficiency to organizing efforts; and building affinity relationships around issue areas across geographic spaces.[9]

Two examples of organizing efforts, one focused on welfare reform and the other on combating sprawl legislation, demonstrate the potential of IT to transform the fields of community organizing and advocacy and ensure greater voice for underrepresented groups in decision making arenas.

The Welfare Law Center's Low Income Networking and Communication (LINC) project was established in 1998 to support the capacity of grassroots organizations to utilize technology to enhance their advocacy work. Founded in 1965, the Welfare Law Center, a national law and policy organization, recognized that information technology could be used as a vehicle to bring low-income groups into the public debate over welfare policies, thereby strengthening democratic institutions. The LINC project uses technology to build and strengthen an advocacy movement around welfare reform by: 1) building a communications infrastructure that allows welfare reform advocates to share information and collaborate; and 2) creating a technical assistance strategy that increases the local capacity of low-income groups to mount their own organizing efforts.

The two components of the communications infrastructure include: 1) a website that provides a clearinghouse of information for grassroots organizations working on welfare reform; and 2) a listserv that promotes dialogue, mutual mentoring for organizers, and a vehicle to

8 Stoecker (2000).
9 Servon and Nelson (2002, forthcoming) provide further illustrations of how IT can be employed toward these goals.

coordinate organizing efforts nationally. Because the Welfare Law Center had deep knowledge about the issue of welfare reform and established relationships with low-income grassroots groups, it was well positioned to organize the field nationally through the use of information technology.

At the same time, the nationally focused Welfare Law Center's LINC project supports local organizing efforts around welfare reform by building the technical capacity of low-income grassroots organizations. One example is Community Voices Heard (CVH), an organization of low-income people, predominantly women on welfare, working together to make improvements in their communities and advance the political, economic, and social rights of low-income people on welfare and other low-wage workers. CVH works locally to ensure that the voice of welfare recipients in New York City informs the welfare reform debate through public and political education, community and legislative organizing, leadership development and training.

With assistance from the LINC project, CVH engages in online activities to augment its offline efforts to promote equity. For example, CVH built a Worker's Computer Center where community members can learn about the Internet and how to use it for research and organizing. Online sample letters, legislative contact information, and instructions on how to download these materials, greatly facilitate public participation in the political process. Most recently CVH has matched its membership database with GIS mapping software to identify the political districts of the group's members. By dividing its member base into political constituencies based on the district in which they live, CVH can quickly identify and efficiently bring constituent members to meet state legislators.

1000 Friends of Oregon provides another example of using IT tools to support advocacy efforts. This nonprofit citizens group, founded in 1975, works to protect Oregon's quality of life through the conservation of farm and forest lands. 1000 Friends of Oregon combines advocacy, education and research. On the advocacy front the organization's efforts include: defending and improving the state's land use laws and regulations before the Oregon legislature and state agencies; developing and advancing new policies and programs that help Oregonians manage growth at the state, regional, and local level; and litigation to establish legal precedents and to enforce existing laws.

1000 Friends of Oregon uses IT tools in a variety of ways to support its efforts. For example, late in Oregon's 1997 legislative session, a bill that would have allowed for the development of Smith Rock, a recreation area, was resuscitated. This happened at a time when notice for legislative hearings was down to less than one hour. Recognizing that they needed to mobilize quickly, and that traditional organizing tools such as direct mail, a phone bank, or door-to-door organizing would be too slow, 1000 Friends of Oregon enlisted the help of ONE/Northwest, to develop an Internet organizing strategy. ONE/Northwest, a Seattle based nonprofit organization that provides technical assistance to conservation activists in the Northwest, utilized its extensive email list and other electronic networking activities to mobilize a legislative lobbying campaign that thwarted the bill. 1000 Friends of Oregon's deep knowledge of local legislative issues, coupled with ONE/Northwest's technical expertise and relationships with the conservation community, created this success.

Information clearing-house

The World Wide Web is extremely useful as a tool for gathering and disseminating information. Some CBOs have begun to use the Internet to develop and share localized and issue specific information with their constituents and other organizations. Some information clearing-houses focus on a geographic area, enabling residents and visitors to find valuable information about institutions, government, events, local history, etc. Other information clearing-houses are issue specific, allowing "communities of interest" to build their shared knowledge base.

One example of an issue-driven clearing-house is the Cleveland Community Development Corporation Network (CDCNetwork), a consortium of practitioners in community development using electronic communications to remove barriers to communication, enhance support, increase access to information, and work toward eliminating the isolation and lack of support that often accompanies community work. CDCNetwork was created by the Center for Neighborhood Development (CND) and the Cleveland Neighborhood Development Corporation (CNDC). The site has three major components: 1) information about CDCs in Cleveland; 2) resources for CDCs; and 3) a CDC forum. The CDCNetwork is also exploring ways in which digital technologies can be employed to increase the effectiveness of community development activities and neighborhood revitalization. Its most recent effort in this arena is the development of the T2K Initiative, a collaborative effort of area CDCs and city agencies to utilize e-business tools to support neighborhood service delivery, program management and communication.

The CDCNetwork uses Internet technologies to build the capacity of community organizations via information sharing. The strength of the CDCNetwork stems from its targeted focus on a specific geography and issue area. Because local practitioners guide the development of the CDCNetwork, the larger organization reflects the priorities and needs of the neighborhood organizations.

Online communications and networking

One of the most logical applications of IT tools is to facilitate coordination of activities. Community serving groups utilize applications such as email, websites, and virtual private networks (VPNs) to work collaboratively with each other and improve service delivery to their constituents. This work facilitates the building of online communities that enhance and support their offline networks. Two examples – one that promotes building relationships between low income St. Louis residents, and the other that facilitates youth-serving organizations in Seattle – demonstrate the utility of these online spaces.

Founded in 1903, Grace Hill is a neighborhood development organization serving disadvantaged communities in the St. Louis metropolitan area. The organization bases its work on the self-help tradition of the Settlement House movement. Grace Hill's Member Organized Resource Exchange (MORE) is an example of the organization's "neighbors helping neighbors" approach to community change. The MORE Time Dollar Exchange is a community-based network of services that can be exchanged like currency between neighbors, allowing participants to earn and save "time dollars" when they volunteer their services to one another. The computerized tracking system allows Grace Hill to monitor and track activity while providing participating residents with a monthly report of Time Dollars earned and owed. Services bartered between neighbors under the MORE system include auto repair, childcare, gardening, photography, tax assistance, transportation, tutoring, and writing. Formalizing and enhancing the skills residents already possess builds on an asset-based approach to community development.[10] Grace Hill implemented its time dollar

10   Kretzmann and McKnight (1993).

program in 1982 using an index card accounting system maintained by staff. In 1985, Grace Hill computerized the time dollar system, enabling staff to more easily update, categorize, and share information about residents' skills and abilities. The automation led to a massive increase in the number of residents participating in the program. In 1998, 10,392 providers and 17,907 consumers completed over 21,000 exchanges generating over $72,000 time dollars. The services that were exchanged ranged from transportation to household chores to childcare. Grace Hill estimates that if a $6 hourly rate was applied to the services that were bartered, over $432,000 in wealth was preserved in participating St. Louis Neighborhoods.

In 1995 a TIIAP grant (now referred to as TOP from the Department of Commerce) facilitated a third upgrade to the Time Dollar system.[11] Grace Hill used TIIAP funds to upgrade existing computer systems and establish a network of personal computers in agencies and public sites throughout the Grace Hill service area. This upgrade led to another significant increase in participation in the Time Dollar program, since residents were now able to access their accounts without the assistance of Grace Hill staff. At the same time, Grace Hill created its Computer Mentor program so that residents with some computer know-how could provide basic computer training to others in their community, enabling all interested residents to acquire the skills necessary to access their accounts online. Although Grace Hill initiated the Computer Mentor program to enable greater participation in the Time Dollar system, residents' initial exposure to computers and the Internet sparked an interest in more advanced IT training. Given Grace Hill's relationships with a network of community serving agencies in the area, Grace Hill is able to connect residents interested in advanced training with other workforce development service providers. Over time, Grace Hill has expanded the Time Dollar system to include a comprehensive online resource bank of services available in the St. Louis metropolitan area as well as a geo-spatial mapping of community resources and assets.

Innovations in service delivery

Just as information technologies are leading to productivity gains in the private sector, IT tools can be applied in the nonprofit sector to improve and expand the delivery of social services. Specifically, the

11 Chapter 4 describes the TIIAP/TOP grants in detail.

strategic use of technology can streamline service delivery, assist social service organizations to serve a larger number of constituents, and facilitate collaboration across organizations. The Sexual Assault Crisis Center is an example of an organization utilizing IT tools to enhance the provision of support services.

Based in Androscoggin, Maine, the Sexual Assault Crisis Center (SACC) is committed to ending sexual victimization and assisting the healing of people affected by rape, sexual assault, child sexual abuse, and sexual harassment. SACC provides an array of services for survivors of sexual violence including a 24-hour hotline, a sexual assault response team, support groups, programs targeted at adolescents, and in-school education programs. Most recently SACC has employed IT to augment its existing services with online support groups. These groups operate on a secure, private, closed site, which can only be accessed by individuals who have been screened and accepted into the group by SACC. These groups allow survivors of sexual violence to connect to each other in a safe way, and often at times when other support groups are not available (for example, late evening hours). A trained staff person moderates the support groups, enabling SACC to maintain control of who participates. Because SACC counselors also maintain offline contact with clients, counselors can contact clients via phone or home visits should an emergency arise during an online support group. This complementarity supports an argument that has been made throughout this book, which is that virtual and face-to-face relationships are mutually reinforcing. The Sexual Assault Crisis Center uses IT tools to *improve* service delivery. Its online support group enhances the other services provided to survivors of sexual violence; technology does not replace these services.

In addition, this tool only works if potential participants are comfortable with the technology and have home access to the Internet. In order to ensure that as many survivors as possible participate in the project, SACC is currently accepting donations of computers. A SACC volunteer, who is also a survivor of sexual violence, upgrades and readies the computers for Internet use. SACC also provides basic training. The computers – and the requisite training – are given to survivors so that they can participate in the online support group.

Interactive database development

The Internet is increasingly moving toward greater interactivity, with complex backend databases allowing users to create individual online experiences by accessing information customized to their needs. CBOs have begun to use interactive databases to assist their constituencies to: find employment; learn about community assets and resources; and access other local information. Two examples, one focused on workforce development, the other on mentoring, illustrate how interactive online databases can forward community development goals. East Bay Works is an online directory of employment and training services available to job seekers and employers in Contra Costa and Alameda counties (CA). Area Private Industry Councils, government agencies, community colleges, educational agencies, and community-based organizations collaborated to create East Bay Works because they recognized that the existing workforce development system was fragmented, duplicative, and difficult to use. The online directory is one component of a larger effort to create a comprehensive and integrated employment and training system that includes the development of 16 one-stop careers centers throughout the East Bay.

The East Bay Works website is an interactive regional directory of employment and training services. The site has a portal for employers which facilitates posting and tracking jobs online. Another portal allows job seekers to post resumes, search for regional employment opportunities, and participate in discussions about training opportunities. Local wage and labor market information, an events calendar, resource listings, links to local training providers and national job banks are also available. Since its initiation in 1997, East Bay Works has provided key information to job seekers and employers in the San Francisco Bay Area. Online job databases have been an essential tool for maintaining the labor pool of the knowledge-based economy. East Bay Works demonstrates how useful this type of online content is for the nonprofit sector.

Formed in 1992, Cabrini Connections provides a framework that enables adult volunteers to provide positive development supports to children in disadvantaged environments such as the Cabrini Green housing development in Chicago. The organization consists of two programs: Kids' Connection and Tutor/Mentor Connection. Kids' Connection combines tutoring, mentoring, and school-to-work approaches to help participant kids complete high school and enter a career or institution of higher education. The Tutor/Mentor Connection (T/MC) was formed in 1993 as a research and advocacy arm of Cabrini Connections. T/MC gathers and organizes information about successful after-school tutor/mentor programs and shares that knowledge to expand the availability and enhance the effectiveness of services for children and youth in the Chicago region. T/MC essentially serves as a clearing-house and roadmap of children and youth services in the Chicago region and has been an invaluable mechanism by which local service providers connect to relevant information and to each other. T/MC uses a range of IT tools to support its work. For example, T/MC maintains a database of over 12,000 volunteers, programs, businesses, foundations, media, and community leaders. This database uses GIS technology to create an interactive map of Chicago with overlays illustrating poverty, poor schools, and locations of tutor/mentor programs. Online versions of this map and database assist individuals and organizations to find programs. The map also serves as an advocacy tool to argue for youth services in underserved areas.

East Bay Works and T/MC highlight the effectiveness of interactive databases to store, share, and disseminate community information. Although databases are hardly a new application, the interactive and online nature of these examples allows larger numbers of people to access information quickly and efficiently. Current applications are also more user friendly than older database software, making it easier for CBOs to integrate them into their work.

Community mapping

Geographic Information Systems (GIS) is a computer application that assembles, stores, manipulates, and displays geographically referenced information. GIS applications are increasingly being used for public policy development, neighborhood planning, advocacy, and research. Although GIS was once used only by universities and policy/research institutes, it is increasingly being used by community serving organizations. GIS mapping enables CDCs to understand the community's assets, provide early warning of community problems, and generate knowledge of local needs. Maps also provide a visual component to sophisticated policy issues, making them easier for lay people to understand. Myron Orfield's use of maps to demonstrate the logic of building a coalition between inner-city and inner-ring suburban residents of the twin cities was instrumental to moving a regional agenda forward.[12]

Neighborhood Knowledge Los Angeles (NKLA), a project of the UCLA Advanced Policy Institute, the Community Development

---

12 Orfield (1997).

Information Coalition, and a host of city agencies and nonprofit organizations, provides residents of Los Angeles with localized information about their neighborhoods. The NKLA website integrates several databases to develop an Interactive Neighborhood Electronic Monitoring System (NEMS), which allows visitors to view comprehensive information on individual properties or neighborhoods. For example, residents can view information about tax delinquencies, code violations, utility liens, and other signs of property neglect, allowing them to develop strategies to improve local living conditions. A community asset mapping component helps residents to identify and build on community strengths. Census demographic information, as well as the ability to conduct advanced queries such as "how many properties in my zip code are tax delinquent and have code complaints" is also available. To ensure broad community involvement and access, NKLA has created English, Spanish, and text-only versions of its website. NKLA also provides training to residents on how to use the community information they find on the website as a tool for neighborhood change. As government agencies increasingly make raw data sets available online, NKLA can localize and contextualize this information in a manner that makes it understandable and relevant to community residents. For example, NKLA, in partnership with community-based organizations, has applied its information on Los Angeles land use patterns in two targeted neighborhoods: Vernon-Central in South Los Angeles and Boyle Heights in East Los Angeles. The project involved using NKLA data to assist local nonprofit developers in the acquisition of distressed properties and to identify home owners at risk of losing their properties so that local organizations could provide necessary counseling and services.

The NKLA project provides rich and detailed information about communities, allows organizations and residents to hold government officials accountable, generates and organizes timely information about neighborhood and enables community activists to craft well-informed strategies for neighborhood improvement. In addition to strengthening community development activities, this project exemplifies a new, community-driven model for research and public policy development. The technical knowledge of the university, coupled with the deep local knowledge of the community partners, have been essential to the collection of targeted, locally relevant, and up-to-date information that is available on the NKLA website.

The Urban Institute, a Washington DC based nonprofit policy research organization, in partnership with local partners, initiated the

National Neighborhood Indicators Partnership (NNIP), a collaborative effort to strengthen the use of neighborhood-level information systems in local policy making and community building. All of the partners have locally self-sustaining information systems that track neighborhood conditions. Some of the neighborhood indicators that local partners track include: births, deaths, crime, health status, educational performance, public assistance, and property conditions. NNIP uses this information to build locally driven strategies to improve distressed urban neighborhoods. The goal of the NNIP is to extend the impact of local partners using information systems by collaborating, sharing best practices, disseminating project outputs, developing creative strategies to support local efforts, and building a National Neighborhood Data System that integrates information from local partners.

One of the local NNIP partners, the Boston Community Building Network (BCBN), works to build on the strengths and assets of the Greater Boston community. BCBN uses IT tools to support several initiatives including the Boston Children and Families Database, the Boston Community Building Curriculum, and the Boston Indicators of Change, Progress, and Sustainability (a civic process cosponsored with the City of Boston's Sustainable Boston Initiative).

Lessons Learned

The examples reviewed in this chapter illustrate the potential of supporting the creation of relevant community content online and of building technology capacity in the community-based nonprofit sector. Addressing these two aspects of the digital divide will facilitate the creation of a comprehensive approach to solving this problem.

Since the emergence of the digital divide as a national policy issue, little has been done to bring technology resources to community-based organizations or to use technology to extend the work of the existing community development infrastructure. These gaps must be addressed as part of a comprehensive approach to addressing the digital divide. This section brings together lessons from the organizations highlighted in this chapter. Employing these lessons will enable a shift from scattered local successes to broader implementation of creative, IT-based community-building strategies.

The culture of use among CBOs must be shifted

In order to develop the content and applications necessary to bridge the digital divide, community organizations must shift their thinking and view technology not as a necessary evil but as a strategic tool. Strategies that promote a culture of use in community serving organizations, and the disadvantaged constituencies they work with, are critical. Some activities that promote a culture of use include:

- Developing stronger and deeper linkages between community technology activists and community builders so that awareness of technological impacts are better understood by community serving organizations
- Creating an inventory of community-based applications, along with technology descriptions, that illustrate how IT tools can be used as a tool for social change
- Generating online and offline opportunities for community serving organizations to share knowledge and experience around developing content and applications

CBOs need to know *why* they should invest the time, energy and money to add technology to what they are doing, and *how* to gain the specific technical capacity they need.

Virtual and physical program components are mutually reinforcing

IT applications such as listservs, email, and databases enable community-based organizations to run more efficiently. In terms of their external work, however, technology does not replace previous systems but rather supports them. In all of the examples cited above, technology complements the in-person, on-the-ground work of community building. IT can be used to extend the work CBOs are already doing, maintain in-person relationships, and enhance outreach effort; IT should not be thought of as a mechanism to supplant existing community-building activities.

Community experience and knowledge must drive the use of technology

A common thread among the examples detailed in this chapter is that a deep knowledge of the issues and constituencies involved drove the organizing/advocacy strategies; technology is employed to strengthen and augment the work that CBOs are already doing. Online strategies must support and inspire offline community development efforts in order for the benefits of technology for community building to be fully realized. Virtual vehicles cannot replace traditional techniques; rather they offer another facet.

CBOs can provide the entry point for building IT skills

People tend to gain technology skills only when they perceive that there is a clear reason for them to do so. Seniors log on in order to stay in touch with their grandchildren. Immigrant communities use email to communicate with relatives back home. The examples illustrated in this chapter show how community-based applications can generate interest in IT that extends beyond the initial reason for logging on. Grace Hill residents obtained basic computer training in order to access their time dollar accounts, and many expressed interest in using computers and the Internet for other purposes. Many SACC online support group participants obtained computers so that they could participate from home. Clearly, these computers will be used for other purposes as well. CBOs are important as bridgers of the digital divide because they know how to make IT directly relevant to residents' lives.

The community technology movement has tended to focus on an equitable diffusion of technology in low-income communities, while traditional community-based organizations have tackled social and economic equity without the help of technology. These two movements, working in partnership, have the experience and wisdom to use technology as a tool to advance an equity agenda. The community technology and community-building movements can complement each other in important ways. CBOs can utilize technology internally to become more efficient and better able to collect and analyze information on their programs. CBOs can also powerfully apply technology to augment and extend community-building activities such as advocacy and organizing. The existing community-building infrastructure can further be used as a foundation for scaling up the community technology movement. Because of their relationships with the individuals and groups that are currently cut off from the information society, CBOs can both reach the people who need to be connected and play a pivotal role in the creation of local content geared toward the specific needs of their constituents. This content can be used as a hook to bring disadvantaged communities more fully into the digital age.

The community-building infrastructure is much more widespread and deeply embedded in community than is the younger community technology movement. As discussed in chapter 3, existing CTCs are currently clustered in and around urban areas, particularly in the northeast and northwest and especially in regions with high-tech economies. Using the existing CBO infrastructure can help the community technology movement to expand more broadly and evenly. Chapters 5 and 6 provide a solid rationale for why the community technology agenda needs to be more broadly implemented. Chapter 5 documented that many youth are not receiving adequate exposure to technology and training in the ways of thinking and skills necessary to prosper in the new economy. Chapter 6 argued that the IT labor shortage will continue to be an issue in non high-tech regions as the world of work continues to be transformed, and as all sectors increase their needs for employees with IT skills. The community-building movement and the community technology movement can partner to ensure that disadvantaged groups and community-based organizations are not marginalized as a result of this economic and social transformation.

As the Internet and other IT tools are increasingly used to support community-building efforts, we must ensure that low-income communities, and the organizations that serve them, have access to and training on these technologies. Although the examples highlighted in this chapter demonstrate that IT tools can be democratizing vehicles, they can reinforce unequal power structures if not in the hands of all communities.

8

Building the Bridge:
Learning from Seattle

In Seattle, many of the lessons laid out in the preceding chapters come together. Seattle, more than any other city, has responded to the new socioeconomic arrangements of the information age by working to become a technology literate city. The City of Seattle has institutionalized its commitment to technology literacy, coordinated its IT work with other public goals, and integrated IT into its mission and into the broader functions of city government. Seattle is an important example because public sector and grassroots initiatives have both been strong and complementary.

The distinctive aspects of Seattle's context, such as its high-tech economy, have pushed the city to deal with its technology gap earlier than have most cities. Employees of the IT industry and IT government employees tend to believe that IT can play a valuable role in addressing social concerns. But other cities, even those that are not dependent on the high-tech sector, have begun to face similar issues. These include the shortage of IT workers – which affects all regions and nearly all sectors – and pressure to figure out how to best connect citizens with IT resources.

Given Seattle's economic base, it is not surprising that the region is also a hotbed of community technology activity and home to some of the most innovative and far-reaching planning initiatives to narrow the technology gap. A recent report issued by the Center on Urban and Metropolitan Policy highlights the concentration of high technology in the Seattle region.[1] The study, which is a comparative analysis of 14 "high-tech" metropolitan areas, reports that the Seattle region has a strong concentration of software, biotechnology, and aerospace

1 Cortwight and Mayer (2001).

industries. The overall high technology location quotient for the Seattle region was 1.7.[2] According to HUD, in 1997 111,938, or roughly 10 percent, of the 1,127,648 jobs in the Seattle metropolitan area were in the high-tech sector.[3]

The strong concentration of high technology and the presence of high-tech firms (for example, Microsoft) has been important in fueling support for public intervention. The industry presence has also provided a vast pool of skilled volunteers and has helped place technology access issues on the agenda of public officials and residents. Many community technology activists, however, believe that the high level of community technology activity and government commitment to universal access is attributable to more than merely the presence of technology-related industries. Activists also point to the strong tradition of neighborhood-based planning and service delivery as well as to the commitment on the part of community technology actors and community leaders to represent the needs of those residents that have been left behind in the city's recent economic growth and prosperity. This activism has translated into an early awareness that the ability for all Seattle citizens to be able to use and access IT is vital to ensure a democratic, just, and economically sustainable city, and local officials must therefore actively promote equitable access to IT. Requests for public intervention into the technology gap problem have come from Seattle's citizens, who expected early on both that important public information be available on the Internet and that all citizens should be able to easily access this information. The city, in turn, has responded to these expectations with action. Seattle is also an extremely community-oriented city. Sixty-two percent of respondents to a recent survey participate in at least one neighborhood or community organization.[4]

The Digital Divide in Seattle

Given the high-tech presence in Seattle, it is not surprising that the city has better-than-average rates of access to IT. More than three-quarters

2   Location quotients are a measure of the concentration of a particular industry relative to the overall economic composition of a given geographic unit. If the concentration of a given industry were similar to the rest of the economy the location quotient would be 1.0. Seattle's high-technology industry has a location quotient of 1.7, indicating a strong concentration of these economic activities within the region.
3   US Department of Housing and Urban Development (2000).
4   City of Seattle (2001).

(76 percent) of Seattle residents have a computer in their home as compared with 51 percent of US households.[5] Groups who do not have access tend to be older, low-income, low-education, and African-American or Latino. In that sense, Seattle's digital divide issue broadly resembles the issue as it plays out nationally. In fact, the recent economic boom had the affect of increasing property values in the City and driving many of the poor out, which may have something to do with Seattle's high access rates. The following statistics illustrate Seattle's specific technology gap:

- Over half (56 percent) of those who do not have access to a computer are 65 years or older.
- More than one out of three (35 percent) African-Americans do not have access to the Internet, compared with 16 percent of Caucasians and 11 percent of Asian-Americans.
- Only half (52 percent) of African-American respondents have access to a computer in their home compared with 80 percent of Asian-American and 70 percent of Caucasian respondents.
- Of those with limited access to technology 68 percent have low or extremely low household incomes.
- Of those with limited or below-average access to technology 36 percent have a high-school education or less.[6]

Rather than remaining complacent about its above average technology diffusion status, Seattle has chosen to continue to work to close its technology gap and move toward the goal of technology literacy for the entire citizenry.

Local government initiatives

Seattle formalized its commitment to narrowing the digital divide in 1994 when the city began funding the Seattle Public Access Network (PAN). PAN was originally established as an electronic bulletin board and is now www.cityofseattle.net. PAN serves as an electronic city hall, allowing Seattle citizens to obtain city information and services electronically and to communicate with city officials.[7] Recognizing

5 City of Seattle (2001).
6 City of Seattle (2001).
7 City of Seattle (2001).

Table 8.1   Development of Seattle's community technology agenda

Date	Activity
1994	City establishes the Seattle Public Access Network (PAN)
1995	Creation of the Citizens' Telecommunications and Technology Advisory Board (CTTAB)
1996	Establishment of the Citizens' Literacy and Access Fund (CLAF)
1997	Technology Access Resource Map created
1997	Community Technology Planner position established
1998	Technology Matching Fund launched
1999	Information Technology Indicator Project launched

that many Seattle residents did not have the computer access necessary to benefit from the network, the city established public workstations with access to the World Wide Web in neighborhood and community centers throughout the city. The city also provides free web hosting for community organizations, viewing them as vital instruments of city policy implementation. Table 8.1 provides key dates in the development of Seattle's community technology agenda.

In 1995, the city created the Citizens' Telecommunications and Technology Advisory Board (CTTAB), a de facto planning body, expanding the scope of the previous Citizens Cable Communications Advisory Board. CTTAB is charged with making recommendations to the mayor and city council on issues of community-wide interest relating to telecommunications and technology. CTTAB members:

- encourage and promote affordable access to and use of telecommunications and technology;
- advocate, solicit, and facilitate citizen participation in telecommunications and technology decision making;
- measure and evaluate the effectiveness of telecommunications and technology policies and programs.[8]

In 1996, the city established the Citizens' Literacy and Access Fund (CLAF), thereby boosting Seattle's commitment to narrowing the digital divide. The city asked CTTAB for initial recommendations on projects and has relied heavily on the citizen advisors for guidance in the development of its subsequent digital divide initiatives. CTTAB's role is advisory only, although the city does listen to it. CTTAB has

8   www.cityofseattle.net/cttab/

used the fund, which is capitalized by a share of the city's cable franchise revenue,[9] to develop projects aimed at improving technology literacy and building public awareness around information-age issues and planning. To implement the projects, the board used a portion of the money to create a planning position within the Executive Services Department Technology Division (now the Department of Information Technology), which is responsible for citywide IT planning. In October 1997, David Keyes was hired to fill the post, making Seattle the first city in the nation to have a community technology planner.

The first CLAF project was to develop a Technology Resource Map, a directory of technology initiatives across the city (see Figure 8.1). Although several CTCs existed when CLAF was established, these initiatives lacked visibility and coordination. The Technology Resource Map publicized existing sites and facilitated coordination between technology initiatives. The City of Seattle Department of Information Technology currently lists 118 community technology sites on its website.

The city has also put together a map of the publicly and privately owned fiber infrastructure. The fiber overlay is an important part of an economic development strategy for attracting new technology businesses into the city and into particular neighborhoods. Moreover, the fiber map illustrates the ways in which the pattern of infrastructure investment, in its current state, exacerbates or potentially diminishes the digital divide. Recently, the city posted signs outside of places where citizens can obtain public access to IT. These signs also increase the visibility of the issue and of the city's efforts to confront it. See Figure 8.2.

The largest portion of the CLAF established the Technology Matching Fund (TMF), which provides resources to Seattle's neighborhood-based and citywide organizations for citizen-driven technology literacy and access projects. Organizations must match the cash contribution from the fund with volunteer labor, materials, professional services, or cash. In order to receive TMF support, projects must: increase points of access to computers and IT; support IT literacy education and training; and/or encourage IT applications that support neighborhood planning and action.[10] Projects must also involve community members in the identification, planning, and execution of the project. Although all projects meeting these criteria are eligible for

9   Chapter 4 discussed such arrangements in greater detail.
10   City of Seattle (1999).

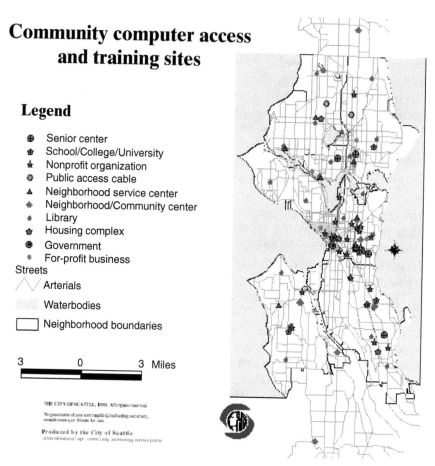

Community computer access and training sites

Legend

- ⊕   Senior center
- 🏛   School/College/University
- ★   Nonprofit organization
- ◉   Public access cable
- ▲   Neighborhood service center
- ♠   Neighborhood/Community center
- ◆   Library
- 🏠   Housing complex
- ◉   Government
- •   For-profit business

Streets

/\/   Arterials

     Waterbodies

☐   Neighborhood boundaries

3   0   3   Miles

Figure 8.1   City of Seattle community technology map
Source: City of Seattle

support, those that address the needs of technology underserved people are given greater priority.

Seattle modeled the Technology Matching Fund after an established and successful matching fund program established by the City of Seattle's Department of Neighborhoods. Aki Namioka, a CTTAB board member and longtime community technology activist who has helped evaluated Technology Matching Fund applicants, recalls that:

> The Department of Neighborhoods' existing matching fund program wasn't funding a lot of technology projects. In addition, they were

Figure 8.2 Seattle public access sign

restricted to funding projects that were neighborhood based. However, we know that technology by its nature is not only creating communities in a physical geographic location, it's also creating communities on line. So we wanted to . . . fund technology-focused projects that were not necessarily neighborhood based.

Many of the projects supported by the Technology Matching Fund have in fact been neighborhood-based, facilitating a collaborative relationship between CTTAB, the Department of Information Technology, and the Department of Neighborhoods and allowing neighborhood organizations that undertake technology initiatives to tap into two funding sources. TMF is a competitive grant program. CTTAB members review proposals, share suggestions and resource ideas with applicants, and make recommendations on projects to approve.

The Technology Matching Fund consists of two categories. One is for large-scale capacity-building projects that take up to 12 months to complete and require up to $50,000 in matching funds from the city. The second category consists of grants for $5,000 or less to fund smaller and less complex projects. The Technology Matching Fund is not meant to provide ongoing support to CTCs. However, in addition to providing hardware and software, city funds can be used to support staff, obtain technical assistance, or to increase outreach. Securing funding for staffing, technical support, and operating costs are some of the biggest challenges facing CTCs.[11] As Keyes notes, the flexibility of the matching fund has been very important in helping CTCs to meet these challenges.

> Our goal for [the Technology Matching Fund] was to increase infrastructure out in the community that helped programs develop greater sustainability, increase access and also provided literacy efforts. We haven't seen [it] as an ongoing support fund . . . But we did make it clear that some of those funds didn't just have to be used for hardware, and that's been an important component working with community groups – work on getting somebody in place, work on helping do volunteer recruitment and so on and help the centers to run. The equipment's easier to come by.

Through CLAF, CTTAB has been successful in helping expand community technology initiatives in the city and has enabled existing programs to develop greater sustainability. In addition, CLAF has also been very important in raising public awareness about the digital

---

11 See chapter 3.

divide and expanding support for community technology initiatives. Through city initiated and supported projects and programs, local officials and community groups see firsthand how technology can be used as a means to help reach community development ends.

Seattle's community technology planner is a key element of the City's commitment to universal technology literacy. The position was created to encourage and foster collaborative relationships among the city's community technology actors. David Keyes, who has held the position since it was created, states that "the advantage of having a community technology planner is having somebody who can step back and have all of those feelers out in the different areas of the community and see what's out there and how we can bridge these things." Greg McDonald, former director of a Seattle CTC, states that:

> Dave is really out in the community getting to know the programs, looking for funding resources, looking for innovative ways to make these centers work . . . Back in January he held a meeting for all the umbrella organizations who are doing multiple centers. [It] was the first time that anybody came together . . . to talk about what their needs are. It was really helpful, just having that link. Having there be a place where people can come together to talk about what kind of training they would need, what kind of resources they need right now is really key.

In addition to coordinating efforts among community-based programs, the community technology planner also works across city departments to share information and help streamline programming. The Department of Information Technology (DIT) has direct linkages to several city offices and departments, including the Department of Neighborhoods, the Office of Economic Development, Department of Parks and Recreation, the Human Services Department, and the Seattle Arts Commission. DIT's relationship with the Department of Neighborhoods is especially close; the Department of Neighborhoods even lists Keyes as a staff member. Table 8.2 lays out the specific ways in which the work of DIT intersects with and supports the work of these other city agencies.

Seattle recently completed the first two phases of its Information Technology Indicator Project, which will ultimately measure the impact of IT on the health and vitality of the city.[12] According to the first report put out from this project:

---

12 City of Seattle (2000: 1).

Table 8.2 Department of Information Technology inter-agency work

Department	Relevant activities	Department of Information Technology role
Department of Neighborhoods	Leadership training	IT training
	Neighborhood Matching Fund	Linked with Technology Matching Fund and used as source of funds
	Neighborhood planning	DoIT staff teach neighborhood actors relevant technology applications
	Neighborhood Service Centers	DoIT operates free public-access Internet terminals
Office of Economic Development	Technology sector development	Fund/initiate CTCs that do job training; create linkages with corporate partners
	Enterprise Zone oversight	Helps to target location of CTCs
	Conduit for Seattle Jobs Initiative (SJI)	Provides tours for students coming through SJI
Department of Parks and Recreation	Community centers	Provide Internet connectivity
	Senior programs	IT programs targeted at seniors
	Youth programs	IT programs targeted at youth
Department of Human Services	Youth	Fund startup and expansion of youth technology programs
	Youth employment program	Creates 10 slots for youth interns in community computer labs
	Aging and disability	Created and maintains STAR community computer center for the disabled
	Aging and disability	Created Seniors Training Seniors in Technology program
	New Citizen Initiative	IT programs targeted at new immigrants
	Homeless and housing	Operates free Internet terminals and promotes use of CTCs by homeless as well as funding homeless organization CTC projects
Seattle Arts Commission		Co-sponsored forum on arts and technology
		Working on creation of artists' resource centers
		Encourages artists to use CTCs
		Funded media arts education projects

The City and people of Seattle want to build a technology healthy community where:

- information technology is enhancing the local economy
- access to technological tools is equitable and affordable
- information technology needs are being met and applied to solving social issues
- technology is promoting relationship-building and community development
- the use of technology supports the sustainability of residents' quality of life.[13]

The creation of indicators will help the city to measure its progress on these goals. From the above, it is clear that the architects of this process see the technology gap as an issue that concerns broader social goals, such as democracy, equity, and efficiency, which will be discussed at greater length in chapter 9.

During the first phase of the Information Technology Indicator Project, indicators in the following categories were created: access, literacy, business and economic development, community building, civic participation, human relationships to technology, and partnerships and resource management.[14] This list illustrates the extent to which the city has integrated IT into a much larger set of goals. It also shows that Seattle, in defining access as only part of the problem, is way ahead of most other public entities.

The city recently conducted a telephone survey of 1,011 residents in order to gather baseline data on: residents' ownership and access to information technology; residents' usage of information technology; levels of technology literacy and fluency; awareness and use of city services online and on cable TV; integration of technology into local community activities; residents' feelings about privacy, security, and safety on the Internet; residents' perceptions of the impact that technology is having on their personal time, quality of life, and the quality of life for the city.[15]

Leveraging federal and state resources

Digital Promise

Digital Promise (formerly the Washington State Neighborhood Networks Consortium) is an alliance of private and public sector

---

13   City of Seattle (2000: 4).
14   City of Seattle (2000: 4).
15   City of Seattle (2001) presents the complete results of this survey.

groups that seeks to establish, maintain, and support CTCs in affordable housing developments throughout the state. NNC was established in 1997 as a consortium of US Department of Housing and Urban Development (HUD) Neighborhood Network centers.

In June 1998, then VISTA volunteer Tobi deVito established NNC as a nonprofit 501(c)3 corporation with a board of directors. Realizing that there were many other actors serving the technology needs of Washington's low-income residents, NNC members broadened the mission of the consortium to allow non FHA-financed properties and other CTCs to participate. To date, NNC has helped establish and/or sustain more than fifty computer learning centers (CLCs) in Washington State.

NNC's long-term goals are fourfold: 1) to help provide every NNC center with Internet access; 2) to form CTC/small business alliances to help center residents enter the workforce; 3) to make all NNC centers accessible to the elderly and residents with disabilities; and 4) to establish a software clearinghouse to complement the already existing hardware clearinghouse.

NNC recently launched a citywide campaign, Connecting Seattle, that seeks to provide computers, connect five sites to the Internet, train residents to be trainers, and provide Internet training and community forums at each site. NNC received a $17,000 technology matching grant for this initiative.

HUD endorses the formation of Neighborhood Networks consortia like NNC because they have the potential to increase the impact of the limited amount of time HUD staff can allocate to the Neighborhood Networks program and leverage intellectual and organizational capital of consortium members. HUD has used NNC as a model for other organizations interested in establishing a community technology consortium. In 1999, NNC received HUD Top 100 Best Practices recognition.

Archdiocesan Housing Authority computer learning centers

The Archdiocesan Housing Authority (AHA) is another example of how the city is leveraging a federal program to extend its own resources. AHA is the largest provider of permanent low-income and emergency housing in the Puget Sound region. In addition to providing affordable housing, AHA is committed to helping residents achieve self-sufficiency so that they can lead fulfilling lives. To help meet these goals, AHA is in the process of developing CLCs throughout King County. According to AHA documents, "the mission of the CLCs is to ensure that all individuals, families and communities have an opportunity to participate and thrive in the new information age – regardless of economic, physical, or cultural differences. CLCs will help us meet this goal by providing free educational and economic opportunities to low-income families, senior citizens, and to the developmentally challenged."[16]

Each of the AHA housing programs serves a unique housing community. The Josephinum apartment building is home to working-class individuals and families; Chancery Place houses elderly and disabled residents; and the Renton Family Housing program provides affordable housing to low-income families with children. Given the diversity of AHA's housing communities, each of the learning centers offers open lab time and a variety of classes, seminars and workshops tailored to meet the specific needs of residents. AHA holds focus groups with groups of residents to obtain information about the kind of services and tools residents would like the CLCs to provide. The Josephinum CLC has emphasized developing job skills and GED exam preparation. The Chancery Place center initiated an intergenerational program in which area high-school students teach seniors Internet and email basics. The Andy Polich learning center offers tutoring for resident children and basic computer classes that address job skill development and résumé building for adults.

Through the HUD Neighborhood Networks program, AHA has been able to use reserve repair funds for the CLCs. AHA has also generated funding from the Boeing Corporation and other area foundations. AHA received $30,000 from the Technology Matching Fund and $9,686 from the Department of Neighborhood's Neighborhood Matching Fund for the establishment of the Josephinum CLC.

Seattle Community Technology Alliance

To help further coordinate and strengthen technology efforts, technology actors established the Seattle Community Technology Alliance (SCTA), which is administered by the Seattle Public Libraries. Funded in fiscal year 2000 with a $300,000 grant from the US Department of Education, SCTA is a consortium of Seattle's Department of

16   Archdiocesan Housing Authority (1999).

Information Technology, the Seattle Public Library, Seattle Public Schools, the Seattle Public Housing Authority, the Seattle Community College District, community-based organizations, and corporate partners funded by a $300 million grant from the US Department of Education.

The aim of SCTA is to ensure that technology opportunities are available to Seattle's underserved communities by improving the impact, effectiveness, and sustainability of CTCs and strengthening the network of public access terminals throughout the city. SCTA has targeted seven CTCs initially.

In most cities, community technology efforts are fragmented. The purpose of Seattle's alliance is to create more formal linkages between community technology actors and initiatives so that best practices can be more easily shared. The proposal laid out a goal of enhancing capacity in each of seven CTCs. All of the sites selected currently operate a technology program but need assistance in making their centers sustainable. Centers were also chosen based on the level of community interest and support. All of the centers are located in low-income neighborhoods and serve low-income populations. Although all of the six initial CTCs are located within the City of Seattle, partners in the alliance have a long-range goal of extending the alliance to serve the greater Seattle region. This regional framing of the issue is important, given that labor markets tend to operate at the regional level.

The partners in the community technology alliance take a multi-faceted approach to capacity building that focuses on hardware and software capacity, technical support, staff training, and curriculum development. Each of the partners will bring some expertise to the alliance. For instance, the library offers Internet training and acts as a repository of community technology information including handbooks and curriculum.

Corporate sector involvement

As mentioned earlier, Seattle's economic base is heavily weighted toward IT, giving the corporate sector a strong incentive to address the digital divide issue. Microsoft, and the Bill and Melinda Gates Foundation, have done a great deal in this area. The Gates Foundation has initiated grant programs that fund a range of activities, primarily in schools and libraries, including providing scholarships to members of underrepresented groups to study IT-related subjects, working with community-based organizations to provide public access to information, and supporting teachers to integrate technology into the curriculum in their classrooms.[17] Microsoft has also contributed over $300,000 in software to the city.

Boeing is another example. Boeing supports the Bellevue Community College worker retraining program. Due to economic shifts and defense downsizing, Boeing has experienced significant layoffs. To assist employees in the transition to the new economy, Boeing supports technology training for dislocated workers. Cisco has donated $30,000 worth of equipment to the city, with commitments to do more. AT&T, via its franchise agreement with the city, has contributed one million dollars in IT initiatives over a three-year period. And Gateway extended the reduced prices it offers to the city to community organizations; Keyes estimates that these lower prices have probably saved these groups $30,000 thus far.

Other key players

Seattle benefits from having a range of other key local players that add capacity to the city's efforts to attain technology literacy. The list below is not comprehensive. Other efforts and organizations also do important work. For example, the Independent Media Center, which was created in the wake of the World Trade Organization protests, is an extremely innovative, nongovernmental initiative that has quickly become a worldwide network.

Bellevue Community College

BCC is recognized nationally as a leading community college in the area of IT education. For example, BCC has partnered with the Seattle-King County Private Industry Council (PIC) to provide technology training to dislocated workers. A key ingredient to BCC's success is strong partnerships with local technology companies. For example, Microsoft has donated both hardware and software to BCC, as well as

---

17 See www.gatesfoundation.org for more information.

assistance with curriculum development. In addition to its efforts to provide IT training to Seattle residents, BCC works closely with the Northwest Center for Emerging Technologies on creating and disseminating national IT skill standards (see chapter 6).

NPower

NPower, discussed in chapter 7, is a leading IT technical assistance provider to nonprofit organizations in Seattle and the Puget Sound region. The organization works with local CBOs to provide: consultations on technology assessments and planning; hands-on assistance with projects such as building a database or launching a website; technology training classes; matches between nonprofits and volunteers; and online and print libraries of technology resources. NPower was initiated through a joint effort by Microsoft, Medina Foundation, the Seattle Foundation, the Boeing company, US Bank, Adobe Systems, and SAFECO corporation. These organizations shared the belief that nonprofits can and should use technology as capably as the most technology-enabled businesses. Chapter 7 illustrated the importance of IT technical assistance to extend the reach of the existing community-building infrastructure. NPower is nationally recognized as a leader in the IT technical assistance field and has helped numerous CBOs in the Seattle region.

Seattle Community Network[18]

The Seattle Community Network (SCN) was one of the first community networks to be initiated, offering free email accounts, listservs, and website space long before commercial providers such as Hotmail. SCN is a comprehensive website devoted to providing information about the Seattle region, and connecting residents to area resources and to each other. SCN hosts neighborhood-focused websites, provides community information by county, and also has invaluable information about state resources for community technology. A range of activities and topic areas are covered including: the arts, cultural activities, employment and training opportunities, housing, social services, and a host of other issues.

18 For a complete history and description of SCN, see Schuler (1996) and Herwick (2001).

Synthesizing Seattle

Seattle is not a typical case. The city is notable for the level and diversity of activity in the community technology arena. The density of high-technology activity in the area clearly feeds the community technology movement in several ways. IT firms have skilled employees, some of whom are interested in supporting social causes, starting social enterprises, or volunteering at CTCs. These employees understand the importance of IT. Whereas many corporations and foundations have been reluctant to fund the community technology movement, IT firms more easily understand the importance of making grants and donations to close the digital divide. Corporate funders have led funding in the community technology field, and corporate funders often weight their funding activity toward local endeavors. Seattle has benefited from this practice.

Yet community technology activists in the Seattle metropolitan region are careful not to overstate the role of the industry in fueling the region's community technology activities. When asked about the role of industry presence in the development of community technology initiatives in Seattle, Keyes replied:

> One of the problems that I see, particularly from some of these technology companies, is that first they'll drop a single grant for a project or donate some software but that's not what's going to help the centers survive in the long run and really make them work. There's still a pretty big disconnect and a lot more room for investment from the companies . . . I've seen some interest from professional associations and employee groups volunteering and donating time and stuff. It seems more ripe on the individual employee level to get support for the community technology centers than it is company-wide . . . There are some companies that have sort of adopted schools. I don't know of any that have adopted community technology centers over the long haul. That's the way to go – see if we can develop some longer-term relationships, partnerships. It's a tougher sell because people want to do a project and get out, you know and move onto the next project. It's a challenge but that's one of the places I think we need to go.

Certainly Boeing, Microsoft, and numerous other firms that produce or rely heavily on technology have provided Seattle with a pool of skilled volunteers. Many community technology activists are connected to one of these firms. Aki Namioka suggests that "It's employees of the company that are helpful. We have a lot of Boeing people working on the Seattle Community Network project. We have had a lot of Microsoft people donate money. It's not the companies, it's the people that work in those jobs that help."[19]

Seattle is the US city that has gone farthest to take on the digital divide. Even so, the city and many of its projects need to continue to push beyond the narrow definition of access, and continue to ask and answer the question, "technology for what purpose?" While continuing to move the access agenda forward, Seattle must also expand its current work on the training and content dimensions of the problem.

It is difficult to separate the government, foundation, private nonprofit, and private for-profit influences on the community technology landscape in Seattle. The corporate sector, coupled with the strong neighborhood planning and community-building traditions, provided a fertile context for the initiation of community technology groups. In addition, there is a strong overlap between the foundation and corporate communities in Seattle – several corporations have established foundations and focus their giving on the technology field. City government also took an early lead and worked closely with existing efforts. At the same time, Seattle is not so unique that its lessons cannot be applied to other places. This case is highlighted in this book because Seattle is an exemplary model that other cities can look to for inspiration and guidance.

Lessons

Seattle's efforts to bridge the digital divide provide an example of how IT tools can be used to work toward larger goals such as democracy, equity, and efficiency. The work underway in Seattle also demonstrates that the public sector must play a critical role in employing IT toward these broad ends, through a process that includes institutionalization, coordination, and integration. The Seattle case provides a range of lessons that other cities – and states and federal entities – can learn from. The following broad lessons have been culled from the Seattle case.

19   It remains to be seen what kind of impact Boeing's move to Chicago will have on community technology in Seattle. The field is probably institutionalized enough to weather such change.

Work to close the technology gap must be institutionalized

Attentive policy makers recognize that digital equity is intimately tied to their economic and community development policy goals. Including this goal as part of government's mission helps to ensure that the issue will not be enclaved. In some cities, such as Seattle, local officials recognize the importance of ensuring access to IT for all of the region's residents. Further, they understand that the issue is more than a problem of access but rather also entails tackling the training and content components of the problem. Seattle has institutionalized its commitment by creating specific government programs, a permanent community technology planner position, and initiating a process to move beyond rhetoric toward the formulation and achievement of measurable goals.

A key piece of this institutionalization has been the inclusion of a broad range of stakeholders in planning processes. The high level of participation in projects such as the Information Technology Indicator Project has surely slowed progress, but it has undeniably resulted in greater buy-in from citizens and representatives of the corporate, public, and private nonprofit communities. Broad participation and accountability increase the potential for digital divide interventions to work. In most places, this level of sophistication and awareness does not exist among government officials. Community activists in many places are working to educate local officials on the digital divide and the importance of providing public support for this issue. Without this institutionalization, such efforts run the risk of being temporary funding fads that will disappear once a new idea surfaces.

Coordination leverages existing work

In many cities, community technology efforts are fragmented. This fragmentation results partly because community technology efforts typically grow up as a set of unrelated grassroots initiatives. Seattle's first task – creating the Technology Resource Map – made all of these efforts visible, and made it easier to create linkages among them. The map also enabled the city to recognize and build on existing capacity rather than duplicating efforts. The Technology Matching Fund created an important incentive for CBOs to expand existing community technology projects and take on new initiatives. In addition, Keyes's work in Seattle to broker relationships, match organizations with resources, and encourage collaboration among existing efforts has been critical to the city's ability to attack this problem at a large scale through coordination of the many small and independent initiatives. The fact that it is the community technology planner's job to connect organizations to each other and to promote partnerships aids overburdened organizational leaders. Not all cities will have the resources and support for a community technology planner. Creation of an interagency task force that integrates technology into existing work can also aid coordination. These kinds of task forces should be considered at the state and federal government levels as well.

IT goals must be integrated into the public agenda

The digital divide issue does not fit easily into any one policy sphere, but rather cuts across a range of local government departments including education, economic development, and housing. Seattle's story illustrates the way a community technology planner can work across local government departments. The creation of this position gives community technology greater legitimacy in the region, with other policymakers and with potential funders. Further, Seattle's IT Indicators Project has formalized buy-in to the goal of technology literacy, not only from the city but also from a range of other stakeholders. In order to make progress on the digital divide issue, policy makers must understand the potential of IT to help them solve the problems they are already trying to solve. Integrating technology broadly into a wide range of public policy interventions will aid progress on the digital divide issue.

Let a thousand flowers bloom

The public sector approach has been one that fosters local innovation, as well as collaboration, creating an environment of inclusion. Seattle city government has taken a very active role in the local community technology movement. However, the way it has done this has been to support and strengthen what works and to fill in existing gaps rather than trying to change or dictate what individual CTCs do. Seattle's approach has been flexible and participatory rather than autocratic. Keyes, in his role as community technology planner, has done a great deal of listening to directors of CTCs about the challenges they face and to citizens about their ideas regarding IT. His planning approach has been participatory, communicative, and focused on equity. As a result, the city has been able to balance strong support with decentralization, enabling creative, neighborhood-focused solutions to the problem to flourish.

Conclusion

CTCs do not have sufficient capacity to narrow the digital divide on their own. They do, when working in concert with others, point the way to an appropriate long-term solution. The Seattle case demonstrates the ways in which the public sector can apply the lessons learned from local CTCs and use its expertise and position as policy maker, incentive provider, and broker of relationships to create a situation in which IT is integral to, rather than marginal to, public goals. Seattle exploits existing policy levers and incorporates learning from grassroots organizations into local government. Over time, these practices have begun to change the structure and process of local government. In addition, key stakeholders in Seattle view the technology gap as fundamentally connected to larger social problems. Rather than feeling pressure to make false choices such as spending on housing versus technology, they are working on ways to do both in an integrated fashion.

But what is the best way to achieve what Seattle has done on a large scale? Does it require that we focus on changing federal policy? Or is it sufficient to support many localized experiments, such as the one that has borne fruit in Seattle? Answering these questions requires an approach that melds feasibility with ambitious goals. The material presented in this book clearly supports the notion that there is room for change that originates from grassroots initiatives. To be sure, an agenda of large-scale institutional change would be extremely difficult to achieve. Most regions possess an infrastructure of community-building organizations that can be harnessed for this purpose. And the recent decentralization of workforce development and welfare policy makes the policy in these two areas much more malleable and potentially responsive. In Seattle, government leverages the existing work of CTCs by helping to eliminate the barriers that prevent them from expanding and then channels the lessons learned from these burgeoning institutions into existing institutions. The key for all regions is to create a process in which these community-based projects can be used to guide policy development.

9

Toward a New Agenda

The community technology movement has grown up at the edges of established institutional arrangements, in the interstices between traditional policy spheres and existing community-based movements. It has incorporated aspects of community development, economic development, education, and organizing. This movement is a response to the larger socioeconomic transformation that has created the information society. The response has resulted in a new set of locally based institutions and programs that act to diffuse technology, engage people in civil society, and connect traditionally disadvantaged groups to the opportunities offered by the new economy.

The preceding chapters have shown the potential of IT as a tool to help lead us closer to an economically and socially just society. Although insufficient on its own, IT can be engaged as part of a larger strategy to break down historic divides such as the inequitable distribution of wealth and discrimination based on gender, race, and location. As such, it is a key second order resource. Thus far, however, this potential has not been realized on a large scale. This chapter pulls together lessons from the preceding ones to make two arguments. First, that advancing the community technology movement necessitates a pragmatic assessment of the potential and limitations of technology. And second, employing IT to achieve broad social goals will require a greater degree of coordination among key actors, as well as a willingness on the part of these actors to take on new roles.

Findings

The following are findings culled from the research presented in preceding chapters.

Access is an incomplete solution

As gaps in access continue to narrow, we must look beyond access to how people actually use technology and for what purpose. Access is undeniably the first step toward creating a technology-literate society. However, statistics that tell us how many people have access to a computer in their household, workplace or school provide us with little information about the actual relationships between different groups and technology. Enough information now exists to warrant support for a more comprehensive solution to the digital divide, one that targets the content and training dimensions of the problem in addition to the access component.

The research presented here shows that when a worker or a student has access to a computer, she still may not be benefiting fully from the information society. It is now imperative, then, that we look beyond gaps in access and ask a broader and deeper set of questions. Why is it that some groups have obtained access more quickly than others, even when we control for variables such as education and income? Who controls the content of the Internet? How can we best provide the kind of training needed to move disadvantaged workers into available IT jobs? How can we deliver new curricula through all of our schools that incorporates the kinds of learning and skills needed to thrive in the information age? A study of technology in the workplace, which grouped users into five categories ranging from "digital exile" to "power users," found that women and people of color were disproportionately represented in the least IT-savvy categories.[1] Chapter 5 also showed that children in poorer school districts tend to use computers and the Internet for less sophisticated applications than do children in wealthier districts. Those who use computers and the Internet for lower-order tasks, such as word processing, do not benefit from the information society in the same way as those who use IT for higher-order tasks, such as analyzing information and design.

The grassroots programs documented throughout this book illustrate the ways in which comprehensive IT programs – those targeted at low-income youth and disadvantaged workers, for example – can open new opportunities to historically disenfranchised groups. These strategies show great promise, and their potential for use on a larger scale must be explored.

1 John J. Heldrich Center for Workforce Development at Rutgers, the State University of New Jersey (2000).

The tech-fix is a myth

Weinberg coined the term "tech-fix" in 1966 to describe the myth that technology is primarily a problem solver. Although the potential of IT to create opportunities for disadvantaged groups must be pursued aggressively, we must also assess pragmatically what it can and cannot do. Technology alone will not level deep historical inequalities. Despite claims that new technology can operate as a "social leveler"[2] with the capacity to "erod[e] the relative power of all kinds of hierarchies structured on the control of information,"[3] significant intervention into the design and deployment of this technology will be required if we are to realize any of its equalizing tendencies. As currently structured and utilized, IT offers freedom, flexibility, and opportunity primarily to already powerful groups.[4]

Technology, then, is one tool, not "the" answer. Deployed wisely, it can significantly advance important human development goals. Without support to make it equally available, and without integrating it into a more comprehensive solution, it will likely aggravate existing inequalities.[5] In order to realize its potential, IT must be combined with other first- and second-order resources to build ladders out of persistent poverty.

Community technology centers are key innovators

CTCs are a growing new form of community organization. Although small and unevenly distributed across the country and around the world, they fill an important niche – delivering the benefits of the information age to those who have been passed by.

Until public sector interventions and partnerships with private sector actors ensure more equitable opportunities for people to benefit from and learn about IT, CTCs operate as important interim measures. Chapter 5 showed that until we determine how to deliver technology equally to students in poor and wealthy school districts, CTCs that serve youth will help to minimize the potential long-run consequences of some children receiving an inferior education. At the same time, CTCs are not merely filling a hole but achieving important status in

2 Pitroda (1993).
3 Builder (1993).
4 Graham and Marvin (1996: 193).
5 Rogers (1995).

their own right. Some have begun to work with existing CBOs to complement the work of both types of institutions, as chapter 7 showed. CTCs are the only institutions with the primary mission to bring technology to underserved communities. They have benefited from the advantage of newness: they tend not to have been bound up in existing bureaucratic arrangements. The lessons learned from them, then, will be key to creating a broader strategy to confront the digital divide.

Virtual and face-to-face activities are mutually reinforcing

Technology does not replace interaction that occurs in physical space. The Internet has not collapsed distance, as some projected. Throughout this book, you have read about community technology initiatives in which IT tools are inextricably connected to place-based community work and face-to-face relationships. In chapter 7, the techno-savvy CBOs that appear to be most successful use technology to supplement and extend the work they are already doing. CTCs, unlike aspatial community computing networks, have an explicit commitment to place. The fact that people come together in a particular place to learn about technology at CTCs is one of these organizations' defining characteristics. CTCs serve the important function of bringing people together, something all communities need. The activity that occurs within CTCs creates positive externalities by initiating new relationships between people who were not previously connected. These connections expand individuals' sets of "weak ties"[6] in low-income communities. And these new ties operate as a form of bridging social capital,[7] helping people to form relationships that provide access to the kind of resources needed to exit poverty.

A focus on youth is key

Youth must be trained now for the future. This means not only training them narrowly with specific IT skill sets but also altering pedagogy and curricula so that they can think and learn in new ways, ways

---

6 See Granovetter (1973).
7 Gittell and Vidal (1998) coined the terms "bonding" and "bridging" social capital to distinguish between the kind of social capital that helps people to get by (bonding) and the kind of social capital that helps people to get ahead bridging.

that will serve them well as demands to adapt to new systems increase. This kind of institutional change will be herculean. Ensuring that youth are able to participate in current social and economic systems must be a primary focus of research and policy efforts. This focus is necessary both for maintaining global economic competitiveness and for ensuring the full functioning of our democratic institutions. A focus on youth will go a long way toward eroding existing inequalities in the span of one generation. Focusing on youth requires patience, because it will take years to realize the payoff. Obtaining a significant public sector commitment to such a strategy may be difficult, given that it requires policy makers to think and act beyond the timeframe of election cycles.

IT aggravates existing spatial inequalities

Early technology theorists projected that new information technologies would have the effect of leveling regional inequalities, that the advantages historically conferred by physical location and infrastructure would matter less. This is not proving to be the case. For the most part, traditionally advantaged people and places continue to be the winners in the information age. Community technology efforts also tend to cluster in wealthier regions along both coasts, in cities, and in areas of high-tech activity. Although IT can be used to lesson geographic inequality – through distance learning, for example – technology will not accomplish this function on its own.

Implementing the Vision: It's Not Just Seattle

The preceding chapters provide many examples of places and programs where IT is being used as a tool to engage low-income individuals and communities. What would it take to scale up these stories, to create the conditions to enable them to happen in more places and with more people? It is too easy to write Seattle off as an aberration or an outlier. Yet all regions possess many of the same resources as Seattle: a corporate sector that will increasingly need workers with IT skills; existing community development infrastructure; schools; libraries; and the ability to divert flexible federal funds into IT programs tailored to the local context. Indeed, we are beginning to see more and more examples of nonhigh-tech cities, such as San Diego, Cleveland,

and Atlanta, that have begun to mount creative initiatives to address the digital divide.

The community technology movement is at a critical juncture, when many of the pieces are in place to bring technology to those regions that do not currently benefit from it. First, a key group of mature CTCs has existed for several years; these organizations have amassed an important body of collective experience. Second, policy makers and funders have begun to recognize the importance of confronting the digital divide. And third, a range of traditional institutions – schools, libraries, CBOs, and community colleges, for example – understand that they have a role to play. Cities and regions that decide to take on the digital divide will not have to travel up the same, steep learning curve that Seattle did. Now that the movement has amassed a significant amount of wisdom, knowledge, and experience, it is time to create a new policy agenda that will leverage this accumulated learning. Although all of the actors mentioned above have begun to gather their own learning within each of their own fields, there has been too little sharing of information and collaboration across fields.

Policy makers

Chapter 2 documented the rapid rise in access to IT across all groups. Policy must work to close remaining divides, focusing specifically on the disabled, African-Americans, Latinos, and those living in rural and inner-city areas. Doing so will require a greater understanding of why these groups have traditionally had lower rates of access. At the same time, as the problem of lack of access to computers and IT continues to diminish, policy makers must create and expand programs to address the training and content dimensions of the digital divide. As access based gaps continue to narrow, the digital divide will be defined much more in terms of what people are doing online and how they are using IT tools.

The Telecommunications Act of 1996 has not sufficiently achieved its goal of making universal service to information technologies affordable to those segments of the population that had previously been denied access to telecommunication networks. As the telecommunications field advances, policy must intervene to ensure that current imbalances between advantaged and disadvantaged places are not exacerbated.

Policy makers at the state and local levels should also continue to use flexible federal funding sources, such as WIA and TANF, to support innovative programs that address the digital divide and simultaneously confront other issues such as the IT labor shortage and persistent poverty. Many examples of such creative use of funds currently exist across the country. These programs, which are effectively demonstration projects, must be studied in order to determine the factors responsible for their success or failure, and the lessons learned should be shared widely. In addition, the public sector should explore ways to create more stable funding streams for those programs that do succeed, while also continuing to fund new, creative solutions to this problem.

Policy makers at all levels of government should view the digital divide as an issue that cuts across departments and programs; failure to do so will have the effect of continued fragmentation and lack of a unified response. The Seattle case demonstrates the benefits of integrating IT goals within a range of existing departments. It is the connectedness of the digital divide to so many other issues and problems that makes it such an important one to confront.

Partnerships between government bodies and other actors will be critical to a successful strategy. Governments at all levels can play a key role by creating incentives for the actors that are separately confronting the digital divide to work together.

The federal government should expand its research agenda to examine the training and content components of the digital divide, as well as the longer-term effects of being connected versus disconnected.

Community technology centers

In the short time they have existed, CTCs have helped countless individuals and communities to harness the power of the information society and reap its benefits. But CTCs are too small, scattered, and vulnerable to the vicissitudes of the funding world to be the answer for society at large. On their own, they are unlikely to make a significant dent in the digital divide problem or to substantially narrow other longstanding divides.

The biggest challenges currently facing these organizations are scale and sustainability. How should we address the digital divide in the many places that do not benefit from the existence of CTCs? Should we devise a way to create CTCs in these places? Replication of those models that have demonstrated success is one possibility, but has always seemed better in theory than it has worked in practices. Locally rooted organizations work because they are rooted in their local context; this makes such models difficult to transfer. Or should we construct mechanisms that enable existing CBOs and other local organizations to build the capacity necessary to address the technology gap? One vision is that of CTCs playing key roles as community institutions of the future, functioning as gathering places, training institutions, and family learning centers. Another vision would position CTCs as stopgap measures, functioning to fill a present void only until existing institutions can gain sufficient capacity to address the technology gap themselves.

The most realistic way for CTCs to achieve scale and sustainability is through partnerships with existing institutions such as CBOs, schools, and libraries. Playing2Win's connections to Boys' Harbor and the Institute for Learning Technologies grounds it in the community and aligns it with a major university. Such partnerships will help to institutionalize the goals of the CT movement and enable it to reach many more people. The community technology movement is also mature enough to have generated a set of intermediary organizations and trade associations. These organizations can help to create scale by documenting and disseminating best practices, educating funders about the digital divide problem and community-based solutions, and connecting with other community-based movements that have complementary goals.

Primary and secondary schools

The existing public school system is clearly the most direct way to disseminate IT to children and to prepare them for work and life in the new socioeconomic system. Taking on this challenge requires schools to be truly responsive to the changes wrought by the information society. This responsiveness may warrant a significant shift in pedagogy, rather than tinkering at the margins of old models. This kind of responsiveness requires leadership – in the federal government and in individual school districts – that understands this problem and believes in its importance.

Numerous local experiments currently exist that may help to guide this process. In order to enable schools to accomplish these goals, they need greater support for equipment, training, and technical assistance. Rather than creating separate computer classes, teachers should be given incentives to learn about IT and integrate it into their existing curricula. Government programs can also create incentives for collaboration between the schools and local CTCs.

Programs such as ExplorNet and Youth Tech Entrepreneurs, which are designed to be scalable and to adapt to a school's needs, should be studied in order to understand and document their potential and limits. Places such as Bellingham, Washington that have taken on the IT challenge in a big way, and high-tech high schools must also be studied. Lessons from federal programs such as the Star Schools program and the 21st Century Learning Program must also be employed to institutionalize programs in schools that not only equalize access but also ensure greater equity in terms of how students across the country are using IT in their classrooms.

Post-secondary education

As chapter 6 showed, although some post-secondary education will continue to be an important requisite for stable employment that pays a living wage, this education need not come from a traditional four-year college. The range of institutions providing post-secondary training has widened and now includes community colleges, community-based training programs, employer-led training programs, and for-profit post-secondary schools, as well as traditional four-year colleges. All of these institutions are training people for work in the IT sector, yet there has been little shared learning among these various categories of institutions. We have insufficient information about who is doing what, and who is doing it well. We do know that, in order to prepare workers for jobs in the IT sector, schools need to have flexible curricula, provide after-program services, and be responsive to employers' changing needs. In addition to learning about the successes and failures of these different types of programs, there must also be greater partnering among key stakeholders. Community colleges in particular can play a key role because of their location in so many communities and their experience serving underserved populations. Those that have successfully altered their bureaucracies in order to train people for the quickly changing IT sector should disseminate what they know broadly.

The corporate sector

The corporate sector has strong incentives to support programs that narrow the digital divide. Doing so creates new markets for their products, produces an appropriately skilled workforce, and builds goodwill. Investing in areas that have not benefited fully from the information society simultaneously promotes larger social goals and enhances corporations' bottom lines. Corporate support is needed to address this problem but is not without complications, as previous chapters showed. Still, the corporate incentive to participate in digital divide strategies makes this problem differ in an important way from most other issues associated with persistent poverty.

Philanthropic organizations

A few key foundations, such as the Kellogg and Markle Foundations, have been front-runners in supporting digital divide initiatives. Given that awareness of this issue is uneven among funders, those that have taken an early interest can help to educate others in order to broaden the base of support for this work. A general critique that has been leveled at philanthropic funders is that they tend to shift funding priorities, moving too quickly from one hot topic to another. All of the actors that support digital divide work – corporate, government, and philanthropic – should share learning more widely and figure out how to complement each other's work. Other funders have created incentives for corporations to increase their work in this area. For example, the Ford Foundation's Corporate Involvement Initiative leverages private sector knowledge and resources to improve income and wealth for low-income people.[8]

Libraries

Libraries were early leaders in the community technology movement and continue to play a large role in identifying and getting resources

8   This initiative is currently funding an evaluation of Fleet Bank's CommunityLink program, which is providing computers, Internet access, financial training, and IT training to low-income Fleet customers in Boston, Newark, and Trenton. Ford will disseminate findings widely in order to share the learning from this project.

and technologies to people. Nearly 14 percent of CTCNet affiliates are libraries. Libraries, like schools, represent a large existing infrastructure investment. In addition, library staff have had training in information science, an extremely important skill set for CTCs; many CTC staff have not had such training. Given this experience, in information science and in the community technology movement, libraries will continue to be key actors in bridging the digital divide. Libraries and CTCs need to engage in information sharing of what they have learned thus far in terms of how to apply IT.

Community-building organizations

Chapter 7 showed that partnerships between CBOs and CTCs can help to extend and institutionalize both movements. Specifically, CTCs can benefit from the connections existing CBOs have to the communities in which they operate. And CBOs can use new technology to increase the scale of their work. The organizations that make up both of these movements tend to work very closely with the complex and multiple issues facing communities beset by persistent poverty. These organizations also have the ability to do creative and flexible programming. One of the most important roles for CBOs will be to document what they do and share these lessons with policy makers so that they can learn from this grassroots work and employ it to influence policy.

The digital divide is one manifestation of an enormous shift currently underway in our society. This shift has made us more global, and our progress more dependent on the facility with which information can be moved and applied. The move to an information society increases our ability to connect to each other, to share information, and to open up access to education and the labor market. At the same time, the digital divide reveals and repeats patterns of inequality that long pre-existed the current problem. These patterns exist not only in the United States but also throughout the world, in developed and developing countries alike. These old divides, which continue to fall out along the familiar lines of race, class, gender, and location, will not be narrowed by a simple tech fix. Rather, addressing persistent poverty and inequality requires a new generation of policy efforts characterized by greater integration, coordination, and, most of all, a willingness to question and change the structures that maintain existing power relations.

IT can support this kind of policy shift, yet policy innovation has not kept pace with technological innovation. Policy directed at the problem of persistent poverty, including digital divide policy, must move toward an investment focus. As long as poverty policy focuses so insistently on first-order resources to the virtual exclusion of second-order resources, existing patterns of inequality will be maintained.

Technology can be a tool of inclusion or exclusion. The question that needs to be answered is: how can we employ technology as a tool of inclusion in a society that is not structured to be fully inclusive? In the end, it is futile to think about either policy or technology in the abstract. Both are driven by people. Both are tools with the potential to create a global society that is more just, more open, and more inclusive – if we can muster the political will to make it so.

Appendix I

Research Strategy
and Methodology

Several separate but integrated research projects fed into this book. This appendix lays out the kinds of research conducted and the methodologies employed. It includes explanations of why the methods used were chosen, what the data consist of, and how data collection was carried out. In addition, it discusses the steps taken to ensure the reliability of the results given the methods chosen.

Research Agenda

This research was intended to provide a fine-grained description of the community technology movement and to understand the potential of this movement to enable progress on the entrenched problems of inequality and persistent poverty. The research is situated within the broad context of urban poverty policy in the US, and more narrowly within the public policy framing and addressing of the digital divide issue.

Choice of Programs and Cities Studied

Initial research for this book was conducted with the purpose of understanding the functioning of the community technology movement within the context of local government. The aim, therefore, was to study cities that had both established community technology movements and innovative local government practices with respect to the digital divide. These criteria clearly eliminated many cities. From those that remained, the aim was to obtain regional diversity as well as not looking only at established high-tech regions. Ultimately, Pittsburgh, Seattle, and Austin were chosen.

Conducting this first level of research provided a solid understanding of the work of CTCs and local governments, and raised additional questions regarding specific program areas in which CTCs are engaged. These questions specifically concerned the relationship between education and technology, between workforce development and IT, and the potential synergies between the community technology movement and the community-building movement.

In order to study youth-oriented CTCs, I selected three programs that I had had previous experiences with – Plugged In, in East Palo Alto, CA; the Technology Access Foundation (TAF) in Seattle; and Playing2Win in Harlem. Again, these programs are regionally diverse. Although all were created specifically to address the digital divide, they come at the problem in different ways.

Addressing the primary question posed in chapter 7 – how can the community technology and community building movements reinforce each other? – required looking at a wide range of organizations that integrate community building and community technology work. For this chapter, innovative examples that use technology to leverage the work of community-building organizations were studied. Again, the examples selected for research are not typical but rather were selected to illustrate innovation and best practices.

The community technology field is relatively new, and therefore it did not make sense to select programs and cities that are representative of the entire field. The intention was rather to gain a better understanding of the *potential* of this field so that creative solutions could be shared across communities and organizations. Therefore, programs and cities that had already traveled a significant distance up the learning curve, that could share their experiences regarding what worked and what did not, were chosen.

Methods of Data Collection

Survey

The survey discussed in chapter 3 was conducted during the summer of 1999. The purpose was to gain a basic understanding of the characteristics of organizations that considered themselves to be community technology centers. Affiliates of the Community Technology

Centers Network (CTCNet), a national umbrella association of these organizations were therefore surveyed. It is important to note that CTCNet's membership is not a comprehensive list of the CTC population. Many CBOs that provide technology services and programs have not joined CTCNet. Some may have opted not to join while others may not be aware of CTCNet. Thus, the sample frame represents an indeterminate portion of the CTC population. However, before the survey, we asked CTCNet staff whether they thought their membership was representative of the field in general; they believe that it is.

The survey consisted of 20 questions, most of which were closed-end questions concerning staff size, target population, services, programmatic uses of technology, and funding sources. A few open-ended questions were also asked about the mission of the organization, current challenges faced, and the type of data collected to evaluate technology programs. Although CTCNet collects basic information on affiliates and has conducted some of the only research in the field, no one has collected descriptive data from the group of CTCs surveyed, rendering the data set particularly important.

The survey sample consisted of 336 affiliates. Although there are affiliates in nearly every state, certain regions of the country, particularly the southeast, have fewer CTCNet affiliates. Of the 336 surveys mailed, eight were returned by the postal service as undeliverable. We received a total of 128 responses, 123 of which were usable. The effective response rate was, therefore, 37.5 percent, based on 123 useable surveys received out of 328 surveys mailed and not returned as undeliverable. The relatively high response rate demonstrates the strong interest among CTCs in learning more about other organizations in their field.

We supplemented survey data with data from interviews with community technology activists, directors of CTC programs and local officials in three case-study cities – Austin, Pittsburgh and Seattle. In selecting our case-study cities we sought out places in which the city government has played a proactive role with respect to IT policy and there are innovative CT programs operating. The goal was to study leading-edge cities in order to understand the *potential* of community technology efforts and draw lessons for local officials and community-based organizations that have not yet progressed as far. The CTCs in the case-study cities, like CTCs more generally, exhibit a wide range of emphasis, but are similar in that their stated mission is to broker access to IT to underserved groups and to provide critical information to the communities they serve. Together, survey and interview data made it possible to put together a broad picture of CTCs and develop a more nuanced understanding of how things work within and between community technology programs.

In-depth interviews

In-depth interviews were used throughout the research process in order to obtain a range of information. Interviews with community technology activists were critical for constructing the history of the community technology movement in chapter 3. In each of the cities in which fieldwork took place – Austin, Seattle, Pittsburgh, New York, and East Palo Alto – interviews were conducted with program staff, program participants, relevant local officials, funders, and officials at connected institutions. Interviews with program staff concentrated on interpretations of programs' mission and goals and assessment of what programs have and have not accomplished, as well as future plans. Interviews with participants (and, at youth-oriented programs, their parents) were broader in scope and depended to some extent on the age range of participants and mission of the relevant program. Questions were formulated to elicit stories about how participants had come to use CTCs and how they felt they benefited from participation in the programs. Interviews with officials at connected institutions were designed to obtain the perspectives of community technology activists and experts, program funders, and other community-based actors. Interviews with public officials were structured to gain a clear understanding of how these officials connected work on the technology gap to other public goals.

The method of interviewing was closely modeled on Rubin and Rubin's concept of interviews as guided conversations.[1] Rather than maintaining a rigid and completely structured interview format, the interviews were shaped in part by the interviewees' responses. Giving back some of the control over the interview situation to the interviewee opens up the potential for learning more and helps to break down the interviewer/interviewee hierarchy. Creating an interaction based on give and take made the interviewees more comfortable with interjecting, offering supplementary information, and redefining issues and questions.

1   Rubin and Rubin (1997).

To minimize the cultural distance between interviewer and interviewee, a graduate student – Raisa Martinez, whose first language is Spanish – was hired to conduct interviews with program participants in Harlem and East Palo Alto. As a native Spanish speaker, Raisa was better able to communicate with these participants. In addition, and in view of the limited time available to establish trust with participants, it was believed that Spanish-speaking participants were more likely to be open with Raisa. This was indeed the case. When we compared notes at the end of the day, we often found that Raisa had learned things we had not learned in other ways.

Nonparticipant observation

I, along with my research assistants, spent a great deal of time at each program. We attended classes, open access hours, and program and community meetings in order to obtain a solid sense of program operations, relationships within the communities, and the ways in which CTCs operated as public spaces.

Existing program data

This category consists of program data such as application and intake forms, grant applications, curricula, historical statistics on client base, internal reports and evaluations, budgets, and organizational charts. Most programs had not kept consistent data on program participants historically. When they did, we collected and analyzed this data.

Expert review

Before the manuscript was finalized, I sent it, in its entirety or specific chapters, to academics, field experts, and others with particularly extensive knowledge about the issues and problems covered in the book. The comments received from these reviewers formed the basis of an extensive revision.

Appendix 2

Community Technology Survey

Name of Organization: _____
Name & Title of Contact: _____
Address: _____
_____

Phone: _____   Fax (if applicable): _____
Email (if applicable):   Website (if applicable):

_____   _____

1. What year was your organization founded? _____
2. What is the mission of your organization (attach extra sheets if necessary)?

3. How many paid staff-persons do you have?

   _____ Full-time   _____ Part-time

4. How many volunteers? _____
5. What kinds of services does your organization provide? Check all that apply

   ☐ Tutoring/homework assistance   ☐ Adult Education/Literacy
   ☐ General youth development   ☐ Adult job training
   ☐ Mentoring   ☐ Community development
   ☐ Youth employment/School to   ☐ Advocacy
     Career   ☐ Technical Assistance
   ☐ Childcare
   ☐ Others (please describe)

6. Who do you serve (target populations)? Check all that apply

☐ Pre-school children   ☐ General Community
☐ School aged Children (5–17)   ☐ Specific neighborhood(s)
☐ Young Adults (18–24)   ☐ At risk
☐ Parents/adults   ☐ Low income
☐ Senior citizens   ☐ Women
☐ Others (please list) _____

7. Which best describes the area you serve?

☐ urban   ☐ suburban   ☐ rural   ☐ mixed

8. What was your budget for the last fiscal year? _____

9. Do you budget for: *Please circle one*

Hardware/software?   Yes   No
Technology support staff?   Yes   No
Equipment upgrades and repair?   Yes   No
Technology Programs?   Yes   No

10. What % of your funding comes from:

_____ Local Government   _____ Private Corporations
_____ State Government   _____ Other (list source and %)
_____ Federal Government   _____
_____ Private foundations   _____

11. Where are your technology services/programs offered? (Check all that apply)

☐ Schools   ☐ Within previously existing
☐ Libraries   community-based
☐ Other; please specify: organization
                                 ☐ Housing project community
_____

12. In what ways does your organization currently use technology in its programs?

Check all that apply:
☐ General (unstructured)   ☐ Communicating with
  computer access   others (email)

☐ Research/Web projects/ online resources

☐ Word processing/ Keyboarding skills

☐ Homework help

☐ Computer-based instruction

☐ Video Projects/Video Production

☐ Job searches/Résumés

☐ Technology oriented business

☐ Other (please describe)

13. Approximately how many computers does your organization have? _____

14. Does your organization have access to the World Wide Web? Yes   No

15. In terms of your organizations priorities, on a scale of 1 to 4 with 4 being the highest, how would you rank the importance of integrating technology into your programs?

1	2	3	4	NA
Not important	Slightly important	Fairly important	Very important	

16. To what extent has technology helped your organization to fulfill it mission/meet its goals?

1	2	3	4	NA
Not at all	Somewhat	Considerably	To a great extent	

17. What percentage of your staff regularly used email or accesses the Internet? _____ %

18. What are the biggest challenges currently facing your organization? Please be as specific as possible; attach additional pages as necessary.

19. How do you know whether your program(s) is (are) successful?

20. Do you collect information to measure success? _____ If so what kind? (attach additional sheets if necessary)

Appendix 3

Analysis of Survey Results

Table A3.1   Analysis of survey results

CTCs	No. of responses 123	Response rate 37.5%
	Total # of responses	Percent of respondents*
Services provided (check all that apply)		
Tutoring/homework assistance	63	51.6
General youth development	65	53.5
Mentoring	43	35.2
Youth employment/school to career	43	35.2
Childcare	19	15.6
Adult education/literacy	69	56.6
Adult job training	50	41.0
Community development	57	46.7
Advocacy	46	37.7
Technical assistance	59	48.4
Others	51	41.8
Target populations (check all that apply)		
Pre-school children	39	31.7
School-aged children (5–17)	91	74.0
Young adults (18–24)	90	73.2
Parents/adults	94	76.4
Senior citizens	73	59.3
General community	85	69.1
Specific neighborhoods	53	43.1
At risk	73	59.3
Low-income	94	76.4
Women	61	49.6
Others	28	22.8

Table A3.1 *Continued*

CTCs	No. of responses 123	Response rate 37.5%
	Total # of responses	*Percent of respondents**
Geographic area served		
Urban	79	64.2
Suburban	10	8.1
Rural	17	13.8
Mixed	17	13.8
How technology is used in programs (check all that apply)		
General (unstructured) computer access	107	87.0
Research/Web projects/online resources	86	69.9
Word processing/Keyboarding skills	101	82.1
Homework help	58	47.2
Computer-based instruction	67	54.5
Communicating with others (email)	97	78.9
Video projects/video production	36	29.3
Job searches/résumés	88	71.5
Recreation/entertainment	71	57.7
Technology-oriented business	30	24.4
Others	22	17.9
Receive funding from		
Local government	62	53.0
State government	52	44.4
Federal government	47	40.2
Private foundations	83	70.9
Private corporations	50	42.7
Other	69	59.0
Largest share of funding from		
Local government	23	22.5
State government	6	5.9
Federal government	17	16.7
Private foundations	25	24.5
Private corporations	12	11.8
Other	19	18.6
Where technology services/programs are offered		
Schools	23	18.9
Libraries	19	15.6
Housing project community	30	24.6

Table A3.1 *Continued*

CTCs	No. of responses 123	Response rate 37.5%
	Total # of responses	*Percent of respondents**
Within a previously existing CBO	70	57.4
Other	47	38.8
Organization has access to the World Wide Web	121	98.4
Importance of integrating technology into programs		
Not important	0	0.0
Slightly important	2	1.6
Fairly important	18	14.6
Very important	103	83.7
NA	0	0.0
The extent to which technology has helped organization fulfill its mission/meet its goals		
Not at all	0	0.0
Somewhat	10	8.3
Considerably	38	31.7
To a great extent	72	60.0
NA	0	0.0
Size of paid staff (full and part-time)		
Less than 5	34	28.3
5–10	30	25.0
11–25	26	21.7
26–50	11	9.2
51–100	8	6.7
>100	11	9.2
Use volunteers	102	89.5
Budget for		
Hardware/software	109	90.1
Technology support staff	97	80.2
Equipment upgrades and repair	101	83.5
Technology programs	86	75.4**

Table A3.1 *Continued*

CTCs	No. of responses 123	Response rate 37.5%
	Total # of responses	Percent of respondents*
Percentage of staff that regularly uses email or accesses the Internet		
0	1	0.8
1–25	17	14.0
26–50	11	9.1
51–75	16	13.2
76–99	15	12.4
100	61	50.4
Biggest challenges		
Funding (explicitly mentioned)	70	61.4
Staffing (paid and volunteer)	41	36.0
Staff development	9	7.9
Curriculum development	8	7.0
Technical assistance	14	12.3
Meeting demand/Managing growth	13	11.4
Outreach/Attracting participants	7	6.1
Maintaining focus on mission	5	4.3
Upgrades/Keeping up with technology	25	21.9
Developing sound evaluation processes	3	2.6
Other	28	24.6
Collect information to evaluate programs	100	84.0

* Percentages are based on the number of respondents to each question.
** 7.3% of survey respondents did not answer this component of the question versus 1.6% of respondents for the other components.

Appendix 4

World Wide Web References[1]

Federal Government Agencies and Departments

US Department of Education, www.ed.gov
US Department of Commerce, National Telecommunications and
    Infrastructure Administration, www.ntia.doc.gov
US Department of Housing and Urban Development, www.hud.gov
Federal Communication Commission, www.fcc.gov

State and City

Iowa Communications Network, www.icn.state.ia.us
Texas Telecommunications Infrastructure Fund Board,
    www.tifb.state.tx.us
Atlanta Community Technology Initiative,
    www.atlantacommunitytech.com
Seattle Public Access Network, www.cityofseattle.net
Seattle Information Technology Indicators Project,
    www.cityofseattle.net/tech/indicators

Umbrella Organizations

Education Development Center, www.edc.org
Children's Partnership, www.childrenspartnership.org
The Morino Institute, www.morino.org

1   Within categories, references are listed in order of appearance in the text.

The Benton Foundation, www.benton.org
Internet and American Life Project, www.pewinternet.org
The Gartner Institute, www.gartner.com
Tomas Rivera Policy Institute, www.trpi.org
National Commission on Libraries and Information Science,
   www.nclis.gov
Alliance for Community Media, www.alliancecm.org
Association for Community Networking, www.afcn.net
Community Technology Centers Network, www.ctcnet.org
National Community Building Network, www.ncbn.org
Information Technology Industry Council, www.itic.org
Information Technology Association of America, www.itaa.org
Northwest Center for Emerging Technologies, www.nwcet.org

Community-level Organizations and Other Projects Discussed

Austin Learning Academy, www.alaweb.org
Hill House Association, www.hillhouse.ckp.edu/
Bay Area Video Coalition, www.bavc.org
Project Compute, www.projectcompute.org
Austin Free-Net, www.austinfree.net
Plugged In, www.pluggedin.org
New Networks Institute, www.newnetworks.com
Playing2Win, www.playing2win.org
HarlemLive, www.harlemlive.org
Technology Access Foundation, www.techaccess.org
Training, Inc., www.traininginc.org
OpNet, www.opnetwork.org
Welfare Law Center's Low-Income Networking and Communications
   Project, www.lincproject.org
1000 Friends of Oregon – ONE/Northwest, www.friends.org;
   www.onenw.org
Cleveland CDC Technology 2000 Team, www.T2K.org
Grace Hill, www.gracehill.org
East Bay Works, www.eastbayworks.org
Cabrini Connections, www.tutormentorconnection.org
Neighborhood Knowledge Los Angeles, http://nkla.sppsr.ucla.edu
National Neighborhood Indicators Partnership, www.urban.org/nnip

Boston Community Building Network,
   www.tbf.org/current/bcbn.html
CompassPoint Nonprofit Services, www.compasspoint.org
National Council of Nonprofit Associations, www.ncna.org
Npower, www.npower.org
OMB Watch, www.ombwatch.org
Progressive Technology Project, www.progressivetech.org
TechRocks, www.techrocks.org
Technology Works for Good, www.technologyworks.org
Cisco Networking Academies, www.cisco.com/edu
DeVry Institutes, www.devry.edu
Alliance for Employee Growth and Development,
   www.employeegrowth.com
International Society for Technology in Education, www.iste.org
Seattle Community Network, www.scn.org
Digital Promise, www.digitalpromise.org
Seattle Community Technology Alliance,
   www.cityofseattle.net/tech/scta
Independent Media Center, www.indymedia.org

Community Colleges

Bellevue Community College, www.bcc.ctc.edu
Iowa Western Community College, www.iwcc.cc.ia.us
De Anza Community College, www.deanza.fhda.edu
Borough of Manhattan Community College, www.bmcc.cuny.edu
Seattle Central Community College, www.seattlecentral.org

Bibliography

Anderson, Robert H., Tora K. Bikson, Sally Ann Law, and Bridger M. Mitchell. 1995. *Universal access to e-mail: Feasibility and societal implications.* RAND Report No. MR-650-MF. Santa Monica, CA: RAND Corporation.

Anderson, Ronald E. and Amy Ronnkvist. 1999. "The presence of computers in American schools." Report No.2 of Teaching, Learning, and Computing: 1998 National Survey. Irvine, CA: Center for Research on Information Technology and Organizations.

Anderson, Teresa E. and Alan Melchior. 1995. Assessing telecommunications technology as a tool for urban community building. *The Journal of Urban Technology* 3(1): 29–44.

Angrist, Joshua and Victor Lavy. 1999. "New evidence on classroom computers and pupil learning." National Bureau of Economic Research Working Paper No. W7424.

Archdiocesan Housing Authority (AHA). 1999. *AHA computer learning centers: Our mission.* World Wide Web page ⟨http://www.ahaclc.org/mission.htm⟩ (accessed August 31, 1999).

Association for Community Networking (AFCN). 1999. Association for Community Networking home page. World Wide Web page ⟨http://www.afcn.net/overview.html⟩ (accessed July 16, 1999).

Atkinson, Robert D. 1998. "Technological change and cities." *Cityscape* 3: 129–70.

Austin Free-Net (AFN). 1999. Austin Free-Net home page. World Wide Web page http://www.austinfree.net (accessed February 11, 1999).

Bailey, Thomas, Norena Badway, and P. Gumport. (2001). "For-profit higher education and community colleges." National Center for Postsecondary Improvement. (Deliverable No.0400). Standford University: Stanford, CA.

Baretto, Matt, et al. 2000. *Latino Internet Use and Online Attitudes.* Los Angeles, CA: Tomas Rivera Policy Institute.

Beamish, Anne. 1995. "Communities on-line: Community-based computer networks." Master's thesis, Department of Urban Studies and Planning, Massachusetts Institute of Technology, Cambridge, MA. World Wide Web page ⟨http://sap.mit.edu/anneb/cn-thesis/html/toc.html⟩ (accessed February 5, 1999).

Becker, Henry Jay. 2000. "Who's wired and who's not." Paper prepared for *The future of children*, issue on children and computers, Fall.

Benton Foundation. 1996. *The Telecommunications Act of 1996 and the changing communications landscape*. Washington, DC: The Benton Foundation.

—. 1997. *The new definition of universal service and the role for public interest advocates to make federal telecommunications policy work in your state*. Washington, DC: The Benton Foundation.

—. 1999a. "E-rate: Closing the digital divide." *The Digital Beat*, March 5: 1–4. World Wide Web page ⟨http://www.benton.org/DigitalBeat/db030599.html⟩ (accessed July 19, 1999).

—. 1999b. "The Digital Divide." *The Digital Beat*, July 8: 1–6. World Wide Web page ⟨http://www.benton.org/DigitalBeat/db070899.html⟩ (accessed July 8, 1999).

—. 1999c. "Broadband and the Future of the Internet." *The Digital Beat*, August. World Wide Web page ⟨http://www.benton.org/DigitalBeat/.html⟩ (accessed March 12, 2001).

—. 1999d. "Native Americans and the Digital Divide." *The Digital Beat*, October 14. World Wide Web page ⟨http://www.benton.org/DigitalBeat/.html⟩ (accessed June 23, 2001).

—. 2000. "Broadband and the AOL/Time Warner Merger." *The Digital Beat Extra*, January 18, 2000. World Wide Web page ⟨http://www.benton.org/DigitalBeat/.html⟩ (accessed March 23, 2001).

Berners-Lee, Tim. 1996. "The world-wide web: Past, present, and future." World Wide Web page http://www.w3.org/People/Berners-Lee/1996/ppf.html (accessed July 19, 2001).

Blakely, Edward J., Stefanus Hadi, and Paul Johnson. 1995. "Information city and the ghetto: The L.A. experience." Los Angeles, CA: The Lusk Center Research Institute, University of Southern California.

Bliss, Steven. 2000. *San Francisco Works: Toward an employer-led approach to welfare reform and workforce development*. Washington, DC: Manpower Demonstration Research Corporation.

Bluestone, Barry and Bennett Harrison. 1982. *The deindustrialization of America: Plant closings, community abandonment, and the dismantling of basic industry*. New York: Basic Books.

—. 1990. *The great u-turn; Corporate restructuring and the polarizing of America*. New York: Basic Books.

Borsook, Paulina. 2000. *Cyberselfish: A critical romp through the terribly libertarian culture of high tech*. New York: Public Affairs.

Branscomb, Lewis M. (ed.), 1993. *Empowering technology: Implementing a U.S. strategy*. Cambridge, MA: The MIT Press.

Breckheimer, Veronica L. and Kevin Taglang. 1999. "Mergers and the public interest." *The Digital Beat*, July 21: 1–7. World Wide Web page ⟨http://www.benton.org/DigitalBeat/db072199.html⟩ (accessed July 21, 1999).

Breeden, Laura, Steve Cisler, Vivian Guilfoy, Michael Roberts, and Antonia Stone. 1998. "Computer and communications use in low-income communities: Models for the neighborhood transformation and family development initiative." Newton, MA: Education Development Center, Inc.

Brock, Gerald. 1994. *Telecommunications policy for the information age.* Cambridge, MA: Harvard University Press, 1994.

Bruno, Ludovica. 2001. *Measuring the evolution of information societies.* IDC report No.W24652.

Builder, Carl H. 1993. "Is it a transition or a revolution?" *Futures* 25: 155–68.

Bush, Corlann Gee. 1983. "Women and the assessment of technology: To think, to be, to unthink, to free." In *Machina ex dea: Feminist perspectives on technology.* Edited by Joan Rothschild. Elmsord, NY: Pergamon Press.

Carvin, Andy. 2000. *The E-Rate in America: A tale of four cities.* Washington, DC: The Benton Foundation.

Castells. 1989. *The informational city: Information technology, economic restructuring, and the urban-regional process.* Cambridge, MA: Basil Blackwell.

—. 1996. *The rise of the network society.* Cambridge, MA: Blackwell Publishers Inc.

—. 2001. *The Internet galaxy: Reflections on the Internet, business, and society.* The 2000 Clarendon Lectures in Management, Oxford University. Oxford: Oxford University Press.

Cattagni, Anne and Elizabeth Farris. 2001. "Internet access in US public schools and classrooms: 1994–2000." National Center for Education Statistics, Statistics in Brief. Washington, DC: US Department of Education, Office of Educational Research and Improvement, NCES 2001–71.

Center for an Urban Future. 2000. "The skills crisis: Building a jobs system that works." New York: Center for an Urban Future.

CEO Forum on Education and Technology. March 2001. "Education technology must be included in comprehensive education legislation." Washington, DC: The CEO Forum on Education and Technology.

Chapman, Gary and Lodis Rhodes. 1997. Nurturing neighborhood nets. *Technology Review.* World Wide Web page ⟨http://www.techreview.com/articles/oct97/chapman.html⟩ (accessed July 21, 1999).

Chapple, Karen and Matthew A. Zook. 2000. "Promising futures: promising practices in information technology training for disadvantaged adults." Paper prepared for the 2000 Association of Collegiate Schools of Planning Conference, Atlanta Georgia. November 1–5.

Chow, Clifton, Jan Ellis, June Mark, and Bart Wise. 1998. *Impact of CTCNet affiliates: Findings from a national survey of users of community technology centers.* Newton, MA: Community Technology Centers' Network (CTCNet), Education Development Center, Inc.

Cisler, Steve. 1998. "Telecenters and libraries: New technologies and new partnerships." Statement written for annual IFLA conference in Amsterdam.

Citizens Telecommunications and Technology Advisory Board (CTTAB). 1999. CTTAB home page. World Wide Web page ⟨http://www.ci.seattle.wa.us/cttab/default.htm⟩ (accessed April 26, 1999).

City of Pittsburgh. 1999. *Department of Economic Development: Industry cluster information.* World Wide Web page ⟨http://www.city.pittsburgh.pa.us/ed/html/hightech.html⟩ (accessed June 26, 1999).

City of Seattle. 1999. *The Seattle technology matching fund program.* World Wide Web page ⟨http://www.ci.seattle.wa.us/tech/tmf/tmfbasic.htm⟩ (last modified September 8, 1999).

—. 2001. *Residential Technology Survey: Summary of Results*. Seattle, WA: Department of Information Technology.

Civille, Richard. 1995. "The Internet and the poor." In *Public access to the Internet*, edited by Brian Kahin and James Keller. Cambridge, MA: MIT Press.

Cole, Jeffery. 2000. *Surveying the Digital Future*. UCLA Center for Communications Policy. www.ccp.ucla.edu (accessed April 20, 2001).

Community Literacy Center. 1999. *The community literacy center: A community–university collaborative*. World Wide Web page ⟨http://english.cmu.edu/clc/⟩ (accessed June 26, 1999).

Congressional Commission on the Advancement of Women and Minorities in Science, Engineering and Technology. 2000. *Land of Plenty: Diversity as America's Competitive Edge in Science, Engineering, and Technology*. Washington, DC: Congressional Commission on the Advancement of Women and Minorities in Science, Engineering and Technology.

Conte, Christopher. 2000. *The learning connection: Schools in the information age*. Washington, DC: Benton Foundation.

Cooper, Mark. 1996. *Universal service: A historical perspective and policies for the twenty-first century*. Washington, DC: Benton Foundation.

Cortright, Joseph and Heike Mayer. 2001. "High tech specialization: A comparison of high technology centers." Washington, DC: The Brookings Institution, Center on Urban and Metropolitan Policy Survey Series.

Cuny, Janice and William Aspray. 2000. *Recruitment and Retention of Women Graduate Students in Computer Science and Engineering*. Washington, DC: Computing Research Association.

DiMaggio, Paul and Eszter Hargittai. 2001. "From the 'digital divide' to 'digital inequality': Studying Internet use as penetration increases." Unpublished.

Doctor, Ronald D. 1994. Seeking equity in the national information infrastructure. *Internet Research* 4(3): 9–22.

Doolittle, David. 1998. High-tech tech. Interview by Jim Lehrer. *Jim Lehrer News Hour*. Public Broadcasting System, July 6.

Edgemont Neighborhood Coalition. 1999. Consumer protections basis of SBC/Ameritech merger case settlement: "Edgemont & others end challenge in PUCO to $73 billion deal." World Wide Web page ⟨http://bcn.boulder.co.us/afcn/maillist/0621.html⟩ (accessed September 19, 1999).

Edin, Kathryn and Laura Lein. 1997. *Making ends meet: How single mothers survive welfare and low-wage work*. New York: Russell Sage Foundation.

Education Development Center, Inc. 2000. *IT pathway pipeline model: Rethinking information technology learning in schools*. Newton, MA: Education Development Center, Inc.

Education and Library Networks Coalition. 2000. *E-Rate: Keeping the promise to our kids and communities*. Washington, DC: Education and Library Networks Coalition.

Famuliner, Charles. 1999. "Opening plenary: Do we have a national agenda? Differing views on policy." Presentation/comments at Community Technology Centers' Network (CTCNet) 1999 National All-Affiliates' Conference, June 18–20, Chicago, IL.

Farley, Dave. 1999. "Operation weed and seed community technology network: Pittsburgh, PA." Paper presented at US Department of Justice, Executive Office for Weed and Seed Annual Conference, Houston, TX.

Foster-Bey, John. 2000. "Has the rise of digital economy reduced employment opportunities for less educated adults?" Oakland, CA: PolicyLink.

Fox, Susannah. 2001. *Seniors online*. Washington, DC: Pew Internet and American Life Project.

Freeman, Peter and William Aspray. 1999. *The supply of information technology workers in the United States*. Washington, DC: Computer Research Association.

Friedman, Robert. 1988. *The safety net as ladder*. Washington, DC: The Council of State Policy and Planning Agencies.

Gittell, Ross and Avis Vidal. 1998. *Community organizing: Building social capital as a development strategy*. Newbury Park, CA: Sage Publications.

Glennen, Thomas K. and Arthur Melmed. 1996. "Fostering the use of educational technology: Elements of a national strategy." Santa Monica, CA: RAND Corporation. www.rand.org/publications. (Accessed October 3, 2000).

Gordo, Blanca Estela. 2000. "The 'digital divide' and the persistence of urban poverty." Planners Network, No.141, pp. 1, 7–8.

Goslee, Susan. 1998. *Losing ground bit by bit: Low-income communities in the information age*. Benton Foundation. World Wide Web page ⟨http://www.benton.org/Library/Low-Income/⟩ (accessed July 10, 1999).

Graham, Stephen. 2000. "Constructing premium network spaces: Reflections on infrastructure networks and contemporary urban development." *International Journal of Urban and Regional Research* 24: 183–200.

Graham, Stephen and Simon Guy. 2001. "Contesting urban network spaces: sociotechnologies of urban restructuring in San Francisco." Unpublished paper presented at international research seminar on the social sustainability of networks, New York, April 2001.

Graham, Stephen and Simon Marvin. 1996. *Telecommunications and the city: Electronic spaces, urban places*. New York: Routledge.

—. 2001. *Splintering urbanism: Networked infrastructures, technological mobilities, and the urban condition*. New York: Routledge.

Granovetter, Mark. 1973. "The strength of weak ties." *American Journal of Sociology* 78: 1360–80.

Grant, August E. and Lon Berquist. 2000. "Telecommunications infrastructure and the city: Adapting to the convergence of technology and policy." In *Cities in the telecommunications age: The fracturing of geographies*, edited by James O. Wheeler, Yuko Aoyama, and Barney Warf. New York: Routledge.

Gruber, David and Brandon Roberts. 2000. *Workforce development: Opportunities and challenges*. San Francisco, CA: James Irvine Foundation.

Grunwald, Terry. 1999. "E-rate – A rejoinder." *Community Technology Review* (summer–fall), p. 15.

Guernsey, Lisa. 2000. "O.K., Schools are wired, now what?" *New York Times*, January 7.

Hafner, Katie. 2001 *The Well: The story of love, death, and real life in the seminal online community*. New York: Carroll and Graf.

Harmon, Amy. 1996. "Daily's Life Digital Divide." *Los Angeles Times*.

Harrison, Bennett and Marcus Weiss. 1998. *Workforce development networks: Community-based organizations and regional alliances*. Thousand Oaks, CA: Sage Publications.

Hauben, Jay R. 1995. "A brief history of Cleveland Free-Net." *The Amateur Computerist* 7(1).

Healy, Jane M. 1998. *Failure to connect: How computers affect our children's minds – and what we can do about it*. New York: Touchstone.

Hecht, Lawrence. 1998. *Community networking and economic development: A feasibility assessment*. World Wide Web page ⟨http://home.earthlink.net/~hechtl/Communities⟩ (accessed February 2, 1999).

Herwick, Mark Steven. 2001. *Sharing public access technology: The development and use of a metropolitan community information system*. PhD dissertation. Portland State University, Department of Urban Studies.

Hill House Association. 1999. *Welcome to the Hill House Community Access Network*. World Wide Web page ⟨http://hillhouse.ckp.edu/hhcan/⟩ (last modified June 16).

Holmes, Steven A. 1996. "Income disparity between poorest and richest rises." *New York Times*, 20 June.

Horwitz, Robert Britt. 1989. *The irony of regulatory reform: The deregulation of American telecommunications*. Oxford: Oxford University Press.

Hughes, David. 1999. Looking at e-Rate. *Community Technology Review* (summer–fall): 14–15.

Hughes, Katherine, Thomas R. Bailey, and Melinda J. Mechur. 2001. *School-to-Work: Making a difference in education*. Institute on Education and the Economy, Teachers College, Columbia University.

Information Technology Association of America. nd. The IT workforce shortage and education. Arlington, VA: ITAA. www.itaa.org/govt/pubs/pprtext.cfm?TopicID=9. (accessed October 12, 2000).

—. 2000. *Bridging the gap: Information technology skills for a new millennium*. Arlington, VA: ITAA.

—. 2001. *When can you start? Building better information technology skills and careers*. Arlington, VA: ITAA.

Information Technology Industry Council. 2000. *2000 High-Tech Education Report*. http://www.itic.org/digital_frontier/iti_educ_rpt2.pdf (accessed March 20, 2001).

Jacobs, Ellis. 1998. *Public utility commissions and sustainable funding for community technology*: 1–6. The Benton Foundation. World Wide Web page ⟨http://www.ctcnet.org/puco1.html⟩ (accessed November 19, 1999).

John J. Heldrich Center for Workforce Development at Rutgers, the State University of New Jersey. 2000. *Nothing but net: American workers and the information economy*. New Brunswick, NJ: John J. Heldrich Center for Workforce Development.

Johnston, Robert C. May 10, 2001. "Money matters." *Education Week on the Web*. www.edweek.org. (accessed May 23, 2001).

Kahin, Brian and James Keller (eds), 1995. *Public access to the Internet*. Cambridge, MA: MIT Press.

Kasarda, J. (1985). Urban change and minority opportunities. In P. Peterson (ed.), *The new urban reality*. Washington, DC: The Brookings Institution.

Keller, James. 1995. "Public access issues: An introduction." In *Public access to the Internet*, edited by Brian Kahin and James Keller. Cambridge, MA: MIT Press.

Kim, Seongcheol and Thomas A. Muth. 1999. "The challenge to local governments: Telecommunication policies in Michigan." *Community Technology Review* (spring–fall), pp. 27–8.

Kleiman, Neil Scott and Andrea Coller McAuliff. 2000. *The skills crisis: Building a jobs system that works*. New York: Center for an urban future.

Kretzmann, John P. and John L. McKnight. 1993. *Building communities from the inside out: A path toward finding and mobilizing a community's assets*. Evanston, IL: Center for Urban Affairs and Policy Research, Northwestern University.

Lazarus, Wendy and Francisco Mora. 2000. *Online Content for Low-Income and Underserved Americans: The Digital Divide's New Frontier*. Santa Monica, CA: The Children's Partnership.

Lerman, Robert I., Stephanie K. Riegg, and Harold Salzman. 2000. "The role of community colleges in expanding the supply of information technology workers." Washington, DC: Urban Institute.

Lillie, Jonathan. 1999. *Possible roles for electronic community networks and participatory development strategies in access programs for poor neighborhoods*: 1–16. World Wide Web page ⟨http://www.unc.edu/~jlillie/310.html⟩ (accessed March 10, 1999).

Lloyd, Mark. 1998. *Communications policy is a civil rights issue*: 1–8. World Wide Web page ⟨http://www.ctcnet.org/r981lloy.htm.⟩ (accessed November 19, 1999).

Mandel, Michael J. 1999. Meeting the challenge of the new economy. *Blueprint: Ideas for a New Century* (Winter): 1–12. World Wide Web page ⟨http://www.dlc.org/blueprint/winter98/thechallenge.html⟩ (accessed March 30, 1999).

Manzo, Kathleen Kennedy. 2001. "Academic record." *Education Week on the Web*. 10 May www.edweek.org. (accessed May 23, 2001).

Mark, June and Kimberly Briscoe. 1995. *The PTW Network: History, change, and opportunities*. Newton, MA: Education Development Center.

Mark, June, Janet Cornebise, and Ellen Wahl. 1997. *Community technology centers: Impact on individual participants and their communities*: 1–29. Newton, MA: Education Development Center, Inc. World Wide Web page ⟨http://www.ctcnet.org/eval.html⟩ (accessed February 16, 1999).

Markusen, Ann. 1999. "Sticky places in slippery place: A typology of industrial districts." In T. Barnes and M. Gertler (eds). *The new industrial geography*. London: Routledge: 98–123.

McChesnesy, Robert W. 1999. *Rich media, poor democracy: communications politics in dubious times*. New York: The New Press.

Meares, Carol Ann and John F. Sargent, Jr. 1999. "The digital workforce: Building infotech skills at the speed of innovation." Washington, DC: US Department of Commerce Technology Administration.

Melchior, Alan, Beata Thorstensen, and Melissa Shurkin. 1998. *The uses of technology in youth-serving organizations: An initial scan of the field*. Waltham, MA:

The Center for Human Resources, Brandeis University. World Wide Web page ⟨http://heller.brandeis.edu/chr/technology.html⟩ (accessed June 1, 1999).

Meyer, Lori. 2001. "New challenges: Overview of state data tables." *Education week on the web.* May 10. (accessed May 28, 2001).

—. 1996. "Requiem for the BCS and NPTN." www.ctcnet.org/requiem.html. (accessed May 25, 2001).

Miller, Peter. 1999. *CTCNet & AFCN: The shared future of community technology centers and community networking.* World Wide Web page ⟨http://www.ctcnet.org/r981afcn.htm⟩ (accessed February 13, 1999).

Mitchell, William J. 1995. *City of bits: Space, place, and the infobahn.* Cambridge, MA: the MIT Press.

—. 1996. *City of bits: Space, place, and the Infobahn.* Cambridge, MA: The MIT Press.

—. 1999a. "Equitable access to the online world." In D. Schön, B. Sanyal, and W. Mitchell, (eds), *High technology and low-income communities: Prospects for the positive use of advanced information technology.* Cambridge, MA: MIT Press.

—. 1999b. *e-topia.* Cambridge, MA: The MIT Press.

Morino Institute. 1995a. *Doors of opportunity for local communities: An overview and framework for the directory of public access networks*: 1–26. World Wide Web page ⟨http://morino.org/pand.asp⟩ (accessed November 19, 1998).

—. 1995b. *The promise and challenge of a new communications age.* World Wide Web page ⟨http://morino.org/promise.asp⟩ (accessed November 19, 1998).

—. 1994. *Assessment and Evolution of Community Networking.* Paper presented at Ties that Bind conference, Cupertino, CA.

Moss, Mitchell L. 1998. Technology and cities. *Cityscape* 3(3), pp. 107–28.

Moss, Mitchell L. and Anthony Townsend. 1999. "Where is the information in urban economic development? Lessons from the Clinton administration." Prepared for Cities in the Global Information Economy Conference, Newcastle, England.

—. 2000. "How telecommunications systems are transforming urban spaces." In *Cities in the telecommunications age: The fracturing of geographies*, edited by James O. Wheeler, Yuko Aoyama, and Barney Warf. New York: Routledge.

Namioka, Aki. 1999, Negotiating open access with AT&T in Seattle. *Community Technology Review* (summer–fall), pp. 9–10.

National Community Building Network (NCBN) and The Heller School, Center for Human Resources, Brandeis University. 1997. *The community builders' guide to telecommunications technology.* World Wide Web page ⟨http://www.ncbn.org/directry/docs/cbgx3.htm⟩ (accessed February 21, 1999).

Negroponte, Nicholas. 1995. *Being digital.* New York: Vintage Books.

Network Democracy. 1999a. *Original briefing paper: Cable franchise renewal discussion points. Proposal for the Institutional Network (I-NET).* World Wide Web page ⟨http://www.network-democracy.org/pgh-inet/bb/redwood.html⟩ (accessed July 29, 1999).

—. 1999b. *Political/franchise questions.* World Wide Web page ⟨http://www.network-democracy.org/pgh-inet/ff/political-faq.html⟩ (accessed July 29, 1999).

—. 1999c. *Seattle and King County, Washington.* World Wide Web page ⟨http://www.network-democracy.org/pgh-inet/bb/seattle_and_king_county.html⟩ (accessed July 29, 1999).

New Networks Institute. "A Broadband Bill of Rights". http://www.newnetworks.com/ (accessed July 20, 2001).

New York Times. 2000. "A governor would give every student a laptop." March 1.

Northwest Center for Emerging Technologies. 1999. *Building a foundation for tomorrow: Skill standards for information technology.* Bellevue, WA: Northwest Center for Emerging Technologies.

Novak, Thomas P. and Donna L. Hoffman. 1998. *Bridging the digital divide: The impact of race on computer access and Internet use*: 1–13. Nashville, TN: Vanderbilt University. World Wide Web page ⟨http://www2000.ogsm.vanderbilt.edu/papers/race/science.html⟩ (accessed February 10, 1999).

Odasz, Frank. 1995. "Issues in the development of community cooperative networks." In *Public access to the Internet,* edited by Brian Kahin and James Keller. Cambridge, MA: the MIT Press.

Oliver, Melvin L. and Thomas M. Shapiro. 1997. *Black wealth white wealth: A new perspective on racial inequality.* New York: Routledge.

Orfield, Myron. 1997. *Metropolitics: A regional agenda for community and stability.* Washington, DC: Brookings Institution Press.

US Congress, Office of Technology Assessment. April 1995. *Teachers and technology: Making the connection,* OTA-HER-616. Washington, DC: US Government Printing Office.

Pew Internet and American Life Project. 2000. *Tracking online life: How women use the Internet to cultivate relationships with family and friends.* Washington, DC: Pew Internet and American Life Project.

Pigg, Kenneth. 1999. "A demand side policy needed to extend the information superhighway." *Community Technology Review* (summer–fall): 45–6.

Pitroda, Sam. 1993. "Development, democracy, and the village telephone." *Harvard Business Review,* (November–December): 66–79.

Pittsburgh Presbytery. 1999. *New Beginnings Learning Center.* World Wide Web page ⟨http://hillhouse.ckp.edu/~nblc/story.htm⟩ (accessed June 26, 1999).

The Planning Partners for a National Strategy for Nonprofit Technology. 1999. *A Blueprint for Infusing Technology into the Nonprofit Sector.*

Putnam, Robert. 2000. *Bowling alone: The collapse and revival of American community.* New York: Simon and Schuster.

Rainie, Lee and Dan Packel. 2001. *More online, doing more.* Washington, DC: Pew Internet and American Life Project.

Rainie, Lee and Tom Spooner. 2000. *African-Americans and the Internet.* Washington, DC: The Pew Internet & American Life Project.

Reid, Karla Scoon. 2001. "Racial disparities." In *Education Week on the Web,* 10 May www.edweek.org. (accessed May 23, 2001).

Rheingold, Howard. 1993. *The virtual community: Homesteading on the electronic frontier.* New York: Addison-Wesley Publishing Company.

Robertson, Bethany. 2001. *Beyond access: How foundations are helping nonprofits leverage the potential of information technology.* Washington DC: National Committee for Responsive Philanthropy.

Rogers, Everett M. 1995. *Diffusion of innovations*. 4th edn New York: The Free Press.

Roos, Jonathan. 1998. "Wired but not inspired." *Des Moines Register*, July 26: 1. World Wide Web page ⟨http://www.icn.state.ia.us/text/News/clips/wired_txt.html⟩ (accessed February 10, 1999).

Rose, Susan. 1997. "The role of community access centers in bridging the technology gap." Master's thesis, Department of Urban and Environmental Policy, Tufts University.

RTPnet (Community Network for Research Triangle). www.rtpnet.org (accessed July 20, 2001).

Rubin, Herbert J. and Irene S. Rubin. 1997. *Qualitative interviewing: The art of hearing data*. Newbury Park, CA: Sage Publications.

Sanyal, Bish. 2000. "From dirt road to information superhighway: Advanced information technology (AIT) and the future of the urban poor." In *Cities in the telecommunications age: The fracturing of geographies*, edited by James O. Wheeler, Yuko Aoyama, and Barney Warf. New York: Routledge.

Sanyal, Bish, and Donald A. Schön. 1999. "Information technology and urban poverty: The role of public policy." In *High technology and low-income communities: Prospects for the positive use of advanced information technology*, edited by Donald Schön, Bish Sanyal, and William Mitchell. Cambridge, MA: MIT Press.

Sassen, Saskia. 1992. *The global city: New York, London, Tokyo*. Princeton: Princeton University Press.

Sbragia, Alberta M. 1990. "Pittsburgh's 'third way': The nonprofit sector as a key to urban regeneration." In D. Judd and M. Parkinson (eds), *Leadership and Urban Regeneration: Cities in North America and Europe*. Newbury Park, CA: Sage Publications.

Schiller, Herbert I. 1996. *Information inequality: The deepening social crisis in America*. New York: Routledge.

Schofield, Rob. 1998. *Comments to the N.C. Utilities Commission*: 1–7. World Wide Web page ⟨http://www.ncexchange.org/US/util-com.html⟩ (accessed February 6, 1999).

Schofield, J.W. and Davidson, A.L. (1998). "The Internet and equality of educational opportunity." In T. Ottmann and I. Tomek (eds), *Proceedings of ED MEDIA & ED TELECOM 98 – World Conference on Educational Multimedia and Hypermedia & World Conference on Educational Telecommunications* (pp. 104–10). Charlottesville, VA: Association for the Advancement of Computing in Education.

Schroerlucke, Kathy L. 1997. *Technical support and training for community technology centers in the Greater Pittsburgh area*. Pittsburgh, PA: Office of the Mayor, Office of Grants and Development.

Schuler, Douglas. 1996. *New community networks: Wired for change*. New York: Addison-Wesley Publishing Company.

—. N.d. *Developing and sustaining community networks*. www.scn.org/ip/commnet/workshop.html. (accessed November 22, 1998).

Schuler, Douglas and Jamie McClelland. 1999. *Public space in cyberspace: Library advocacy in the information age*: 1–28. World Wide Web page

⟨http://www.lff.org/advocacy/technology/public/entirepublic.html⟩ (accessed September 12, 1999).

Servon, Lisa J. and John B. Horrigan. 1997. "Urban poverty and access to information technology: A role for local government." *Journal of Urban Technology* 4(3): 61–81.

Servon, Lisa J. and Marla K. Nelson. 1999. *Creating and information democracy: The role of community technology programs and their relationship to public policy.* Washington, DC: The Aspen Institute Nonprofit Sector Research Fund.

—. 2001. "Community technology centers and the urban technology gap." *International Journal of Urban and Regional Research.*

—. 2002. Forthcoming. "Why planners must work to close the digital divide." *Journal of the American Planning Association.*

Shapiro, Andrew L. 1999. "The net that binds: Using cyberspace to create real communities." *The Nation.* June 21.

Shaw, Alan and Michele Shaw. 1999. "Social empowerment through community networks." In *High technology in low-income communities: Prospects for the positive use of advanced information technology,* edited by Donald A. Schön, Bish Sanyal, and William J. Mitchell. Cambridge, MA: MIT Press.

Shorters, Trabasin. 1999. *A case for: Technology works for good.* Washington, DC: Technology Works for Good.

Skocpol, Theda. 1995. *Protecting soldiers and mothers: The political origins of social policy in the US.* Cambridge, MA: Harvard University Press.

Smolenski, Mark. 2000a. *The digital divide and American society: A report on the digital divide and its social and economic implications for our nation and its citizens.* Stamford, CT: Gartner Group.

—. 2000b. *Living with the digital divide.* Stamford, CT: The Gartner Group.

Spooner, Tom and Lee Rainie. 2000. *African-Americans and the Internet.* Washington, DC: Pew Internet and American Life Project.

Stern, Christopher. 6 February 2001. "FCC's Powell Discusses TV, 'Digital Divide.'" *Washington Post.*

Stoecker, Randy. 2000. "Cyberspace vs. face to face: Community organizing in the new millennium." Paper presented on COMM-ORG: The On-Line Conference on Community Organizing and Development. Http://commorg.utoledo.edu/papers/htm (accessed September 10, 1999).

Stoll, Michael. 2000. "Workforce development policy and the new economy: Challenges, tensions and opportunities in connecting low-skill workers to IT jobs." Paper prepared for PolicyLink and the Bay Area Video Coalition.

Tascarella, Patty. 1998. Local foundations gave nearly $300 million in '97. *Pittsburgh Business Times,* June 15, pp. 1–2. World Wide Web page ⟨http://www.amcity.com/pittsburgh/stories/061598/story3.html⟩ (accessed September 1, 1999).

Tech Law Journal. 2001. *Summary of H1-B Visa Bills.* www.techlawjournal.com (accessed June 16, 2001).

Teitz, Michael and Karen Chapple. 1998. "The causes of inner-city poverty: Eight hypotheses in search of reality." *Cityscape* 3, pp. 33–70.

Temin, Peter and Louis Galambos. 1989. *The fall of the Bell system: A study in prices and politics.* Cambridge: Cambridge University Press.

Turner, Ryan. 2001. *Bush FY 02 budget and community technology centers.* Washington, DC: OMBWatch.

21st Century Workforce Commission. 2000. *A nation of opportunity: Building America's 21st century workforce.* Washington, DC: US Department of Labor, Office of Policy.

United Nations Development Program. 1999. "New technologies and the global race for knowledge." United Nations Human Development Report, *Globalization with a human face,* United Nations.

——. 2001a. *Making new technologies work for human development.* United Nations Human Development Report, United Nations.

——. 2001b. *Human development report 2001: Making new technologies work for human development.* New York: United Nations Development Programme.

US Department of Commerce. 2000b. "US Secretary of Commerce William M. Daley kicks off 'closing the digital divide' tour in New York City." Press release.

US Department of Commerce, US Department of Education, US Department of Labor, National Institute for Literacy and Small Business Administration. 1999. "21st Century Skills for 21st Century Jobs." Washington, DC: US Government Printing Office.

US Department of Commerce, National Telecommunications and Information Administration (NTIA). 1995. *Falling through the net: A survey of the "have nots" in rural and urban America.* Washington, DC: National Telecommunications and Information Administration. World Wide Web page ⟨http://www.ntia.doc.gov/ntiahome/fallingthru.html⟩ (accessed November 19, 1998).

——. 1998. *Falling through the net II: New data on the digital divide.* Washington, DC: National Telecommunications and Information Administration. World Wide Web page ⟨http://www.ntia.doc.gov/ntiahome/net2/⟩ (accessed November 19, 1998).

——. 1999a. *Falling through the net: Defining the digital divide. A report on the telecommunications and information technology gap in America.* Washington, DC: National Telecommunications and Information Administration. World Wide Web page ⟨http://www.ntia.doc.gov/ntiahome/fttn99/contents.html⟩ (accessed July 8, 1999).

——. 1999b. *How access benefits children: Connecting our kids to the world of information.* Washington, DC: US Department of Commerce, NTIA.

——. 2000a. Falling through the net: Toward digital inclusion. A report on Americans' access to technology tools. Washington, DC: National Telecommunications and Information Administration. World Wide Web page http://www.ntia.doc.gov/ntiahome/fttn99/contents.html

US Department of Education Planning and Evaluation Service. 2000. "E-Rate and the digital divide: A preliminary analysis from the integrated studies of educational technology." Washington, DC: US Department of Education Office of the Under Secretary, Doc No.00–17.

US Department of Labor. 1999. "Futurework: Trends and challenges for work in the 21st century." Washington, DC: US Department of Labor.

Wilhelm, Anthony. 1999a. "E-rate: Don't let the flame expire." *Digital Voices,* May 24: 1–3. World Wide Web page ⟨http://www.benton.org/Digital Voices/dv052499.html⟩ (accessed July 1, 1999).

——. 1999b. Mergers offer opportunities to invest in communities. *Community Technology Review* (summer–fall): 11–13.

Wilson, William Julius. 1987. *The truly disadvantaged: The inner city, the under-class, and public policy.* Chicago: University of Chicago Press.

—. 1996. *When work disappears: The world of the new urban poor.* New York: Alfred A. Knopf.

Wired For Good A Joint Venture of Center for Excellence in Nonprofits and Smart Valley, Inc.® February 1999. Report produced by Applied Survey Research and Center for Excellence in Nonprofits. Copyright © 1999, Center for Excellence in Nonprofits.

Wyatt, Sally. 2001. "Living in a network society: The imperative to connect." Unpublished paper presented at international research seminar on the social sustainability of networks, New York, April 2001.

Index